E.K. JONES

HOLZ

Too young to be a hero

LARGE PRINT   £16.99

B. HOL

L 5/9

TOO YOUNG TO BE A HERO

Rick Holz was born in a small town in Germany in 1924, to a father who told him glorious stories from the Great War, and a mother who never understood him. When his father dies on the first day of school, little 'Ollie' feels deserted in a harsh world. He joins the Hitler Youth at ten and begins to greet his mother with 'Heil Hitler' instead of 'Good morning'. At seventeen, the young patriot can barely wait to sign up for the infantry and fight for his beloved Führer. But his years of brainwashing quickly wear off as he reaches the brink of insanity defending a corridor west of Stalingrad.

RICK HOLZ

TOO YOUNG TO BE A HERO

Complete and Unabridged

ULVERSCROFT
Leicester

First published in Australia in 2000 by
HarperCollins Publishers
Sydney
Australia

First Large Print Edition
published 2002
by arrangement with
HarperCollins Publishers Pty Limited
Australia

British Library CIP Data

Holz, Rick
    Too young to be a hero.—Large print ed.—
Ulverscroft large print series: non-fiction
    1. Holz, Rick
    2. Soldiers—Germany—Biography
    3. World War, *1939 – 1945 —*
Personal narratives, German
    4. Large type books
    I. Title
    940.5'482'43

    ISBN 0–7089–4667–4

Published by
F. A. Thorpe (Publishing) Ltd.
Anstey, Leicestershire

Set by Words & Graphics Ltd.
Anstey, Leicestershire
Printed and bound in Great Britain by
T. J. International Ltd., Padstow, Cornwall

This book is printed on acid-free paper

I would like to dedicate my book to all the unarmed, unfortunate men, women and children who suffered and died as innocent victims of the atrocities of a war that should never be forgotten.

I would also like to express my gratitude to my dear friend Anne, who encouraged me to write my story; to Henry Rosenbloom, who gave me invaluable advice; and last but not least to my wife Corazon, for her unconditional love and trust.

Preface

I had no say in it at all. I prefer to believe that I was a product of my parents' love. Yet countless times I thought of myself as an accident and a living disaster and most likely I was. I know, that's not a flattering thought. I know now it isn't — I didn't know then. In my early days I had aspirations of being a fireman, a policeman, the Kaiser, a warrior or a hero like my father.

I was too young when my father died — too young when a migrant from Austria called Adolf Hitler set my mind and heart on fire and opened a door to fame and glory for me. I know, I shouldn't make excuses. On the other hand, I can't see how a young kid like me could be blamed for the outbreak of World War II — though I admit that I used to be what one might call a perfect, two-legged, double-jointed, pig-headed example of a Heil Hitler-screaming German son of a bitch. I know I was. But then the war made me grow up in a hurry. I volunteered to die for my country and I was accepted.

On the very day I realised that I was fighting for my own life instead of dying in a

1

blaze of glory for my beloved Vaterland, my Fatherland, I volunteered for immediate discharge from the army. I would have walked all the way home on my hands, but they wouldn't accept my resignation.

'Mitgefangen, mitgehangen.' Caught together, hanged together. I didn't mind being caught so much. It was the hanging bit that didn't appeal to me. 'Mitgefangen, mitgehangen' — what a ridiculous way to look at things. But then, more often than not, life *is* ridiculous. Dying is ridiculous. War is ridiculous. And fighting a war for the sake of peace and the preservation of freedom really makes no sense to me at all. Isn't freedom, like beauty, in the eye of the beholder? Lots of people, I know, can't cope with freedom. And me? I couldn't cope with anything. Caged birds almost always die when they are set free; I died a thousand times without ever leaving the cage.

I keep telling myself that I should have kept a diary, a kind of gloom-and-doom account. But I guess I would have lost it along the way, together with my anguish, my hatred, my virginity, my adversities, my obsessions, my stupidity and all the many and various things that can warp one's mind and steer a naïve young man towards self-destruction.

For so many years I tried to write this

memoir but it just didn't come together. I found that it was much easier to write about my life under a different name. 'Ollie Weiss' helped me get down exactly what I thought and felt.

I chose the name Ollie because it is related to my real name, Ulrich. For much of my childhood I was known as the black sheep. Perhaps this is why the surname Weiss (White) was so appealing.

My story is not about the rise and fall of the Third Reich. My story is about me. I am neither famous nor infamous, neither a dazzling success nor a dismal failure. I am gentle and I am rough. I am cunning and I am gullible. I am some of the things one wants to be, and some of the things one abhors. I am a plain and ordinary human being who was too young to be a hero. I am the shy, polite guy from next door, the quiet fellow who you can't quite figure out. And being a product of my own experiences, I have become a dyed-in-the-wool pacifist. The hard currency of war is human blood and I believe strongly that winners as well as losers are hapless victims.

I have all I could ever wish for now — well, almost all. I am at peace with myself. Yet, after so many years of tranquil life, I still draw the curtains when storm clouds rise on the horizon. And when the first clap of thunder makes the window panes rattle, I pray to God and beg Him to give freedom and peace to me, my children, my grandchildren and all the people who share the privilege of living on this magnificent planet of ours.

1

I am still convinced that my mother picked the wrong time of year to bring me into the world. If I'd had a say in the creation of my own flesh, I would certainly not have chosen the last month of winter, when the majestic whiteness of snow blanketing the small country town in Germany was destined to turn, sooner or later, into a grey, slithering ocean of slush. I would have been born in spring, sprouting and growing in sweet unison with the trees that lined our cobblestoned street, with the shrubs and the maybells that flourished in our garden. Is it a blessing or a curse that one can't make one's own choice in the matter of conception and birth?

My mother said I duly cried, as all healthy babies do, when I received that first slap on my newly-born backside. I have an inkling that I cried because I'd been forced to leave the comfort of my mother's womb and realised there was no way of going back to where I'd come from. I'd only just been born and I was already a refugee. The cord that tied me to my short past had been expertly cut, and apparently it took me no time at all to do what baby and man alike enjoy doing for sustenance and recreation: I searched for a soft breast. And when my lips brushed against a hard nipple I sucked on it as if my life depended on it, and I suppose it did.

At the time I was conceived my father was a millionaire many times over. He used to bring his rucksack home full of money on every payday. He earned billions of marks a week. He was employed by the local gas company and made a fortune reading the meters. And that's the truth.

By the time I was born, my father had nothing left to show for all those billions he'd earned. The Great Inflation had passed by. When I saw the light of day, food prices were back to normal. An egg, which cost 1900 million marks in October 1923, retailed for a mere 15 pfennigs only five months later. And that's the truth also.

I know I must have been present at my christening, but I guess I was too young at the time to slot the event into my memory bank. Isn't it amazing what a few drops of water can do when they are dabbed onto your innocent, heathen brow with your head firmly held over a font in the local church. And, abracadabra and bumderasassa, long before I could say 'Amen' I became, by some inexplicable miracle, a Protestant.

It took me more than the whole duration of childhood to realise that, at some stage in life, one gets into situations where one has no choice but to pray like hell for sheer survival. But then, of course, it wouldn't make a scrap of difference if one prayed to Muhammad, Jehovah, God or the Pope, as long as there was some kind of solace or miracle forthcoming in as short a time as possible.

At times the choice of where to direct one's prayers is somewhat narrowed down through experiences one never really wishes to experience. In my late teens, in those daunting days when I desperately needed to pray to somebody — because I felt that I had no chance of survival at all unless I tossed in the odd 'Our Father Who Art In Heaven' — I was extremely choosy about whom I should pray to. Hard as I tried, I couldn't forget the pastor who'd taught religious instruction for an hour a week for the whole of two years before confirmation. Although there was a convenient arrangement in place — convenient for us, the confirmees, as well as for our pastor — my own sense of values told me that it was not right, within the walls of our holy church with all its symbols of righteousness, to lift the right hand at examination time if I knew the answer to a question, and to lift my left hand if I didn't. Perhaps a smart pastor could cheat a congregation of parents. But could he cheat God? Of course he couldn't. He did try. He got himself caught for misappropriation of church funds and even Jesus Christ Himself couldn't keep him out of gaol.

Maybe I should have been born a Catholic, a Muslim, a Jew or even a Jehovah's Witness. As things were, I really didn't know whom to pray to when it really mattered.

Anyway, I'm getting too far ahead of myself. First things first. Looking back to those early days in my life, things were pretty well in the balance. Mum and Dad took me to church every Sunday. I didn't mind being forced to go to church and sit there for the best part of an hour trying desperately not to go to sleep or break wind, because Lieselotte, my sister who was four years older than me, was not given a second choice either. She had to accompany the rest of us. And to my heart's delight, she hated going to church even more than I did. I relished that thought. Did I ever!

I'm sure I would have liked my sister if she hadn't been such a snob. She pretended to know all the facts of life but, for reasons unknown to me, she would not share any of that knowledge with me. She got a kick out of teasing me until I was blue in the face. But most of all I hated her for getting me into trouble.

'Come here, little brother.'

'Do this, little brother.'

'Do that, little brother.'

'I've kissed a boy, but don't you tell Mother, little brother . . . '

Jesus Christ, I was sick of being her Little Brother. I didn't want to know her. Who in his right mind wants a sister anyway? I certainly didn't. Whether right or wrong, she always blamed me for everything that shouldn't have happened but did, like rain at a picnic or failing her school exams. She also blatantly denied that she'd ever played 'Doctors'. You'd have to be an idiot to believe that!

I remember playing 'Doctors' with Helga. She lived with her parents in an upstairs unit in the apartment block my father had invested in when he inherited some money on his father's death, a few years before inflation ruined the value of the Reichsmark.

Helga was a sweet little girl. She had long blonde hair and the bluest eyes I'd ever seen. She had a dimple in each rosy cheek when she smiled, and her teeth were as white as snow and as shiny as pearls. I fell in love with her long before I knew anything at all about falling in love.

Helga's father was a Baptist preacher or something like that. Always dressed immaculately in a grey flannel suit, white as white shirt, black tie and shiny patent leather shoes, he never missed giving me a kind of mellow, well-wishing smile whenever we passed one another on the stairway. I'm not so sure that he would have smiled as nicely at me had he known that his beloved daughter and the wicked son of the landlord indulged quite regularly in the exciting game of 'Doctors' in the privacy that lay within the old brick walls of the wash house, which stood neatly tucked away in the far corner of our backyard. I learnt a lot about human anatomy in those cosy one-to-one consultations. The most puzzling thing I learnt was that Baptists don't have doodles like Protestants do. I didn't believe Helga until she took her panties off, lifted up her frilly skirt and said to me, smiling from ear to ear: 'See, Ollie? I haven't got one. And I know that my Mama hasn't got one either. Do you believe me now?'

'Gee, I'm glad I'm not a Baptist,' I replied, quite bemused. 'I'd rather be a Protestant any day. How can you do your wee-wees without a doodle?'

'I'll show you,' she grinned. And she did.

For weeks on end afterwards, I tried to talk

my sister into showing me her doodle. I was sure she had one just like mine, but she never gave me a chance to find out. Told you she was a snob!

★   ★   ★

It snowed during the night preceding my fifth birthday. The three-storey block of apartments, built in bright red brick on the outskirts of town, stood there like a fortress, braving the howling northerly breeze. In a belated show of strength, winter had spread a last fresh carpet of snow all the way across the streets and gardens of my home town. White tufts, like fairy floss, balanced precariously on the leafless branches of our dormant fruit trees in narrow strips of the whitest white — the white that meant winter in my home town.

The spacious area under the tiled roof of our apartment block was divided into storage attics for the tenants, each section separated from the next by a network of wooden lattice. A lock for his or her attic door was provided for each of the tenants together with the rent book.

In the corner of our attic stood the bed box, a huge wooden crate used for the storage of spare feather quilts, blankets and winter

11

clothes during the warmer part of the year. A thick layer of oat straw, which provided a soft bed for last season's apple crop, covered the remaining floor space.

Lieselotte and I had to climb up to the attic every Saturday afternoon to turn the apples one by one, so they wouldn't rot, before Mother turned them into apple sauce or apple jelly. If we were extremely lucky, Mutti would throw some into the oven to bake as a special treat for us when we managed to be 'good children'.

With my fifth birthday falling on a Saturday, Mutti granted us a special and rare privilege. Instead of having to wait till later in the day — as per the normal scheduled routine — we were given permission to turn the apples as soon as Lieselotte came home from school at noon. Did I mention that my mother really had a heart of gold? I'm sure she had. What a pity it was that she hardly ever bared her precious, loving heart to me. I loved the woman, I really did. But she was one of those old-fashioned people who thought that stern, unyielding discipline was the only necessary requisite to raise a child, especially one of the male species. She was so frighteningly strict that she made me feel as though I had to ask permission before I sneezed, and then apologise to her afterwards.

God only knows why so many apples decided that year to go rotten all of a sudden. We knew we had a disaster on our hands as soon as we opened the attic door.

'If Mutti catches us with a bucketful of rotten apples it'll be the end of a birthday party for you,' said Lieselotte, gazing at the rotten mess.

Just for once, I agreed with my sister. And I found myself in yet another of those tricky and ominous 'Hey, little brother' situations. One moment I was gathering rotten apples from the straw, and the next I stood at one of the large attic windows, throwing missiles at anyone who passed by on the street three stories below.

'Hey, little brother,' said my big, ugly sister. 'I bet you couldn't hit that man down there if you tried.'

On my first attempt I missed the target by a couple of metres. I tried harder. I concentrated. I had a point to prove to that smartypants sister of mine.

Gradually I transformed the pure white snow on the footpath down below into something that my father would have described as a battlefield in the Somme.

I finally scored. I hit the brim of a brown

felt hat — perfect target, perfect hit.

'I did it! I did it!' I shouted triumphantly, as I watched the apple drop and disintegrate on the man's patent leather shoe. I was still jumping up and down with joy as the victim gathered his toppled hat from the ground. He looked up suddenly, his eyes stabbing at me like a thousand daggers.

'You stupid little idiot,' Lieselotte hissed, panicking. 'Now that you've got us into trouble, how are you gonna get us out of it? Did you have to jump up and down in front of the window like a madman? He's spotted us. He's coming to get us. Don't just stand there. Do something!'

'The bed box,' I whispered. 'Quickly! Come on, we'll hide behind it. It's the only choice we've got.'

Lieselotte pushed me out of the way in the race to the hiding place. 'You stupid little idiot!' she screamed, her voice raging out of control. 'Look what you've done. I told you not to throw the apples, didn't I?'

There was no time for arguments. I should have known that she'd put the blame on me to save herself. We pulled the lattice door firmly shut behind us and hid behind the large crate.

'Dear Jesus,' I prayed. 'Don't let that nasty man find us. I promise, if you help me now

I'll stop hating this sister of mine and, dear Jesus, that's the most difficult pledge I've made in my whole life. And I promise to say my prayers every night without being told to. And I'll even eat cabbage soup, and you ought to know how I hate that stuff.'

Lieselotte, crouched next to me, was shaking like jelly. I must admit that I got some kind of sadistic thrill out of watching her cower like that. She had her eyes tightly closed and her thumbs were buried in her ears. I could have gladly choked her to death, but I whispered, 'And, dear Lord, I'll pray for my sister too.'

I kept on praying like hell. I promised all the things I could think of, things I hadn't promised before, things like not stealing money from my mother's purse any more.

Footsteps came closer and closer. Attic doors rattled louder than my teeth. Then a sharp cough, much too close for comfort; a flood of angry words. And then footsteps fading away in the stairwell.

We wiped the sweat from our brows and waited for about ten minutes until we found the courage to leave our hiding place and make our way downstairs. Lieselotte tried to hand me the almost empty bucket.

'You take it,' I told her, shoving my hands into my pockets. 'I don't want to get myself into trouble on my birthday.'

'Who cares about your birthday! I didn't throw a single apple anyway. You'll be in trouble all right.' Her grin stretched from ear to ear. I looked up to where I thought God might be. I seethed with anger and said: 'I hope You didn't listen, God, when I made all those stupid promises. Give me a fair go, man. I'll never be able to stop hating my sister.'

When we got to the first-floor landing, we saw that the door to our flat was wide open. Mutti stood in the doorway. She was talking to a man whose right shoe was decorated with the remnants of a very rotten apple. My sister, rising to the occasion, just kept on prancing down the stairs with the bucket.

'Ollie did it,' she said, without turning her head. 'I told him not to. But he wouldn't listen to me.'

I wanted to die instantly but I couldn't. Before I knew it, my mother grabbed me by the ear and pulled me towards her. I knew that I was in more trouble than an ice-cream on a stove.

'I trust you'll give the little scoundrel the punishment he deserves,' said the man with the dirty shoe.

'Don't you worry about that,' replied Mother, shaking the stranger's hand. 'By the

16

time I'm through with him, he'll be more than sorry for what he did.'

I looked at my mother, pleading silently with her. She was still holding me by the ear when she dragged me down the hallway. I knew that my pleas fell on deaf ears. I was in for a very special birthday present indeed.

I surrendered. I cried without shedding a tear. Like a robot, I went through the usual routine. I pulled a chair from under the polished table and put it in the middle of the polished kitchen floor. Everything in that kitchen of ours was polished. Without further ado I fetched the cane from behind the cupboard, where I'd hidden it the previous day after yet another belting, and handed it dutifully to her. I lowered my pants, far enough to expose my bare bottom, then bent across the leather-covered seat. The scene for corporal punishment was set.

'All I want is a hug and a cuddle and a friendly word, Mutti,' I whispered quietly. 'Don't make me hate you.'

The cane came swishing down, bruising my skin. Down it came again and again. The only pain I felt was in my heart. I glanced sideways at my sister. The smug grin on her face made me wince just once — just for one brief moment.

When a few invited friends arrived in the

mid-afternoon to celebrate my birthday, my mother was the most perfect, friendly, smiling and generous hostess any child could have wished for.

Naturally, all my guests thought that my mother was the best and nicest mother in town. But of course they didn't know her as well as I did. They didn't know that my bottom was a very painful maze of welts, which ran crisscross all over my backside. I found it hard to move on my chair without flinching but I managed. I was much too proud to mention to anybody what had happened to me just a couple of hours before. And my much admired mother didn't want to make it public either.

On the following Sunday, Mutti and Papa took us to church again, so that I would emulate my peers and grow into a God-fearing, honest and decent German. Many people said hello to us and we said hello back to them, and my bottom still hurt just as much as it had at my birthday party. And just to show God and the world how I felt deep inside, I did what I'd wanted to do for a long time in the hallowed realms of the church. I farted. I let a silent one go that smelt like rotten eggs. And all and sundry around me sniffled and snuffled in disgust. I snuffled with them, and even the best of them

18

couldn't point an accusing nose at me. I said
to myself, 'Jesus Christ, I love you today!'

★　★　★

Spring arrived earlier than in most years. The
ice-crystal flowers on the outside of the
double-glazed windows had melted into
obscurity, and the iron-clad wheels of
horse-drawn wagons had lost the noiseless-
ness of winter, clattering once more across
the shiny cobblestones.

The snowman I had lovingly built in the
front garden wouldn't listen to me any more.
His arms had melted away. His head had
slipped into a precarious angle, and his nose
had turned back into a carrot. Herr
Snowman had been my close confidant for
almost three months. He'd made me feel
understood when I'd bared my soul to him.
Unlike my father, who was either at work,
busy in the garden or doing repairs in one of
the apartments, my snow-white friend had all
the time in the world and all the patience to
listen to my problems and, most importantly,
he never sent me away. And it was so easy to
make him smile. Almost anyone could draw a
smile on a snowman's face.

The sun came out with the might of a
thousand vultures, and it consumed, greedily,

the carrion of winter. A few weeks later the daffodils flowered in our garden.

Out in that beautiful, life-giving sun, my father chopped firewood one Sunday morning after we returned from church. It was a pity that he was always so busy. I loved him dearly. I admired him so much, I wanted to grow up to be exactly like him. I was grateful for every minute he spent with me. My father was a wonderful man. He never laid a hand on me, except when he put it on my shoulder to reassure me of his love.

At lunchtime he dropped the axe; at coffee time the doctor called; by dinnertime the ambulance arrived to take him away to the hospital. And all the neighbours whispered into each other's ears as they watched the spectacle.

I stood wide-eyed, tight-lipped and perplexed, reaching out for a hand that wasn't there for me. I could not understand why my father was too lazy to walk by himself. Sure, I'd heard of other children having sick mums or dads. But my father was different. He'd never been sick in his whole life. He'd never had time to be sick.

My mother took me to the hospital to see him, but he was asleep whenever I tried to talk to him. I thought I was having a nightmare each time I held his hot, sweaty hand. Everything would be all right next morning, I thought. But it wasn't all right at all.

Three days later, my mother dressed me up in my favourite sailor suit, put a brand new school bag on my back, a huge paper cone filled with sweets into my hands, and walked me to school. My first day at school! Hurrah! Not long to go now to be a man. One day a useless little kid, and the next day an aspiring scholar. Very soon I'd be a real man.

I loved the first lesson in the classroom. 'Wait till I get home,' I whispered to myself. 'I'll tell you all about it, Papa. I want you to be so proud of me.'

And then I remembered that my dad wasn't at home. He was 'playing sick in hospital' on my first day at school. Now that wasn't a very nice thing to do, was it? So what, if he didn't come home today, he'd be home tomorrow.

I cavorted down the stairs with all my new schoolmates after the first lesson. I was happy. I liked school.

And then I spotted Aunt Martha. She wasn't smiling. She was waiting for me at the bottom of the steps. Her eyes were all red as if she'd been crying. 'Come here, Ollie,' she said, her voice trembling. 'I've come to take you home. Go fetch your bag.'

'No, I won't,' I parried quickly. 'I like school. I want to stay here.'

My teacher caught me halfway up the steps. He was carrying my school bag. 'Run along and be a good boy,' he said. 'When you come back tomorrow you can draw as many pictures as you want on the blackboard.'

'You promise?'

'Trust me,' he said.

When we arrived at home, my mother wasn't there. Neither was my father. But Lieselotte was there. She sat slumped over the kitchen table, sobbing her heart out. Our Uncle Willi was also present. I'd never seen him shed a single tear, but he was crying now. And the whole apartment was filled with people, neighbours and all. I was more confused than I'd ever been. What the hell was going on? Would somebody please enlighten me.

I opened the flap of my school bag, reached inside and groped for one of the lollies I'd deposited there. I couldn't make up my mind — peppermint or raspberry? It didn't really matter. Rolling the bonbon around inside my mouth, I just sat there like a statue and tried to figure out why everybody was crying and tiptoeing through the crowded apartment.

After a while, all the crying around me made me so sad that I also broke into tears.

Suddenly, somehow, it dawned on me that all of us were crying for my Papa. All of a sudden I had this nagging, horrible feeling that my Papa would not come back from that awful hospital they'd taken him to. But I still refused to believe that I would never again sit next to him on the couch on a Sunday after dinner, watch him smoke his fat cigar and blow smoke rings into the air. And I simply couldn't cope with the idea that I'd never again listen curiously to his fascinating stories about the Great War and the tales about the Kaiser's heroes who, just like my father, had fought many great and victorious battles in France for his beloved Deutschland. Perhaps, quite innocently, he ignited the blazing torch of undying patriotism within my receptive mind.

Somehow I knew that I would not see him come home from work again, have him muss up my hair and say to me, 'Hallo, mein kleiner Spatz.' Kleiner Spatz, little sparrow, that's what he used to call me. I don't know why. Perhaps I was so small and frail and vulnerable. Oh, my God, how I wished right there and then to be a little sparrow. I'd fly far, far away, so far that nothing could reach my aching heart.

My father, my hero, my Papa was dead. Dead, dead. Nobody had to tell me, I *knew*.

23

Do people have to die before they go to heaven? Did I have to die to feel my Papa's guiding hand on my shoulder again, or to sit in his lap? Hey, Papa, lead the way!

My Papa was dead. They would put him into a box and take him away for good. Oh, Papa, I still had so many questions to ask, and you still had so many stories to tell. Why? Why, Papa? Why did you have to die? Who can I talk to now? Snowmen only live for three months of the year. Jesus Christ, I'll miss you, Papa. I'll miss you.

I hated my mother for taking me to the funeral. Funerals make death appallingly final. A little boy, six years of age, should not have to suffer the horror of parading past an open coffin. He should not be compelled to look at a dead part of himself lying inside a lacquered black box, lined with shiny white satin. Nor should he look at a pair of closed eyes — eyes that would never open again to reveal the love and the warmth and the strength and kindness and wisdom I'd come to depend upon so very much.

And then there were all the relatives and the nosy neighbours and lots of people I didn't know from a bar of soap. They all cried their hearts out and lamented and went on about what a good man he'd been, and what a great tragedy his death was for his grieving wife, Frau Weiss. All the men wore black as a sign of respect. All the women wore fancy new hats and pearl necklaces. Nobody, but nobody, seemed to care about me. Yet somehow I thought that I *was* important on that very special occasion. One only buried one's father once in a lifetime.

Two weeks later, back at school, my classmates started to tease me, giggling and sniggering, shouting things at me like 'Ha ha ha! Poor Ollie Weiss hasn't got a father. Ha ha ha!'

I ran away to seek refuge in the nearby park and cried my heart out. With the tears running freely, I promised myself that I would run away to America. What else could I do? I was the poorest boy in all of Germany. I had a mother who flogged me, a sister who hated my guts, and a father who'd died on me. I was certain that even Jesus and the Holy Ghost didn't want to have anything to do with me. For a while I had this great idea of killing myself, so I could be reunited with my father. But I didn't know how. So I went home, told a fib about school being out early, had lunch, and felt better.

2

Heil Hitler, Mutti! Heil Hitler, Lieselotte! Heil Hitler, Deutschland! Sieg Heil, mein Führer!

Oh, those were great and adventurous times for a thirteen-year-old boy with three wonderful, proud years of Jungvolk training already under his belt. Soon, on my fourteenth birthday, I would be old enough to be transferred into the ranks of the Hitlerjugend. Dressed in my brown shirt and black shorts, I was ready to conquer the world. You could bet your bottom Reichsmark on that. Nobody had to tell me that Germany was the greatest country on earth. I knew that already.

My beloved Adolf Hitler had appeared from heaven like a merciful angel and, with wisdom, swiftness and efficiency, had changed our Vaterland almost overnight. If ever a man had performed miracles, our Führer was that man. He'd brought smiles back onto the faces of our people. He'd chased the shadows of economic depression into oblivion and he'd put honest and well-earned money back into the wallets of the working men. Factories, houses, whole suburbs were sprouting like mushrooms after a thunderstorm.

My heart went out to the English and the French and all other foreigners who were not fortunate enough to be German, to all strangers who could not take part in the miracle that raised my Vaterland from the dust and sludge of despair and the doldrums of stagnation. I wanted to invite all the boys from all over the world to come and march with me through the streets of Prenzlau, singing songs like 'Our flag leads the way; our flag is the new era . . . ' with vibrant, joyful voices and hearts filled with gratitude and pride.

Our sleepy country town had risen from a long, bad dream. No more crippling poverty, no more despair. The sugar mill was working full steam again and soon unemployment was a thing of the past. And those antisocial stragglers who refused to work were drafted into the newly formed National Labour Service, put into brown uniforms, housed in barracks and put to work with pick and shovel. Mein Führer was a true genius.

On Labour Day the streets were transformed into oceans of flags, wrapping me into a sea of pride and indescribable joy. Joy to the world, our saviour Adolf Hitler was born!

Heil Hitler and Sieg Heil! Down with the communists and the capitalists, whoever and wherever and whatever they were.

I was wrapped from head to toe in the Jungvolk, Hitler's youth movement. The coyness and the shyness, which had been so much a part of my psychological make-up as far back as I could remember, gave way to brashness and cockiness. Although I might still have had trouble spelling the word 'arrogance' correctly, I certainly knew how to adopt it. Especially where my mother was concerned.

After my Papa took leave of absence and left me to stumble through the rest of my childhood as a half-orphan, my mother had it in for me. Shortly after I turned ten, my sister finished school and started work in a solicitor's office, which left me to the mercy of my mother's moods and whims. I suppose she tried honestly to be a mother as well as she could. But she certainly hadn't served an apprenticeship. I guess no mother does. I had a love/hate relationship with her. I am certain that she loved me, but she wasn't happy with who I was. I suppose that in her dreams she wanted me to be like the husband she'd loved and lost. I was much too young to fill my father's boots. If only she had learnt to love me half as much as she punished me, I would have been putty in her hands, to be shaped into anything she wanted me to be.

Instead of love she gave me discipline. I remember her coming to my bed one night, asking me, 'Are you sick, Ollie?'

I told her I wasn't.

'Strange,' she muttered. 'You didn't get a spanking today. I'm sure there must be something wrong with you.'

'But Mutti ... ' That's all I could say before she turned away from me.

'Good night, Ollie.' No cuddle, no kiss, nothing. Just the sarcastic question, 'Are you sick today?'

I did get a spanking almost every day. Mutti and I played a sort of 'catch as catch can' game. She tried to find a reason to give me a workout with the well-worn cane, or simply a swift backhander across the visage, and I tried to do something wrong like lying or stealing, so that I'd have the satisfaction of knowing that I wasn't bashed up for nothing.

In fact, my mother was an expert in all kinds of physical abuse. If one method didn't hurt me enough, she'd have another one up her sleeve. I still think that her worst and most devastating punishment was making me stand in a corner, facing the wall for hours on end, and even forbidding my sister to speak or to listen to me. Being ignored must truly be the most hurtful and degrading punishment a child can suffer.

After one such rather lengthy session at home I attended a training session with the Jungvolk and I asked my Scharführer, the leader of our patriotic group of thirty, what a good German boy should do if he suspected his parents of being Communists. 'Just curious,' I said.

'Denounce them, of course,' the 20-year-old Scharführer told me. 'Denounce them and let them burn in hell.'

From then on my mother lost control over me completely. Every time she belted me or violated me in any other way, I smiled defiantly and felt no pain. 'If I want to, I can destroy you,' I said to myself over and over again. 'Perhaps tomorrow I'll use my power and have *you* stand in a corner, facing the wall. Heil Hitler to you.'

Of course, there were some sunny days in the Weiss household as well. Sometimes Mutti was almost human. Like the day she gave me my one and only sex education lesson.

'Sex is a sin unless you're married,' she lectured me, when the mass of pimples on my face conveyed the message to her that my hormones were on a rampage inside my adolescent body. The nasty little critters certainly gave me a confused mind and itchy balls.

'And if you play with yourself you'll go blind.'

Well, Mutti, I can let you into a secret now. Only the weekend before you talked to me about the facts of life, I formed a big circle with ten of my friends under that huge old chestnut tree at the far end of the park. We all wore our uniforms. And we opened the flies of our black shorts and masturbated like hell. And I came first and scored ten cigarettes for my effort. And I didn't go blind after all.

Oh, Mother dear, you were born so upright and so square and so righteous and so innocent. Didn't you have any fun at all? What a boring life you must have had.

Looking back at things now, I really can't blame you for wanting to jump out of the kitchen window to kill yourself a couple of weeks after Papa was buried.

You tore my heart to shreds when I found you crouching on the window sill, your legs dangling in the air, your voice piercing and shrill: 'I can't take it any more! I want to die. I want to die. So help me God, I want to die!'

Jesus Christ, Mutti, didn't you have any consideration at all for your son, for the little boy who struggled with you and dragged you back from the brink of your death? You brought me into this world. Wasn't I reason enough for you to go on living? *Wasn't I, Mutti?*

Maybe I should have let you jump, maybe I should. At least I would have escaped punishment when I hitched a ride home from school, hanging on to the tailboard of a truck until I fell off and my head hit the cobblestones and I blacked out. When I regained consciousness I was lying in the lounge and you were belting the living daylights out of me, screaming: 'Do as you are told! Do as you are told!'

Come to think of it, I'm really glad that I broke into the locked drawer of the china cabinet in the lounge room and stole all that rent money you'd tried to hide from me. You know what I did with it, Mutti? I took it all to the fowl yard at the back of our garden. And I lit a bonfire with all those bank notes and I chanted: 'I hate you. I hate you. Dear little innocent mother, I hate you!'

Well, those days were history. Now I was a proper and likable Hitlerjunge. I was convinced I could not only fill my father's shoes, I could fill anything I wanted to fill.

Which brings me to my childhood sweetheart, Helga. While I, out of straight-out defiance, greeted my mother and my sister with a crisp 'Heil Hitler' instead of a 'Good morning' or a 'Good day', with Helga I turned into the very timid and polite boy I used to be during those good days when she and I played 'Doctors' in the wash house.

No 'Heil Hitlers' for Helga. 'I love you,' I would whisper to her, feeling myself drawn to her more and more. The great thing that drew us closer together was that we could not only talk to each other, we could listen to each other as well. And nobody else in the whole world had any ambition to listen to Ollie Weiss!

Helga had her problems too. Her father hated to see her dressed in the white blouse and blue skirt of the BDM, the pretty and becoming uniform of the League of German Girls. Apparently he, as a Baptist preacher, had no time for our beloved Führer at all. No matter how much Helga tried, she couldn't convince him that he should pray to the Führer instead of wasting his time on God.

Nevertheless, Helga and I lived in our own little world. We built our own castles in the sky and, at least in my corner of the ring, friendship evolved into something that gained more and more momentum.

The buttons almost burst off the fly of my Jungvolk pants when we cuddled and petted and hugged in the dark hallway of our tenement block for the first time, both of us wanting to make love, needing each other and shamelessly acknowledging our needs, and trying, for the sake of each other, to keep our sanity intact and our once in a lifetime friendship untarnished.

Mothers are a vital part of a growing boy's life. My Mutti was a good cook, she made sure that I always had decent clothes to wear, and she even washed and ironed the uniform I wore so proudly, although she hated the sight of it.

'Your Papa would turn in his grave if he could see you parade around in that silly uniform of yours,' she would tell me every now and then. 'Your Führer isn't even a German. How can you idolise a foreigner who knows nothing about us? You might as well have Napoleon running the country. Hitler is up to no good.'

'I'll denounce you to the Gestapo if you keep on talking like that,' I'd threaten her. 'Fancy my own mother being an enemy of the Third Reich. Papa would be ashamed of you, that's for sure.'

I was convinced that my dead hero, my Papa, was on my side.

★ ★ ★

34

People who live in large cities may think that life in a small country town is nothing but a surrender to insipidity and ennui. Those people are wrong. Something exciting was always happening in our community of Prenzlau, which hugged the shores of the Uckersee, a beautiful and tranquil little lake that was covered with ice in winter. Ice thick enough to skate on, or to dance on under the silvery moon.

Who, I ask you, who in our peaceful town could have possibly imagined that a mere eight years later, the clean, transparent water of our lake would turn red with the blood of innocent children, women, grandfathers, grandmothers and all the others who hadn't qualified for service in the Wehrmacht and gone off to the war? In the spring of 1945, when the Russian war machine came to swallow up our town, which was over eight hundred years old, most of the inhabitants fled to the shores of the lake, seeking open spaces rather than the prospect of being buried under the rubble of their homes. It was a sensible choice which proved to be fatal for many.

As they celebrated the end of the war, they uncorked bottles of homemade red currant wine and thanked the Lord for their survival. And when the Russian artillery opened fire from the opposite shores of the lake, the revellers died with a song on their lips as the shells exploded among them and tore their flesh to shreds.

Perhaps it was just as well that I couldn't gaze into the future. Besides, I was too busy shouting 'Heil Hitler'. Too busy trying to be a good German in those great days.

★   ★   ★

When I came home from school one day my mother looked quite flustered. 'Dr Rosenbaum was picked up by the Gestapo this morning,' she informed me, as soon as I walked through the front door.

I laughed in her face. 'One of these days you'll be arrested if you go on spreading rumours like that. Who, for God's sake, would want to arrest poor old Dr Rosenbaum? He's a good doctor.'

'He's a Jew,' Mutti snapped. 'Hitler wants to get rid of them. He hates Jews.'

'What if he does?' I parried smartly. 'What if he does? He'll certainly know the difference between a good one and a bad one. Jesus Christ, Mutti, Dr Rosenbaum was an officer in the Great War. He was decorated for bravery — I've seen him with all his medals on Remembrance Day. And he said hello to me only the day before yesterday. If you don't stop spreading gossip like that, the Gestapo will come and get you one day. And I for one won't feel sorry for you.'

Mother just didn't know when to call it quits. 'They got the gypsies too,' she said, staring straight into my defiant face. 'At least we can keep the clothes on the line now, with that thieving lot gone. Good riddance!'

'Bullshit,' I swore. She was really starting to get under my skin. 'Unmitigated bullshit! If you weren't my mother I would tell the Gestapo about you. And you know what they'd do with you.'

'Same as they did to Dr Rosenbaum and your gypsy friends, I guess.' Mother didn't flinch for a single moment.

I knew what would happen, even before I said it. But I couldn't help myself. 'You're a bloody Communist!' I yelled at her. 'Why am I stuck with a horrible mother like you?'

I had no time to duck. She was fast. She didn't strike me with an open hand either. The clenched fist that struck my face almost knocked me to the ground. 'Why didn't you die instead of your father?' she gasped. And I was out the door and jumping down the stairs, three steps at a time.

'I hate you, I hate you, I hate you.' I couldn't think of anything else. Not until I arrived at the camping ground of my gypsy friends, just on the other side of the railway bridge that spanned the highway leading out of town.

I loved the happy gypsies. I'd found refuge, kindness and all the cuddles I needed whenever Mutti punished me for something I didn't do. My gypsies always made me smile when I was down. Many a time they had to drag me all the way back to our front door because I wanted to spend the rest of my life with them. I wanted them to initiate me into the same life of joy they lived, wherever they were.

But there was no joy in my heart when I came to their campsite. I hated my mother for being correct. I couldn't believe my eyes. I sat on the charred remains of a wagon wheel. Stricken with grief, tears running down my cheeks, I stared at what used to be the home of my friends. I watched a falling star cut through the dusky sky, made a wish and hoped it would come true. I knew it wouldn't. Not this time.

I carried the blackened neck of a violin in my hands as I walked home. A lone string was dangling from it like a rope from the gallows. The stars brightened as the sky darkened and I whispered, sweet memories crowding my mind: 'Play the mazurka again,

Maestro. Please, Umberto, play it for me.' I strained my ears and tried for one more time, just for one more time, to hear the happy sound of tambourines and the clicking of castanets, but heard nothing but my own heartbeat. Farewell, my friends, I thought, wherever you are.

I couldn't bear the thought of facing my righteous mother there and then. I stole a few flowers here and there on the way to the cemetery, where my father was waiting for me. He was as good a listener today as he'd been yesterday and yesteryear. I could talk to him about everything. My deepest secrets would be safe with him. Even if I couldn't put my arms around him and hug him, at least he didn't send me away as Mutti did. I was quite certain that he enjoyed our meetings as much as I did.

I talked until I ran out of words. I thought until I ran out of thoughts. By the time I climbed up the steps to our apartment, I felt a hell of a lot better.

Two days later, when I came face to face with my Scharführer from the Hitlerjugend, I grabbed the opportunity and asked him about the sudden disappearance of the gypsies.

'I don't know why you're interested in bastards like that,' he said. 'I hope they hang them from the trees instead of wasting a bullet on them. There's no room for riffraff like that in the Third Reich, that's for sure.'

'Heil Hitler, Herr Scharführer,' I said, hiding my true feelings behind a smug grin. 'To hell with the gypsies and all other enemies of the Third Reich.'

I could have killed myself for saying it, but I didn't. The Führer already had me in the palm of his hand.

Propaganda is a very subtle tool of deception. It gets at you slowly and inconspicuously. And if you happen to open your mind just a fraction, you've lost the battle long before you take up arms to fight it. What the hell did I know about propaganda? What did I know about politics?

I didn't have to know anything about shit like that. I had eyes in my head. I could see. Wasn't it much more credible to sing hymns of praise to Adolf Hitler, the man whose strong, resonant voice I could listen to on the radio, whose image I could see on the cinema screen in magnificent magnitude, than to worship someone, something way up in the sky, some mythical figure which, most likely, wasn't even of Aryan descent? If God really existed, would He have taken my father away from me when I needed him more than mother who couldn't or wouldn't let me love her the way I would have wanted to?

Oh yes, there were times when I thought that all my problems would go away if I really tried hard to be a good Christian. So I tried, and I was not alone. As a matter of fact, half of our school class got together during recess time for inspirational meetings in the far corner of the school yard. It was a squeaky-clean fellowship — Catholics, Jews, Jehovah's Witnesses and the like had no hope of being admitted.

After half a dozen exciting meetings we settled on the most interesting way of committing Christianity. We formed a plan.

Although the government had tried its utmost to get rid of a filthy slum area on the fringe of town, where no decent German would want to be seen, the no-hopers still lived in their slimy, louse-ridden environment. What more Christian thing could we do than to help those who were very much beyond helping themselves?

Working in groups of three, we used half of our pocket money to purchase inexpensive items in the shops. One of us would divert the attention of the shopkeeper by choosing something cheap from one of the rear shelves, and the other two would cram everything within reach into their pockets and the front of their Hitlerjugend shirts.

At an arranged time we'd meet after each foray just outside the slum area, march in together and play Santa Claus to the children of drunks and derelicts.

Of course, our benevolent deeds of Christianity didn't get us any points of merit from God, but they did get us a dishonourable mention in the local paper and a firm promise from our school principal that all of us would be expelled should we ever try to indulge in committing Christianity again.

It would have been nice if Dr Rosenbaum had come back from his holiday trip or whatever he'd gone on. He'd helped my mother to bring me into the world. He'd been our family doctor ever since. But, alas, dear old Dr Rosenbaum did not return. His surgery remained closed, and the smashed window pane of the waiting room was never replaced. His conspicuous absence made me feel uneasy. It bothered me because there were still many other Jews who were allowed to stay and go about their daily chores. Some of their shops were still open, though always empty. It just wasn't proper, it was outright unpatriotic, to buy anything from a Jew. Maybe that was progress. Who knows? And come to think of it, perhaps I wouldn't have ~~~~ ~~ ~~~ Dr Rosenbaum — if he had returned to open his practice again — for fear of being seen to associate with him.

★　★　★

By now, my friend, you might be thoroughly disgusted with some of the things I've been telling you. But I set out to tell the truth, and that's what I'm doing. I was a well-indoctrinated little bastard. I make no excuses and no apologies for that. If you'd been in my place, maybe you wouldn't have been quite as gullible, but neither you nor I know that, do we?

I didn't really understand what this business with the Jews was all about. But I felt that my Führer, my teachers and my superiors in the Hitlerjugend were much better informed than my mother who, in my opinion, had lost all touch with reality. If Jews and Communists were a threat to the Third Reich, then I for one wanted to have nothing to do with them.

The Jews who were still living in Prenzlau now wore the Judenstern, the Star of Israel, with the word 'Jude' on it. But even before they had to wear the identification tag I never had any difficulty in picking out a Jewish kid in a crowd. Jews ate garlic. The rest of us in our town hated garlic. But then, I really hated

Catholics a lot more than the Jews, but they were more difficult to identify, because they didn't have their rosary beads sewn on the lapels of their coats.

Living in a mostly Protestant town, we would resort to calling somebody a Catholic pig if we ran out of swear words. Catholics could lie in your face one day and go for confession the next, and then tell lies all over again. How could you trust someone like that? Maybe if I'd been born a Catholic, my life would have turned out differently.

The general feeling towards Jews kept on worsening and became more apparent from month to month. Our propaganda machine was running smoothly and full steam ahead. The only two people I'd hated so far were my mother and my sister. Oh yes, there was someone else, my French teacher, who all the kids suspected to be a Communist.

Now such phrases as 'Don't worry about him, he is only a Jew' came rolling across my lips without a second thought.

There was no time for any of us to reflect on happenings in the past. Events, much bigger than a synagogue on fire on Kristall-nacht, the Night of Broken Glass, were already in the making. As 1939 approached, Germany rejoiced in an avalanche of success. Our beloved Führer was making huge inroads towards the creation of a United States of Europe under his command and at his feet. Our history teacher was jubilant and said, over and over again: 'We are making history! The East was German and the East shall be German again!'

Our borders began to expand to the east, the south and the west without a single angry shot being fired. We were pushed from high to high by a mountainous wave of euphoria. Weekend after weekend I joined the queues at the movie theatre, but not to watch Tom Mix slaughter hordes of wild Red Indians. We had our eyes glued to the silver screen watching the flag of the Thousand Year Reich rise over Sudetenland, Memelland, Saarland, Austria. The sky was the limit. And all the lost pigeons came home to roost. All the land that had been stolen from us was German once again.

For the first time since 1918, our national anthem told the truth: 'From the Maas to the Memel, from the Etsch to the Belt, Germany above everything in the world! Deutschland über alles!' The Thousand Year Reich was well on its way. We were growing; we were strong; we were invincible. And I, together with millions of proud Germans, said 'Heil Hitler' instead of 'Amen'.

The Jews had now almost vanished from

the streets. Those who ventured out walked with their eyes fixed on the ground, stooped and frightened. To hell with them, I thought. If they still opposed the upward surge of our new Reich they should do what the many slogans, painted in huge letters on countless walls, told them to do: 'Juden raus!' I turned fifteen in February — my first birthday without a birthday cake, without a birthday party. Mother didn't bother. It wasn't worth the effort, she said. I was pleased in a way. I didn't feel like saying thank you to her anyway.

And when Easter came, there were no Easter eggs hidden in the garden. Lieselotte, who was now engaged, spent the break with Hans and her future in-laws. Who cared? Easter eggs were strictly kid's stuff. I had better things to do than worry about crummy Easter eggs. That's what I told Mutti anyway, though it was not what I felt.

My mother did sew another golden braid on my school cap, though, without my having to ask her. And after the Easter holidays I started my last year in school. Thank God, only another twelve months for me to put up with Mutti's tantrums.

What would I do once I'd finished my education, I wondered. I might join the army; or perhaps the navy, so as to get as far away as humanly possible. I was absolutely wrapped in the Hitlerjugend. I was sure that I would enjoy army life. My Papa loved the army. Why shouldn't I?

During the summer break I went to a Hitlerjugend camp together with three thousand proud boys. We lived in tents, played war games, attended lectures every day, competed in a lot of physical contests and sat around the camp fires at night, dreaming of our Thousand Year Reich. From the third day onwards we were taught how to handle a small-bore rifle, and how to aim at cardboard cut-outs of enemy soldiers which popped up from among the trees. 'Got you, you Communist bastard!' I'd shout with unbridled enthusiasm. I thought about my Papa and all the Frenchmen he'd killed. I wanted him to watch me and be proud of me as I aimed and hit target after target. 'Bang, you're dead! Bang, you're dead!' How am I doing, Papa? Who says that I'm too scared to be a soldier? Watch me, Papa!

★   ★   ★

On the first day of September 1939 the sun rose in the east, just as it did on any other day. Nature's discerning brush was already busy painting the trees in the most beautiful autumn colours. And our mighty army marched into Poland.

During the first eighteen days of September the first soldiers of my home town died a hero's death on foreign soil, died to defend the freedom of our Third Reich. And the multicoloured flowers, which had flourished in the green wooden boxes on the balconies, died with them.

Some weeks later the men from our garrison arrived back home, their proud features still encrusted with Polish dust. Some of the truck canopies were torn, and the tatters fluttered in the breeze like victory banners.

Pride, joy, shock and relief were etched deep into the faces of our very own heroes, as they passed slowly through the streets of Prenzlau in their battle-scarred trucks. The autumn leaves that had fallen during the night were covered with a carpet of flowers. Huge throngs of happy onlookers lined the streets, laughing and shouting and rejoicing. 'Welcome home! Sieg Heil! Hip, hip, hurray!' The army band played the Radetzki March and I was fiercely proud of being a German.

During the night following that very special day all the restaurants stayed open until dawn, all the dance halls and ballrooms opened their doors, and scores of enthusiastic and patriotic girls opened their slender legs to accommodate the returned heroes.

However, a silent minority of grieving parents, whose sons had not returned, took no part in the wild celebrations. Nobody seemed to notice that they were crying their hearts out, cursing the war, envying the lucky ones who had no reason to mourn.

The day following the homecoming of the troops was declared a public holiday and the schools remained closed. With my blood still running hot from excitement, I went to the recruiting office in the town hall and joined the long queue of volunteers who'd come to enlist. I felt somewhat strange among the older men.

Some made fun of me. 'Go home, Junior,' they jibed. 'Come back when you're dry behind the ears.'

I felt like sneaking away quietly, but then I spotted a few comrades from my Hitler-jugend unit. It was too late to back out now. I pushed my little chest out, waved to them and made sure that they recognised me. After all, wasn't I volunteering to become a hero?

For a moment it passed through my mind that I was standing in this queue to escape an unhappy life at home rather than to volunteer for something that would gain me a cross of distinction — either an Iron Cross for bravery or a wooden cross with my helmet on top. But it was only a fleeting thought. I was a German. I was proud of my heritage. I adored my Führer. Did I need any other qualities to stand up and fight for my country?

It seemed that I did. The recruiting officer took a brief look at me, tried to keep a straight face, and waved his hand in my direction. 'Go home, do your school work, sonny,' he said. 'Come back in three years' time. You're not old enough to die a hero's death.'

I had no other place to go but home. Mutti wanted to know where I'd been. So I told her the truth. 'I went to join the army,' I said, feeling rather proud of myself.

Like so many other times before, she caught me by surprise. She hit me twice before I had a chance to duck out of reach. 'You stupid little idiot,' she scolded me. 'Have you gone crazy? Don't you think you're a bit too young to die for that Führer of yours? You've got a head on your shoulders, haven't you? Try using it. It'll be for your own good.'

I almost called her a bitch or something like that. She knew exactly how to deflate my bloated ego, and I really wanted to stand up to her now. But it had taken me all of my courage to stand in line at the recruiting office; I didn't have enough strength left to stand up for myself. I wanted to tell her that I was sick of being treated like a nincompoop, but the words got stuck in my throat.

Being the son of my mother was not the easiest thing in the world. I got walloped for telling lies and flogged for telling the truth. I wished I was dead.

3

Frederik Schuster was one of those people who never stood out in a crowd. If I'd bumped into him on the street, I would have said 'Pardon me' and walked on without noticing the shape of his nose or the bushy eyebrows. He would never have become a force to be reckoned with in my life if Mutti hadn't put an advertisement in the local newspaper: 'Full board and lodgings for refined gentleman.'

After Lieselotte got engaged she'd spent little time at home. Hans, her husband-to-be, had been called up for active army service and Lieselotte spent most of her spare time with Hans's parents, maybe because she wanted to avoid confrontations with Mutti. Perhaps her future in-laws didn't criticise her for wearing lipstick or painting her finger-nails.

I also spent as little time as possible at home, because I was thoroughly sick of being told that I'd have a very bleak future unless I changed my attitudes. As far as I was concerned, Mutti was barking up the wrong tree. She didn't know me. I had no attitudes.

My life consisted of likes and dislikes, of black and white. There was no space for grey areas in my young mind. I loved or I hated, simple as that. Compromise was for the weak-minded, not for me, an aspiring young German who, at the tender age of fifteen, had already tried to volunteer for active service in the Wehrmacht.

In a way I was glad that Mutti had put that advertisement in the paper. Maybe it was a good idea to have a referee on hand, someone who'd give me some credit.

Seeing that I had slept in the corridor for longer than I liked to remember, and that the spare room was only used on odd occasions to accommodate visitors, it didn't really matter to me whether somebody rented the room or not.

We lived within a handy distance from Prenzlau's new airport, and many single men looked for board and lodging in our area. Mother could do with the extra money. The company would be good for her and, hopefully, for me. Perhaps Mutti would eventually soften her attitude towards me and my ideas.

When Herr Schuster knocked on the front door, my mother rushed to open it for him. She must have liked the dapper little man, because she didn't hesitate to invite him into the kitchen for a cup of coffee and a piece of cake. Normally Mutti was very wary of strangers.

It turned out that the stranger worked as a mechanic at the airport. He was a widower after many years of childless marriage. I had a sneaking suspicion that he was more intent on looking at my mother than on viewing the room he came to rent. At long last he did have a quick look at my favourite room in our apartment, nodded and said quickly, 'I'll take it, if it's all right with you.'

Mother told him that she'd have to think it over, and would he call back tomorrow. They shook hands and he left.

'What do you think of the man?' Mutti asked me after closing the door. 'Would you mind if he moves into the spare room? He seems a nice enough man.'

I was flabbergasted. Mutti actually asked me for an opinion. I told her I didn't mind. 'If I can't have the room, you might as well make some money out of it. I don't mind him living here as long as he doesn't try to run my life.'

So it was settled. Frederik Schuster paid a month's rent in advance and moved into the nicest room with the largest windows and the most picturesque view.

He sipped a cup of coffee in the kitchen while he waited for his new landlady to take the dust sheets off the furniture and make the bed. I stood in the doorway and watched Mutti, and I said farewell to the room that should have been mine but never was.

So the corridor was still my bedroom. It had no windows at all; only doors, doors everywhere, all opening out into it. And each one of the doors took away a little of the privacy I craved. From now on even the new boarder had to walk across 'my' corridor to use the toilet.

Don't we all need some place, somewhere, where we can be undisturbed for a minute or two, where we don't offend anyone with anything, where we can be ourselves and take a good look at who we are; a place where we can try to assess what we want out of life and what we are prepared to put into it? Don't all of us deserve a window in the bedroom? A window that lets the morning sun shine through to warm the heart; a window you can stand by to watch your anxieties drift away into thin air?

I promised myself that, should I ever be fortunate enough to buy my own house, I would have a huge, arched window in my bedroom. And I vowed that my house wouldn't have a damned corridor at all.

From the moment Frederik Schuster stepped into my life, I dubbed him 'Frederik the Great' — partly out of sarcasm but mostly because he did resemble the famous Prussian king, whose troops would gather after each battle and, lose or win, sing, 'We thank Thee all, my God.'

I certainly thanked God for sending us a peacemaker. Our lodger brought a change of climate into our home. After a chilling ten years of winter, it seemed that spring was just around the corner. My mother stopped being angry with the whole world. She got off my back and stopped trying to change me into what I didn't want to be. Going home from school without fear of what might happen was a strangely comforting feeling. I stopped telling lies and searching for excuses, because my mother focused more and more on the little man with the grey eyes and the warm smile.

Heil Hitler to you, Frederik. Welcome!

★　★　★

Lieselotte told me one day that she'd run into Mutti and the boarder hugging and kissing. Mutti hadn't been embarrassed at all. She'd said that we'd have to get used to having Herr Schuster around for a long, long time, because they were planning to get married soon.

I welcomed the news, even though it came via Lieselotte. If Frederik the Great could keep on making my mother as happy as she'd been since he moved in, she might even stop victimising me and give up punishing me for Papa's death.

It was Frederik, and not my mother, who gave me the news officially. It would have been nice if Mutti had approached me first. But it didn't really matter. I told him exactly how I felt. 'Your marrying my mother has nothing to do with me. If she wants to marry you, that's her business. It's no skin off my nose. I'll be joining the army soon. Maybe it's a good thing to know, that Mutti won't be left all by herself.'

My stepfather-to-be gave me a friendly slap on the shoulder and smiled. 'That's the spirit, son. You'll see, I'll be a good father to you.'

At first I thought I'd misunderstood him. Had he really called me 'son'? He shouldn't have. He had no right to call me 'son'. Next up he might expect me to call him 'Papa' as well! We had got on so well together for quite a while. Now he'd caused irreparable damage to what could have turned out to be a reasonable relationship. No man was good enough to emulate my father. No one could fill his shoes. Nobody could ever take his place.

'Fuck him,' I said to myself. 'Who the hell does he think he is?' It didn't bother me one iota that he would be sharing my mother's bed. If it made her happy, if her conscience could hack it, it was all right with me. But as for myself, I had Adolf Hitler for my God and my Papa for my hero, and no other man could push his way into my heart.

I cried myself to sleep that night, and I played truant from school the following day. We'd already finished our final exams, and I saw no point in going to school red-eyed. I hid my school bag in the cellar and walked to a secluded spot on the shore of the Uckersee. The water's surface was like glass. I turned my back to the town and pondered my future. What would I do? What *should* I do? So far there hadn't been a straight stretch of road ahead; just crossroads, nothing but a maze of crossroads taking me nowhere. Sure, the choice was mine to make. But it wasn't an easy task for a boy of sixteen.

I was dying to get into the army. Jesus Christ! Wasn't it easier to live for one's country than to die for it? Why did my hands always get clammy and sweaty when we were told at our meetings that it was an honour to die for the Third Reich? What was *happening* to me, the boy who chose to play chess rather than cowboys and Indians, the kid who wrote poetry in praise of all things beautiful?

I hated violence because I'd grown up with a violent mother. I'd never had a fist fight. I'd never dared to retaliate. Anybody could hit Ollie Weiss and get away with it. I'd just put my hands deep into my pockets and refuse to hit back. I knew that my lack of reaction infuriated my mother. Maybe that was a good enough reason for me not to defend myself.

I was no hero. Holy hell, what was I? *Who* was I?

Every time I listened to a speech of Josef Göbbels on the radio, I would burst with patriotism and laugh at the funny jokes and ditties about Churchill and his fat cigars. I wanted nothing more than to be a hero, a hero who would do his father proud. I was no longer a school kid. A schoolboy one day, a public servant the next. My meddlesome mother had my whole life already arranged for me some months before I completed my education. Instead of walking to school every day, I walked to work six days a week with my lunch packed in Papa's old briefcase. Against my own better judgment I did try to please my mother and found myself nailed down to a straight-backed wooden chair, locked in between greyish, drab, suppressive office walls for forty-eight hours a week, sitting listlessly behind a manual calculator and assessing dog taxes. What a wonderful and fulfilling job that was for an ambitious young man almost old enough to fight for the freedom of his country!

Thank the Lord the war wasn't quite over yet. I still had a slight chance of dying a hero's death and doing my father proud. I'd been assured that I would be accepted for active service as soon as I turned seventeen; only eight months more to wait, after our victorious troops had brought my father's arch foes to their knees. France, the land of Napoleon the Great, had been absolutely trounced in a most remarkable six-week battle.

Serves you right, you Frog bastards! You shouldn't have declared war on Germany. Didn't you know that our Thousand Year Reich is invincible? Now you know, don't you!

Lieselotte's wedding was postponed. Hans was in France and couldn't get leave as planned. Jesus Christ, did I envy Hans.

Frederik the Great got hitched to my mother in a private function at the registrar's office. The unsentimental ceremony meant nothing more to me than Frederik's not having to sneak into Mutti's bed for a cuddle any more when he thought I was asleep. Legally, he could scratch Mother's back now whenever she felt an itch.

I felt sad because I couldn't even remember the last time I'd slipped into Mutti's bed and snuggled up to her. Gee, I would have really liked that.

Of course, Mother didn't know that Helga and I were doing our own lot of cuddling. And the very things I wished for more than anything were that my Führer would not invade England before I was allowed to prove myself to him and to my Papa, and for Helga to agree that our platonic relationship needed urgent progress towards a joint orgasm. Next to Hitler and my father she was the most important person in my life. I loved her with all my heart, and my whole body ached for her. But she kept on begging me to wait. I got thoroughly sick of fantasising and dreaming of her with each climax I gave myself, and I was positive that it took two to tango to experience the ultimate satisfaction. I thought, many times, that it was stupid for me to waste my precious sperm the way I did. Helga and I would make beautiful Aryan children together in times to come.

I saved enough money from my meagre salary to take a course in ballroom dancing. I pleaded with Helga to come along, but her parents thought that in times of war praying was much more important than waltzing across a dance floor.

'I'll have to go on my own, then,' I told her.
'You don't know what you're missing.'

'We have a whole life ahead of us to dance
together, Ollie,' she whispered in between
kisses. 'You know what my parents are like. If
they say no it means no.'

Girls, girls, girls, flippant and flitting,
flurrying and fluttering like a flock of
swallows. Oh, dear Jesus, I thought, wouldn't
I like to get my hands under one of those
frilly, starched dresses in soft pastel colours.
There they were, all lined up against the
opposite wall of the dance hall like sparrows
on a power line, each of them looking
irresistibly delectable. Help, Helga! Help!

Regrettably, or perhaps fortunately, Helga
was *not* there to take care of me. But
Brigitte was. Her hair was as red as my
flushed cheeks when I asked her to dance
with me.

'Take your partners for a waltz, gentlemen,'
said the instructress.

I said 'You are beautiful' to the redhead, as
I took her out onto the slippery floor with my
sweaty hands shaking and my head filled with
outrageous, raunchy ideas.

The teacher counted: 'One, two, three
. . . one, two, three . . . ' And my little
member of Parliament stood up in all his

glory, straining to make a statement. I forced myself to move away from her a little, embarrassed by all the commotion that was going on inside my confirmation pants — the only long pants I possessed. But she kept herself at close range. Each time the teacher turned her back on us, Brigitte's knees would brush against the inside of my legs. 'Do you like it?' she flirted, her white, glossy teeth just centimetres away from my parched lips.

'You're driving me insane,' I said, savouring the sweetness of her breath and the ever so smooth touch of her hands. 'Do you know what you are doing to me?'

'Sure I do,' she whispered, her burning eyes driving me nuts. 'Sure I do. Are you going to take me home tonight?'

It's the Gospel truth, Helga: I honestly didn't want to say yes. But you weren't there! And this was one chance in a lifetime I didn't want to miss. 'Even if you live on the moon I'll take you home,' I said, and I actually meant it. It is incredible what a pair of knobbly knees and inviting eyes can do to a young man's brain.

We danced on and on, right through the two hours of the lesson, and all the time we danced I contemplated very carefully every one of the moves I would make to sacrifice my virginity to the hottest redhead in Prenzlau. How come that, at given opportunities, a man's brain short-circuits, goes haywire and slips all the way down to his doodle?

We had to cross through the dark central park on the way to her home. We stopped under an old oak tree. I pulled her towards me and kissed her, a hot and passionate smacker right on those hot, cherry-ripe lips of hers. She pulled away and gazed into my bloodshot eyes. 'Don't you know how to kiss a girl properly?'

Before I had a chance to work out what she was talking about, she shoved her tongue way past my shivering lips, and my whole body exploded with unbridled passion as I experienced the exquisite sensuality of a French kiss for the first time in my adolescent life.

I pushed my tongue all the way towards her tonsils. Animal or human being? Human being or animal? Angel or devil? Oh my God, who am I? Probing fingers straying slickly, unrestricted, uncontrollable, towards an undefended goal. And her skin is as silky as the panties she wears. The devil holds my hand and guides it expertly towards the ultimate destination. My burning fingertips reach the wiry curls of her pubic hair and she clings to me as if I am the only man on earth and says, 'Yes, yes, yes, yes!' I lose control of my senses and a million sperm come gushing out. Brigitte turns away in disgust and complains: 'What a waste. What a bloody waste!' She leaves me standing there, wet pants and all, and her laughter echoes through the trees of the park. I am quite convinced that I am the greatest fool on God's earth.

Cross my heart, I never told Helga about that experience. And I never did another one-two-three with Brigitte either. I'd learnt my lesson. My heart still belonged to Helga, though I did suffer from a nasty case of bad conscience. I shouldn't have worried. I'd done nothing wrong. If girls sleep around they are sluts. If boys go on a spree of one-night stands it's called 'getting experience'. Lots of water has gone under the bridge since, but I have never forgotten Brigitte, nor have I expelled from my mind that wonderful and memorable occasion when I first found out that masturbation might not be the ultimate sexual high.

Were love and sex the same thing? I'd find out one day.

★ ★ ★

Christmas 1940 came much too quickly. The snow almost arrived too late. But when we went to church on Christmas Eve the first snowflakes swirled from the grey sky to lay a soft, white, glistening carpet beneath our feet, just in time for the festive season.

The church bells pealed through the wintry air, and I honestly didn't know whether to walk with God or to march with my Führer, Adolf Hitler. I knew Hitler. I'd witnessed many miracles he'd performed. Germany was prospering. Germany was conquering the world!

Of God I knew little. Maybe Jesus *could* walk on water. Even if the Gospel was true, it didn't connect with my life. Whatever I knew of Him was only hearsay. Our Führer was forging us into the mightiest nation on earth. And God? What had He done for me? Fuck all, that's what! Heil Hitler to You, you old legend up in the sky that was supposed to be heaven.

Four candles spread their flickering yellow glow from each of the pine wreaths which hung suspended from the lofty ceiling above the aisle of the church. The Christmas tree, sparkling in splendour, decked out in silver and white, tried its utmost to send the message of Christmas into all our hearts: May peace dwell within you. May peace and sanity and compassion prevail for ever and ever. Humble yourselves, for the meek shall inherit the earth. Christ the Saviour is born.

With the solemn hush of Christmas capturing soul, body and mind, our old pastor, grey hair, black robe and all, stood in his pulpit and proclaimed blatantly: 'May the Lord be with you all. May the God Almighty bless the Führer and bless the Third Reich, and all the good people of Germany. May God bless you all.' And I said 'Heil Hitler' instead of saying 'Amen', as did most of the congregation. Hell! Facts spoke for themselves, didn't they? Jesus in his day had made big speeches about peace on earth. And how many wars had we had since Jesus was nailed to the cross? Our Führer didn't make hollow promises, did he? Shit no! My Führer was a greater peacemaker than Jesus could ever have been. My Führer was the true God.

Nobody, but nobody, stood up to dispute the facts. The ones who knew the truth were too frightened to speak up. As time went by, hour by hour, the *Hakenkreuz* flag, the object of my unqualified admiration, gathered more and more friends as it kept on casting its spell over a trusting, proud nation.

Hans arrived home the day before Christmas. He'd been granted only a fortnight's leave, too little time to organise his wedding. I looked at Hans with envy. He'd already earned himself the Iron Cross Second Class while serving in France. He wore his decoration with pride. Yet, no matter how nicely I asked him, he refused to tell me how he had earned his medal. Nor would he even hint at how many Frenchmen he'd killed. For the life of me, I couldn't understand that. If I ever got awarded a medal, I'd boast about it to the whole world.

I played 'Silent Night' on the violin that was a legacy from my Papa. That's all he'd left me, a violin and a bicycle. I liked my bicycle though I still couldn't comfortably reach the pedals. And I'd cherished my violin. But now I hated it, because it kept reminding me of my gypsy friends. I only brought it out on special occasions like Christmas.

I played out of tune, but I played just the same: 'Vom Himmel hoch, da komm 'ich her . . . From high in the heavens I come . . . ' My emotions were running wild inside me and I couldn't hold back the tears any longer. I wished that the old, wise God somewhere up in the sky would come down from his perch one day, just for a day, for a minute, for a moment, for the length of a heartbeat, to hold my hand.

Dreams come cheaply, don't they? Lieselotte and Hans were holding hands. Mutti and Frederik the Great were holding hands. Nobody held my hand, nobody.

Helga would be holding hands with her mother and father, especially with her father, he being a preacher. But Helga wasn't here, where I needed her. I knew that her heart was with me. Yet her hands weren't, and I needed her hands for reassurance, for comfort and for courage.

Frederik sang louder than all the others put together. I stopped fiddling with my ill-tuned violin, put it back into its black case, retreated to the unprivate privacy of the dark passageway that was my bedroom, with a handful of ginger nuts, and I did what I wanted to do more than anything else. I cried. Boys don't cry? Well, let me enlighten you, my friend, they do.

4

Roses are red, violets are blue.
If you don't kill the Russians,
The Russians kill you!

Hurrah! Hurrah! Heil Hitler and Sieg Heil, all rolled into one! After weeks and weeks of worrying about failing my medical examination, the mailman came to deliver my yearned-for call-up notice. There was no prouder man in town than me, Ollie Weiss, a hero in the making. The fact that I'd be the first of my old school class to wear the traditional grey cloth of the Wehrmacht made me feel extra special.

My legs could hardly keep up with me as I hurried from place to place to spread the marvellous news. Ollie Weiss, standing a hundred and sixty-five centimetres tall — a full five feet, five inches — was about to join the mighty German army!

I would have loved to train as a fighter pilot, but the air force regulations stipulated that volunteers with eye defects, such as the myopia I had, could not be accepted for flight training. Wearing spectacles made no difference. I was terribly disappointed. The enrolling officer suggested that I join the ground staff of the air force, because I would stand a good chance of being stationed right there in Prenzlau.

To a proud and eager man like me, such a proposition was an outright insult. 'I don't want to polish propellers, sir,' I retorted cheekily. 'I have volunteered to fight a war for my Führer. I want to see the white in the eyes of our enemies, sir.'

Hell, what would my Papa think of me if I shirked fighting the Russian Bolsheviks who were threatening the freedom of our Third Reich? It wasn't only my duty, oh no, it was my privilege to protect my Führer and my people from those who were trying to destroy us.

'I want to join the infantry,' I insisted. 'If I can't be a pilot I want to be an infantryman like my father.'

The only prerequisite for foot soldier volunteers was a stupid, suicidal yearning to die in a flash of glory for the Vaterland. Needless to say, I qualified without any hitches.

It never occurred to me during those days of euphoria that I had been carefully programmed all through that wonderful time in the Hitlerjugend. Führer befiel! Wir folgen!

71

Leader gave orders! We follow!

Being so cocky, I boasted that I could win the war single-handedly. I shouted my message much too loudly — I had to drown out the voice that rose whispering from inside me, asking, 'Have you gone stark raving mad, Ollie Weiss?' I would think of all the war stories my father had told me, and I would look at myself in the mirror and yell at my image at the top of my voice: 'Heil Hitler, mein Führer! Oh yes, I am proud to be a German. I shall fight like a German. And if need be, I shall die like a German. Hell, yes, Papa, yes, Herr Hitler, you shall be proud of Ollie Weiss. I promise!'

A week before I had to leave home I told my boss that I wouldn't come back to work any more. I relished the very moment when I told him exactly what he could do with his adding machines and those never-ending pages of dog tax assessments. The well-bred bureaucrat's eyes almost popped out of their sockets and his face burned as red as the ripe tomatoes in Mutti's garden.

Being rude and crude and telling him in exact words what I would have liked to tell him on the day I first met him at my job interview gave me tremendous satisfaction and a feeling of strength and power, which in turn kept the nightmares from reaching out to me during the day.

My mother didn't treat me all that badly during my last few days at home. She even cooked all my favourite meals for me. And she tried hard to tolerate my coming home late from yet another farewell party. One evening I found her sitting on her own in the kitchen, listening to the radio and knitting a pair of socks for anyone who needed them. If no one wanted them now, they'd come in handy some day for somebody. That's what she wanted us to believe. The fact was that she simply could not sit still for a minute without doing something. Knitting seemed to be her panacea.

Despite all those hostile vibes between us, I still longed for her to reach out and give me a hug, and I told her so. She didn't even look up from her knitting as she growled: 'Can't you see I'm busy? Make yourself a sandwich and go to bed. It's getting late.'

For a brief moment I wanted to walk up to her and give her a cuddle, but I just shrugged my shoulders and said: 'I'm not hungry. I think I'll go and talk to Papa for a while.'

'That won't do you much good,' she muttered. 'He's been dead for over ten years. Can't you let him be?'

'No, I can't,' I replied. 'Papa is still very much alive for me.'

'Lucky for you, he isn't,' said Mother quietly. 'Your father wouldn't be very proud of you, that's for sure.'

If she didn't know how to love me, she certainly knew how to hurt me. I turned abruptly and stomped out into the corridor and slammed the door behind me.

'Sorry, I couldn't bring you any flowers tonight,' I apologised to my father some time later. 'But I shall water the ivy before I sit down and talk to you.' I grabbed the watering can, which lay hidden behind the headstone and filled it from a nearby tap.

'There you are, Papa. Mustn't let your blanket wither. The nights will get cooler soon.' I filled the can again and poured it over the ivy-covered grave. Then I sat down and did what I could do better than anything. I talked to my father. 'Papa,' I said, 'Mutti thinks I'm crazy because I come here and talk to you. You know I'm not mad, don't you? I don't want you to be dead. You are the only one who really understands me and listens to me. Except Helga of course. But I need you, Papa, and I won't let you die. I need you.'

I don't know for how long I'd been sitting there. Time is nothing when one talks to a loved one. Suddenly I felt a soft hand on my shoulder. For a brief moment I thought that Papa had risen from his grave. Jesus had, hadn't He? To me my father was more important than Jesus.

I turned my head and saw Helga standing behind me. 'Hello,' I said, astonished. 'What are you doing here? How did you know where to find me?'

'Your mother told me, Ollie. I asked her. I had to find you. I don't know what to do.' She sounded very depressed and extremely miserable.

The moon hung large and bright in the clear sky. It provided more than enough light for me to see Helga's reddened and swollen eyes. 'What's the matter?' I asked. 'Looks like you've been crying your heart out. Why? What has happened? I've never seen you so upset.'

'It's my father,' she cried. 'Oh God, my poor father.' With her tears glistening in the moonlight, she told me that her father had been taken away for questioning on the previous day, and he hadn't come home. 'Mother has been running all over town trying to find him or to find out why he's been arrested. She is convinced that the two men who picked him up are from the Gestapo. They never said a word; just walked in and took him away. It's driving us crazy. My father hasn't done anything wrong. He wouldn't hurt a fly. What would the Gestapo want with him?'

I tried to allay her fears. 'Don't give up hope, Helga. I'm sure that they'll let him go. You'll see, he'll be back home tomorrow.' That's what I told her, and I felt like a hypocrite. I'd said the same to Mutti, when she'd told me about Dr Rosenbaum's arrest. Of course, Dr Rosenbaum was a Jew, and lots of Jews had vanished during the last few years. Nobody seemed to worry much about them. Nobody wanted to know where they'd disappeared to. 'But your father isn't Jewish, is he?' I said, trying to answer my own questions. 'Of course he isn't.'

Helga was sobbing her heart out. 'How could he be Jewish? He is a Baptist preacher. Surely that can't be the reason behind his disappearance. If my father is Jewish, so are you and I. It's preposterous even to think like that. Mother has different ideas though. She thinks that the Gestapo is rounding up all the Baptist preachers to send them to those awful concentration camps. What if that's the truth? What if, Ollie?'

'It can't be true,' I insisted, 'it simply can't be. It's nothing but Communist claptrap. Our Führer wouldn't stand by and let that happen.'

I wished I could have spoken with some power of conviction, but I couldn't. My reasoning sounded stale and hollow. I'd used empty phrases like that much too frequently already. But no matter — the Führer was right, wasn't he?

It was utterly absurd. The two of us, with a whole, wonderful future ahead of us, were sitting here in the last resting place for the dead, crying for the living.

Joy shared between two people is twice the joy. Yet shared sorrow never halves the pain. It just makes it a little bit easier to bear.

It was late when we walked out of the deserted, silent resting place for the dead with our hands entwined. As we passed through the large open gate, I said to her: 'I know what it feels like to lose a father, Helga. I do hope with all my heart that you haven't lost yours. Neither God nor the Führer will let that happen to you.'

We would make it, Helga and I. We'd build a future together. I didn't know how to go about it yet, but I knew we would succeed, no matter what. We were not little children any more. We were young and responsible adults now. We deserved a happy future.

After a short walk through deserted streets, we arrived at the tiled front steps that led up to the apartment block where both of us lived since we'd been brought into the world. Helga wasn't ready to front up to her grief-stricken mother. She drew me down onto the steps. Putting her arm around my waist, holding me close to her, she kissed me on the cheek and sighed. 'Two more days and you'll be off. What will I do without you, my love?'

'You'll manage,' I assured her. 'Can you imagine it? In two days from now your Ollie is going to be a soldier. It's hard to believe, isn't it?'

'I'll be so proud of you.'

'And I'll be proud to wear the uniform of the legendary Wehrmacht . . . ' A little bit of quivering falsetto crept into my voice. Think positive, Ollie Weiss. Think positive. Heil Hitler and up yours, you rotten Bolsheviks. I'll make you shrivel in your boots.

I was so full of my own bullshit that I almost didn't hear Helga's question: 'Aren't you scared?'

In all of my life, as far back as I could remember, I'd never told a lie to Helga, and I didn't intend to start now. That's why I replied: 'I guess I'm a bit scared. I've never lived away from home. It'll be a big change.'

Helga smiled. Whenever she smiled at me, all my worries paled into insignificance. 'I'm prepared to die for you,' I whispered, my fingers tracing the contours of her face. 'If need be, I'll die for you tomorrow.'

'Hey, hey, hey,' she said, wiping the tears

from her cheeks. 'I don't want you to die for me. I want you alive. When you get out there into the fighting, don't you try being a hero, just keep your nose to the ground and stay alive, ja? I'll be praying for you every day. Just don't forget that I'm going to marry you, and I can't marry a dead hero, can I?'

'Are you proposing to me?'

'No, Ollie. I leave that up to you.'

'All right then. Will you marry me?'

'You know I will.'

'Tomorrow?'

'The day after we win the war.'

'You'd like to have children?'

'Two would be nice — one of each, don't you think?'

'Can we commence with the production right here and now?'

Helga laughed for the first time that evening and I laughed with her. She wound her fingers out of my hand and reached across to the mass of sweet peas that hugged the picket fence of the front garden. She looked at me and her still wet eyes sparkled like the stars above, only brighter. She picked a long, curling tendril from among the sea of sweet pea blossoms and put it into the palm of my hand. She then trimmed the young green shoot until there was nothing left but a single curl.

'Well?' she challenged. 'What are you waiting for?' She pointed her ring finger at me.

'With this ring I thee wed,' I told her, all of a sudden feeling hot and cold at the same time. I slipped the tough little curl onto her finger and repeated my vow. 'With this ring I thee wed.' I knew that this was one moment in my life I'd never forget.

'You may kiss the bride now, Ollie Weiss.'

Our lips touched, and life stood still for a long, long time. And no, there was none of that uncouth tongue-shoving going on between Helga and me. Maybe slobbery kissing like that was all right to do with cheap, teasing, hot-stuff trollops like Brigitte, but not when it came to the pure as pure girl I was in love with. Though I could still hear Brigitte's derisive laughter echoing through the park from tree to tree, I knew that I belonged to Helga, lock, stock and barrel. I would never again yield to temptation, never again.

'I love you,' said Helga, as we climbed the stairs. 'I love you, and don't you ever forget that.'

'How could I?' I replied. I cupped her face in my hands and kissed her on the forehead. 'How could I ever forget the most beautiful girl in the world?'

With my little cardboard suitcase packed and a snapshot of Helga safely tucked away in my wallet, I stepped out into the unknown.

Mutti walked me to the station. We didn't talk much. We really had nothing to say to each other. Instead of lying to me and telling me that she would miss me, she bought coffee for us both from the kiosk on the platform. The train pulled in shortly after we'd gulped the terrible brew. I clutched the handle of my suitcase and braced myself for a farewell kiss from Mutti. Aren't mothers and sons supposed to hug each other on occasions like this? I didn't expect my overly inhibited mother to go overboard with her emotions. She didn't. It must have been a real effort for her to put her hands on my shoulders, give me a bit of a squeeze and brush her cold lips across my forehead.

'Goodbye, son, and good luck,' she said. Her words sounded as if she was trying to absolve herself from all responsibilities.

Well, at least we didn't part in anger. If only Helga could have come to say goodbye.

The locomotive strained to get on its way. The couplings clattered as they took up the slack. Groaning, as if under protest, the iron wheels began to turn slowly.

I leant out of the window. And I saw her, pushing through the crowd. With almost half of my body protruding from the window, I waved my arms through the air and shouted: 'Here, Helga, here. I'm here. Hurry!'

She was running and approaching the end of the platform before she spotted me. It was a hopeless chase. The train kept on moving away from her, slowly at first, then picking up momentum. Yet, despite the distance that yawned between us, I could read her lips. 'I love you!' she shouted.

And I screamed into the noise: 'I love you too! Wait for me, the war will be over soon. I'll be back.'

★　★　★

The Free City of Danzig didn't exactly roll out the red carpet for me. This was perhaps the most exciting day of my life, and the army hadn't even sent a welcoming committee. What an anticlimax!

I wasn't the only recruit-to-be who'd come to Danzig on this beautiful, sunny morning in July. And judging by the weary faces around me, I wasn't the only one who'd spent a sleepless night on a crowded train.

I guess if I had known what I'd let myself in for, I would have put my Hitlerjugend uniform in mothballs and run a thousand miles to where I could never be found. But it was too late for me to back out now.

I learnt a hell of a lot on my first day in the army, and I didn't like any of it. A recruit is just that, a recruit. He has no rights. He has no privileges. He is a nitwit who salutes not only Tom, Dick and Harry but everything that has two legs and walks and resembles a human being or a gorilla. I was so muddled up and mentally disturbed that when I looked into a mirror I saluted my own image. A recruit never ever salutes any living being with a fag dangling from his lips. I tried once, and it cost me twenty-five push-ups. A recruit follows not only blindly but obediently like a dog. He does not show any feelings because he's not allowed to feel anything. A recruit doesn't think. He leaves the thinking to the horses that have bigger heads than his own. He hurries when he's told to hurry. He waits when he is told to wait. When he is forgotten he just stands there and salutes everything that moves until, hopefully, somebody will come along to unforget him.

To sum it up, a recruit is an annoyingly useless thing, a disgrace to the country, a dead loss to Germany, a disgrace to himself, and he should be shovelling shit somewhere else instead of wearing the proud cloth of the army. Yes, sir!

The only bright moment for me on the first horrible day of my army career was when I discovered that there was a window in the dormitory allotted to me and nine of my fellow sufferers. My first bedroom with a window, after so many years of toughing it out in a dark corridor. Hey, life in the army might not be so bad after all.

The quartermaster stocked only two sizes of clothes in his store. For a little fellow like me even the small size was too large. As we queued up for our regulation issue, the man in front of me complained about the sleeves being too long. The corporal in charge grinned at him and handed the complainant a coat of the larger size. 'Nothing wrong with the coat,' he said exaggeratedly. 'It fits. You are just too small for it.'

I couldn't help laughing out loud. But my short burst of Schadenfreude was shattered when my new platoon leader saw me and said: 'Jesus Christ, look at yourself, Weiss. If they put you on a flagpole and sent you to the Russian front, you'd scare hell out of the Russkies. You'd have them running all the way to Siberia.'

It took less than a week for me to lose all my enthusiasm for the Wehrmacht. The prospect of assessing dog taxes for the rest of my living days didn't seem to be such a shit job after all. Perhaps being a soldier wasn't quite as easy as I'd imagined. I couldn't help wondering how much harder it would be to turn into a hero like my father.

Sharing a dormitory with nine other people, aged between seventeen and forty, from all walks of life, was not an easy task. If one of us broke any one of the strict rules, all of us would be punished. The hardships we endured built a bridge across political, social and age differences. The motto 'One for all and all for one' forged us into a unit of comrades.

As much as I appreciated the bond that developed between us, I found it almost impossible to cope with the strict discipline. For seventeen long years my mother had preached to me that I was less than nothing, that I was the black sheep of the family, that the world would have been a better place if I hadn't been born. And now the army dished out the same kind of cruel treatment. Maybe Mutti had been right in the first place when she told me that I wasn't cut out to be a soldier.

In my heart I was still a Hitlerjunge, shouting 'Heil Hitler' to the world — brash, obnoxious and defiant. But in my mind, with my enthusiasm and my dreams of grandeur shrivelling away from day to day, I was a terribly frightened and confused boy of seventeen, a boy who pondered the thought that he might not have time to grow up to be a man before getting himself killed.

Hit the dirt, Weiss! Down, Weiss! Crawl, Weiss! Keep your arse to the ground, you stupid little bastard! — Yes, sir! Jawohl, Herr Gefreiter! Jawohl, Herr Unteroffizier! — You are a soldier, Weiss! You are in the infantry, Weiss! Keep on marching! Soldiers don't get blisters on their feet! Grenade! Take cover, Weiss! Shoot, Weiss, shoot! Pull that damned trigger, Weiss! Shoot! Kill! Fix bayonet, Weiss! See that bale of straw? It's a Bolshevik, Weiss. Kill him, damn you! Kill him! Charge! Kill him with your bayonet, Weiss! That's what a bayonet is for, you stupid idiot. Kill him! Kill, kill, kill!

Jesus Christ, I thought to myself, what the hell am I doing here? Boy, did I want to go home.

Karl de Blanche wanted to go home too. He told us that he came from a respected lineage of French aristocrats. Karl was the odd man out in our little group of ten. He was either a complete nutcase or an extremely clever malingerer who'd set his mind on getting out of the army as soon as humanly possible.

We had some extremely funny and some not so funny experiences, courtesy of M. de Blanche, who loved nothing more in his simple life than chewing big chunks of reeking tobacco, which had stained his teeth and left indelible yellow marks in the corners of his forever moving mouth. One morning at muster time our company commander spotted Karl's mobile mandibles, walked up to him, confronted him and shouted, 'What the hell have you got in your mouth, soldier?'

'Tobacco, sir.'

'Spit it out at once.'

'No, sir. With all due respect, sir . . . '

'I said, spit it out. That's an order!'

Karl took one deep breath, flicked his tongue, and the sticky piece of tobacco came out like a bullet, just missing the officer's ear by the tiniest fraction.

I stood behind Karl on that morning. I heard him whisper into the ear of the comrade next to him, 'I could've plugged him right in the ear if I'd wanted to.'

Karl got a week of kitchen duty out of that. It wasn't punishment for him, he said. He'd rather peel potatoes than run around all day long with half a dozen bricks in his backpack or climb up the flagpole singing

87

'I'm a soldier and I love it'.

Maybe Karl should have stayed in the kitchen for one more day, because the day they let him loose we were scheduled to learn how to throw hand-grenades. The practice grenades didn't have a full charge of explosives in them, but they were still potent enough to kill a man at close range.

We marched for an hour to get to the restricted area used for practice with live ammunition, where we had to observe strict safety measures. The army wanted us to kill a few Russians first before we blew our own brains out.

We assembled about a hundred metres away from a foxhole, where the drill sergeant waited for us as we approached one by one. He took each one of us separately into the foxhole and explained the whole procedure very carefully before handing us a grenade. We had to hold on to the deadly thing for three seconds, then throw it into no-man's land, take cover in the foxhole, and walk back to safety after the grenade exploded. The instructions were precise and easy to comprehend.

Well, that's what all of us thought until Karl de Blanche had better ideas when it was his turn to lower himself into the protective foxhole. Who knows? He might have had trouble counting to three after pulling the pin. What we watched was like a movie running in reverse mode. The drill sergeant came flying out of that foxhole like a rocket and flattened himself on the ground. Karl made it in the nick of time. He just stood there, flabbergasted, innocent, his thumbs buried in his ears, waiting for the hand-grenade to explode. And it did, right inside the safe confines of the foxhole.

Long before the sergeant could catch his breath enough to scream, Karl came ambling back to the rest of us, smiling from ear to ear. 'Told you it would be a piece of cake, didn't I?'

On that very evening we took Karl to the canteen to celebrate. He hated drinking alcohol, so we opened his mouth and poured the shots of brandy down his throat. He didn't even have to swallow. We had sworn to get him drunk so that he would tell us the truth: Was he faking or wasn't he? Was he playing a deadly game? Faking insanity to get out of active service would have earned him a bullet in the head if he'd made the slightest mistake.

Karl just kept on chewing and swallowing and told us nothing at all. When he was too drunk to talk and too drunk to sing, we carted him back to barracks, tied him up in his cotton sleeping bag and dumped him on his cot.

He must have had one hell of a hangover when he woke up the next morning. Considering the ordeal he'd gone through, he was happy and chirpy and fresh as a daisy. He even offered to go to the kitchen to pick up the coffee and the rations for our 'Stube' of ten. How could we have refused such generosity?

After a couple of days we just took it for granted that Karl would get the large can of coffee, butter and jam and whatever else they gave us.

It was hard for us to get back into some kind of morning duty routine after Karl was transferred all of a sudden. Rumour had it that he'd been sent to a mental hospital.

Four weeks later we received a letter from him. He'd been discharged from the army and was back enjoying his civilian life as a stable hand in Strelitz, his home town.

'By the way,' he wrote, 'I hope your coffee tastes a lot better now that I've stopped pissing in it every morning after you took me to the canteen and got me drunk. Enjoy life in the army. Heil Hitler to you all!'

Was there any truth in Karl's letter? Had he really urinated into the coffee we drank? Was he clever? Was he crazy? He was the only one who knew the answers.

Karl de Blanche had beaten the system, and we were the wankers who didn't know any better than to follow orders. We were zombies in the making. Carefully, systematically trained robots, that's what we were. Cannon fodder to be sacrificed at any given time for any given reason, or for no reason at all.

'You are an idiot, Weiss. Repeat!'

'I'm an idiot, sir.'

Humiliation upon humiliation, executed to perfection by the butchers of human spirit.

A whole company — two hundred and twenty grown and half-grown men — standing on a parade ground like battery-operated dummies. 'Do you want to be soldiers?' shouts the lieutenant.

Two hundred and twenty voices shout back, 'Yes, sir!'

'Are you ready to fight to the death for our Führer, our Reich and our people?'

'We are ready, sir!'

★   ★   ★

'Ready for a game of chess?' Rudi would ask every now and then. A couple of years ago I would have ignored Rudi altogether. He was twice my age and he was not a member of the

Party. Perhaps I would have approached him with extreme caution just in case he was a Communist. One never knew with people as quiet as he was. Now we wore the same uniform and slept under the same roof. And both of us had been drinking the same suspect coffee, compliments of Karl de Blanche.

Rudi Krüger was not a volunteer. He was married, had two children, and a career he'd had to leave behind when he was drafted into the army. He was a nice, quiet fellow who minded his own business, wrote to his wife most evenings and played a mean game of chess.

Rudi and I went out to paint the town red when we were let loose for the first time on a Sunday afternoon. Beer and schnapps were still freely available in all the watering holes. And we had saved all our army pay — one Reichsmark a day — a king's ransom for devoted service! Now we were bent on blowing the lot. We had a ten o'clock curfew, but poor old Rudi excused himself much earlier than that.

'Sorry, comrade,' he said, 'I think I've got to throw up. Gotta go, Ollie.'

I couldn't go anywhere at all at that stage. I had a hot, very much alive female sitting in my lap. I had my hands full as well. But the devil called 'curfew' caught up with me sooner than expected. Although it was a tremendous effort to take my eyes off the extraordinary cleavage right under my nose, I managed to check my watch and I knew I'd be in deep shit if I didn't catch the right tram to take me back to the barracks.

I got to the stop just in the nick of time. If I'd missed the nine-thirty I would have had to wait a whole hour for the next one, and I would have broken the curfew and got myself into more trouble than I could cope with.

The rambling, rattling carriage was crowded with soldiers and civilians. I stood in the aisle and the people around me held me upright. I'd had a good night. Everything had gone exceptionally well. But then disaster struck. My bladder was screaming for attention. I am one of those fellows who can't cope with pressure in the waterworks department for very long. If I'd got off the tram to water a tree, the driver wouldn't have waited for me. Besides, I didn't fancy having a hundred-strong cheer squad watching me do a very private thing. After considering my options rather quickly, I pushed my way through the crowd to the back platform, where a few old ladies were chatting about what life used to be like when they were young. I whistled 'Lili Marlene' to cover up my embarrassment. The old ladies smiled at me, and I prayed that my boots wouldn't overflow as I emptied my bladder.

Fifteen minutes later I waddled past the sentry at the gate. It was ten to ten. I'd made it back just in time. Rudi was sitting at the far end of the long table that was the centrepiece of our room. He had a writing pad in front of him and was looking at the pencil in his hand as if it was something from outer space. I knew that he wanted to write to his wife but didn't even know why he was sitting there. However, despite the stupor he was in, his bleary eyes fastened on my rather wet pants.

Anticipating his next question, I defended myself vigorously. 'No, it's not what you think, Rudi, honestly.' A man has got to tell a white lie every now and then. 'That nice blonde girl that sat on my lap all evening,' I said. 'When I told her I had to catch the next tram home, she poured a whole glass of beer all over my pants.'

I mustn't have sounded very convincing, because, as drunk as he was, Rudi grinned at me and said: 'Yeah, Ollie, I know. That's what they all say. Never mind, it's better to piss in your pants than to catch syphilis or crabs or something.'

Before I went to bed, I stuffed my boots with newspaper and hoped that they'd be dry when I woke up in the morning. And they were. Luckily they didn't squeak any more either.

So it was back with our noses to the grindstone again. No rest for the future heroes of the Thousand Year Reich. No rest for the imbeciles of today. As Rudi said so aptly one day: 'Jesus Christ, all of us know that we are in a big, damned zoo. Trouble is, we don't know if we're the monkeys inside the cage, or the people on the outside looking in.'

Maybe we were the monkeys, because we didn't act like human beings any more. We ate like animals because we were treated like animals. We drank like drunkards because we hated to be sober. And we talked about nothing but sex. We didn't talk about politics because we were rather scared to voice an opinion. And we didn't talk about the war because none of us were really all that keen about dying a hero's death.

★　★　★

Army life got pretty boring after we completed our initial training. We waited from day to day for something to happen but nothing ever did. Idleness is the most serious threat to body and mind. The only thing that kept me firmly anchored to sanity were Helga's letters, which arrived regularly twice a week. Mother's letters never reached me in those days of anguish and uncertainty. I guess they were neither written nor posted. Even a game of chess with Rudi was not a challenge any more. Boredom was nagging at me like a cancer that was slowly destroying my brain. I knew that something had to be done to put some kind of meaning back into my life.

5

Apparently, the evening before a convicted murderer is to be hanged, he gets the meal of his choice. A recruit in Adolf Hitler's army, as I knew it, was given two weeks furlough after completion of basic training, before he was sent out to fight and to die in glory or in vain for his much treasured Vaterland.

I couldn't get home fast enough. As soon as I boarded the train my ego began to inflate. By the time I stepped out onto the platform at the railway station in Prenzlau, I was so full of hot air and bullshit that I bounced like a balloon through the small crowd that treated me with undeserved lack of attention. Wasn't I one of the youngest sons of Prenzlau to wear the prized field-grey uniform that made heroes out of nincompoops and snow-white lambs out of black sheep? Hey, Prenzlau! Look at me. Can't you see? Here comes Ollie Weiss.

Thinking of it now, I wondered how for God's sake could a wonderful girl like Helga have fallen in love with a conceited jerk like me.

Anyway, on this November morning in

1941, Helga came running towards me. I spread out my arms and I saw more crystals of love in her glowing eyes than there are stars in the sky on a cloudless midsummer night. Suddenly, with my heart jumping for joy, I was not only the proudest but also the most fortunate human being within the vast and spreading boundaries of the new Thousand Year Reich, the greatest empire ever.

'I love you!' I shouted at the top of my voice. 'I love you, I love you, I love you.'

I'd been somewhat disappointed when I realised that Mutti hadn't come to welcome me home. But now I wasn't any more. Honest to God, I just wanted to drop my kitbag right there and then and make love to the most beautiful girl in the world. And judging by the way she looked back at me, she wouldn't have stopped me either. But sanity prevailed. I was extremely glad that my rather foolish escapade with Brigitte had turned into a major disaster, curtailed by what the specialists call 'premature ejaculation' — or was it 'premature evacuation'? I was as white as a lily, and as pure as the girl I was in love with — well, almost as pure.

I was just about to complain about Mutti's failure to show up at the railway station when Helga said: 'Your mother was very nice, Ollie.

When I talked to her about meeting you at the station, she said: 'By all means, you go. He'd much rather see you first than his mother.' So don't you be angry with her for not rolling out the red carpet for you. She is looking forward to seeing you too. She is not as bad as you make her out to be. Take my word for it.'

On the way home Helga told me that her father had not returned from wherever he'd been taken. Her mother had gone from authority to authority to find out what had happened to him. But as far as the bureaucrats, the Gestapo and the police were concerned, a Baptist preacher called Schneider didn't exist.

We walked home, hand in hand, dreaming the same dreams, thinking the same thoughts.

Prenzlau hadn't changed, of course, since I'd volunteered to turn into a hero. Yet, after having seen a big city like Danzig, my home town seemed to have shrunk a little. But it was still the same beautiful and historical old town.

My mother still looked the same when she opened the door for us. And, may God strike me dead if I lie, she put her arms around me, squeezed me and planted a kiss fair smack on my mouth. 'Welcome home, son,' she said.

I bit my tongue just in time to stop myself

saying, 'I love you too, Mutti.' I should have said it, but I didn't.

Mutti put an arm around each of us and walked us through 'my bedroom' to the kitchen, where the breakfast table was set for three. 'Frederik is not home from work yet. The poor man is working his fingers to the bone, with the shortage of labour and all.'

Mutti served thick omelettes and mustard sauce, one of my favourite meals. 'It's a lot better than the breakfasts we get in the army,' I said, to keep the conversation going.

'Don't speak with a mouthful of food,' she replied, scolding me. 'Don't they teach you any manners in the army?'

I bit my tongue once more and kept on chewing. I knew that I'd rather die than turn out to be as hard and unloving as she was. But the last thing I wanted was an argument with my mother on the dawn of my furlough. Come to think of it now, perhaps that's the last thing my mother wanted as well.

Inquisitive by nature, Mutti wanted to know what life in the army was like — and so did Helga. I talked about Karl de Blanche and all the funny things that happened and didn't happen. I made things up as I went along, and I hoped that neither Helga nor Mutti would get the slightest suspicion that my army life wasn't exactly as I'd expected it to be. I even pulled the wool over Helga's eyes for a couple of days.

I didn't see much of Frederik the Great. Either he was asleep or I was. I stopped hating him because my mother looked a lot happier since he'd taken care of things. Maybe he was handy in more things than replacing blown fuses. But I didn't want to know. It was none of my business, just the same as my Papa was none of his damned business.

On the first Sunday of my leave Helga's mother invited me for dinner. I liked Frau Schneider very much and I liked the two poodles that were part of the Schneider household. They'd do the shopping at the butcher's and the baker's, and I wouldn't have been surprised if they'd had their special seat in the church or chapel or whatever building the Schneiders did their worshipping in. On the other hand, I doubted very much that there was a dogs' heaven right next door to the one for us humans.

Helga was neither a Catholic nor a Jew nor a gypsy. Her parents were as Aryan as I was. Helga's mother looked very distressed. She tried to manage a smile, but the tears just kept on rolling down her cheeks. Helga and I tried our best to cheer her up. After all, both of us were convinced that the preacher's arrest was nothing but an unfortunate mistake. We knew that it was only a matter of time before Herr Schneider would return to his well-respected family.

My future mother-in-law just shook her head, played nervously with the golden wedding band on her finger and said: 'It was no mistake. My husband won't come back. If only half the rumours are true, he might be dead already. I'm sure he wouldn't want us to sit here, moping and crying our hearts out, though.' She wiped the tears from her face with the back of her hand, told us to sit down at the table, and prayed, 'Dear Lord, bless this food . . . ' I felt so helpless. To me it was as clear as daylight that an unfortunate error had been made. My beloved Führer would never dream of harming a good, God-fearing man like Helga's father, especially not if he was one hundred per cent Aryan, just like Hitler himself. I wanted to tell her that she should put her trust in the saviour of Germany, more so than in God. But I had a funny feeling that my hostess could well do without my advice. I shut up and busied myself with the nice meal she'd put in front of me, and obeyed my mother's teaching: Keep your mouth shut while you're eating.

After dinner I thanked Helga's mother for an enjoyable meal and she told me that she was quite happy to have me for a son-in-law. I was flattered. At least one adult in Prenzlau didn't see me as a black sheep.

Buoyed by her confidence in me, I pledged in all sincerity that I would love nothing more than to be part of her family. 'Trust me,' I vowed, 'please trust me. I shall never hurt or harm your daughter in any way. I love her more than my own life.'

Frau Schneider found a bottle of Cognac somewhere and handed it to me to uncork while she went to the kitchen to get some glasses. 'Prosit!' she said. 'May you and my daughter find all the happiness you deserve.'

In response I said: 'There's a war that's got to be won first, Frau Schneider. Your husband will come home soon, and all of us will be happy, you'll see. Our fate is in the Führer's hands. Everything will be all right.' I almost finished my little speech with a heartfelt 'Heil Hitler', because I knew from the bottom of my heart that I spoke the truth. Frau Schneider was such a nice woman that she pretended to agree with me, because she was not going to disillusion me and spoil my holiday.

As far as I could see, she had absolutely nothing to worry about, if she'd only come to grips with the fact that the rise of Adolf Hitler was indeed the second coming of Christ. If somebody had told me right there and then that God was of Aryan, German or even Prussian descent, I would have agreed wholeheartedly.

I really was a conceited bastard. Bragging like the truth had gone out of fashion, I attained celebrity status among ignorant snotnoses, brainwashed Hitler youths and classmates alike during those two weeks of glorious leave; and if ever a young man behaved as though he would soon be the sole saviour of Germany, then I was that man.

Thank God, Helga knew me a lot better than most people. When I was with her I didn't have to pretend, not to her and not to myself. Maybe I didn't know yet what real love was, but I did love her with all my heart. Of that I was certain.

Helga knew that I was simply putting on a big, brave show for the sake of all and sundry, so no one could look past my armour of arrogance and all the grandstanding. She was the only person I was honest with. I made her promise me that she would never reveal the truth to anyone, not even her mother, before I confessed that I was shit-scared and very much confused about the army, the war and all the bloodshed and suffering that was necessary to secure the freedom of Germany. 'I hated to stick a bayonet into a bale of hay,'

I confessed. 'How will I be able to poke it into a human being, even if it's only a Russki? I don't like pulling a trigger at the practice range. I couldn't even shoot a sparrow. How the hell could I kill a real human being? Maybe some people are cut out to be soldiers. I'm sure I'm not.'

Helga was brainwashed too. She said the same thing that Hitler and Göbbels and my drill sergeant tried to make me believe: 'It's a man's duty to fight for his country!' But she didn't say, 'Fight to the death and die like a hero.'

'Keep your head down,' she begged me. 'Don't get yourself killed. I want to marry you, and I can't marry a dead hero.'

★ ★ ★

Later in the evening, Helga came with me to the cemetery to visit the resting place of my very own hero, my father, the man I idolised almost as much as my Führer. We opted for the long way to get there. When we returned, we took a shortcut that led us past Mutti's pride and joy, her garden. The lilac bushes had shed all their foliage and gone into hibernation. The air was still and all the birds had either gone to sleep or migrated to the south. I was almost as close to heaven as I

105

could ever get. Being together like this, walking hand in hand, was what I wanted to do for the rest of my life — feeling close, feeling loved, feeling grateful and happy.

Each spring, for as long as I could remember, Helga and I had played hide and seek among the lush foliage. We'd picked thousands of the white and pink and mauve blossoms and sucked the sweet nectar out of them.

Now our steps slowed. We turned towards each other. Helga came into my arms. There was no need for spoken words. Our heartbeats said it all. Suddenly we were the only two people in the whole world. Nothing would stand in the way of our happiness, nothing and nobody, not even the great war I still had to fight.

I gathered her into my arms. She was the sweetest load I'd ever carried, sweeter than a myriad of scented lilac blossoms, sweeter than the nicest dream. I lifted her across the fence into our garden, then followed her. And the glow of the moon bathed her features in pure silver.

'Oh, my God, how beautiful you are,' I whispered, wishing that time would stand still forever. 'I love you.'

'I love you too,' said Helga.

We were virgins no more. From now on we

would belong together, heart, body and soul, on earth and in eternity. And when the girl I loved more than my own life begged me to make us a child, she made me the proudest man on earth. I screamed in ecstasy: 'Yes, mein Liebling. Yes, yes, yes!'

I forgot that we were still children ourselves. I was seventeen; Helga, just sweet sixteen, was still going to high school. And I still had a war to fight.

The remaining days of my furlough passed all too quickly. Why is it that the happiest days always turn out to be the shortest? Helga and I had so much to talk about, so many plans to make, and so many embraces and aspirations to share. All the time as we built dream castles in the sky we banished the harshness of reality from our intimate and happy world. We were young and we were strong and we were certain we could jump any hurdle that might stand in our path to bliss and everlasting euphoria.

Sure, my mother wouldn't jump over the moon with joy once she found out that Helga was carrying my baby. None of the older generation thought that it was all right for a sixteen-year-old girl to have intercourse, let alone have a child. 'Save yourself for the wedding night.' That's what my mother told me. Sex was a dirty word to her. Sex was disgusting. Could a gold band on a finger make a dirty word squeaky clean?

Anyway, Helga and I didn't *have sex*. *We made love* when we gave ourselves to each other. Even the Führer would give us his blessings, as long as we were both members of the Aryan race. And we most certainly were! We would proudly produce as many pedigreed babies as we possibly could.

It was a bit of a worry to both of us, Helga and I, that many of her school friends had turned away from her since her father's arrest. Well, friends in need are friends indeed. The war would soon be won, and we were strong enough together to face the world.

★ ★ ★

While memories can last forever, holidays don't. The dreaded moment of saying goodbye came much too soon. I travelled back to my garrison with a broad, contented, permanent smile plastered on my face. Three miracles had happened within a short fortnight: Helga and I became lovers; Mutti and I managed to live under the same roof for two whole weeks without a harsh word said by either one of us; and even Frederik, whom I addressed as 'Herr Schuster' just to keep him at a fair distance, hadn't called me 'son' once during the brief moments we were forced to spend together. I'm sure he harboured the same thought as I: If you can't beat him, ignore him. And we both made a splendid job of it.

I certainly found army life much easier to cope with when I returned to Danzig. Helga sent me three letters a week. The radio played my favourite pop song at least once a day: 'I dance with you into heaven, into the seventh heaven of love . . . ' I sang that song every day from sunrise to sunset, and I lost every game of chess I played with Rudi, which didn't worry me at all.

When the first snowflakes tumbled from the sky, I received the one letter I'd been longing for. 'I've missed my period for two months, mein Liebling,' she wrote. 'You can go to the canteen and celebrate our good fortune. We are going to have a baby.'

The very next day, with Rudi and me blurry-eyed and nursing debilitating hangovers, we marched through the cobblestoned streets of grand old Danzig for the last time. Seeing that we were a whole battle-strength battalion of new and well-trained heroes-to-be — and first grade cannon fodder to boot — headquarters spared no expense in bidding us a fitting farewell. The big brass band, playing the Radetzki March and everything else short of the National Anthem, led the way to the railway yards, where a smoke-belching locomotive shunted an assembly of goods wagons from track to track.

After a final roll-call, just to make sure that none of us had slipped away into the sewers or hidden in the brothels of Danzig, we climbed aboard, fifty to a wagon, no more, no less. The band played 'Muss i' denn zum Städtele hinaus?', which was the favourite farewell song in Germany until a fellow by the name of Elvis Presley came along and butchered the lyrics. None of us had a 'Wooden Heart' when the train began to move. Our hearts were right up in our throats, racing like crazy, as our journey to the unknown began.

As for my own feelings, and palpitations, I couldn't help thinking that fat cattle were taken to slaughterhouses all over Germany in the same type of wagons. It wasn't a thought I relished. I was glad that none of my comrades could see the shivers that ran down my spine.

God works in His own mysterious ways, and so did Hitler's army. I'm quite sure that God had nothing at all to do with mapping out our lengthy journey. It was common knowledge among us that we would be sent to the battlefront in the east. Yet our engine driver took us due west right across the top of Germany, pausing every now and then to add another few wagons to the train. A week after we left our garrison near the Polish border, we gazed in disbelief at the tall steel structure of the Eiffel Tower. But we didn't quite make it all the way into Paris. We were shunted from track to track as if our locomotive couldn't make up its mind where to let us set foot on French soil for the first time.

With the permission to leave our carriages and to stretch our legs on the platform came strict orders forbidding us to stray from the vicinity of the station. Of course, orders are given to be broken. A few adventurers simply couldn't resist the temptation of exploring a bit more of France than the strange-looking pissoirs on the platform.

Two hours later, with all our valiant explorers safely aboard, our train did a big loop and then headed back towards Germany again. With the kerosene lanterns swinging from side to side from the curved carriage roof, I entered a whole new phase of totally despicable sex education. I had known for a long time, of course, that French letters were not the kind of missive one would proudly send to his parents. And, thanks to Helga, I

111

knew now how to make a baby. It was only when I was invited to play a game of cards that I realised how little I knew about sex.

Fifty-two cards, all of them portraying fornicating men and women, black, white and brindle, in seemingly impossible positions on each of the glossy cards — filthy, obscene, disgusting, despicable, deplorable, detestable, vile, lewd and very, very interesting. Despite one or two horrid if unfruitful experiences I'd had in Danzig's red-light district, my curiosity was still very much alive.

Who is the imbecile who claims that all a man needs is a roof over his head, three square meals a day and a wife to keep him warm? And who is the wise guy who claims that variety is the spice of life?

Our rattling train kept on rattling along the rails for a whole week more, finally crossing into Poland and disgorging its volatile cargo in the drab-looking, deserted railway station of Cracow.

Many of us were still bursting at the seams with curiosity when we marched, burdened with backpack, rifle and sundry war equipment, through the streets of a beaten nation. I was once again on a spirit-raising ego trip. Reliving the proud days of Jungvolk and Hitlerjugend, I conveniently forgot that in those times I actually was someone to be counted, while now, dressed in field-grey, I was nothing but a paltry and insignificant arsehole.

I experienced true euphoria as I walked as a victor through enemy country. I had indeed come a long way since I'd stood by the roadside and cheered our victorious soldiers on their return from the Polish battlefields. I reckon I strutted along like a peacock on heat.

The handful of onlookers obviously didn't share my feelings of elation and exhilaration. Eventually the Poles, together with countless other nations, would all become part of the emerging Thousand Year Reich. They didn't know how lucky they were.

Before dismissing us to our new quarters, our CO laid down the rules for us in plain language.

Do not fraternise with the enemy.

Never leave the barracks on your own.

German soldiers don't rape women, not even Polish scum.

If a pretty girl on the street invites you to screw her, don't. If you're lucky she'll give you VD. If you're unlucky she'll bury a knife in your back.

Don't take unnecessary risks. Sex in enemy territory is hazardous. That's why the army provides a brothel for you. All the whores are young, pretty and under doctors' supervision.

Is that understood?

Dismissed!

It took me a couple of days to say fluently: 'Hotch, hotch, Panienka, alle ya nie mam pinienze', or something like that, which was Polish for 'Come on, girl, but I haven't got any money'.

It took one more day for the ever so reliable Feldpost to deliver half a dozen letters from Helga to me. After reading her letters it took me a mere second to decide that I would be the last person on earth to say to any girl but Helga: 'Hotch, hotch, Panienka.' Maybe my slow process of growing up had just begun.

But there were still a hell of a lot of things that didn't make any sense at all to me. Like why a whole battalion of unblooded heroes-to-be was wasted and apparently forgotten for the rest of the winter. While most of us pretended to be ready for the ultimate sacrifice, hoping that the opportunity would never arise, we were given the arduous task of protecting a huge motor-pool, something like a vast second-hand car lot with nobody interested in buying and no one wanting to go for a test drive. Two hours on, four hours off, and the seventh day set aside for copulating or whatever else one fancied.

Oh, Jesus Christ, was it any wonder that the unfortunate conscripted whores of Cracow were working overtime?

Unlike others who made a habit of screwing everything that wasn't nailed down, Rudi remained faithful to his wife and his children. 'I don't want to wake up one morning, look in the mirror and hate the face that looks back at me, Ollie. If I lose my life in the war it's tough luck and I can't do a thing about it. If I lose my self-respect I'd be ratshit. And I can do something about that!'

I felt the same way. That's why Rudi and I became better friends. We sat side by side writing letters to our loved ones, or we faced each other across a chessboard. The only arguments we had were about my being too obstinate to realise that Helga and I were much too young to have a baby.

'It's all right for you,' he kept on telling me. 'Nobody gives a shit about you here in the army anyway. But how about your girlfriend? She's just turned seventeen, unmarried and pregnant. You know what people are like, especially in a small place like your home town. They'll crucify the poor girl. And if they don't, then Hitler's mob will give her hell. Don't you realise that you've got the law and the whole flaming hypocritical society against you?'

The only thing I could say for myself in defence was that Helga wanted us to have a baby. 'And so did I,' I said. 'Is it so bad if two people love each other and have a baby? Isn't that what life is all about? What's wrong with evolution, Rudi?'

At some stage, sooner or later, Rudi would just point at the chessboard, shrug his shoulders and say, 'It's your move and your funeral, Kamerad.'

In April, when the snow began to melt and the rays of the sun lost their winter chill, Helga wrote saying that she'd been kicked out of school and the BDM, Hitler's League of German Girls. 'I'm at my wit's end,' she wrote. 'I wish you were here. I don't know what to do. I love you always.'

I took the letter straightaway to my company commander and asked for compassionate leave, which was refused. I felt like walking out of the barracks to go AWL and hitching a ride all the way back to Prenzlau.

'Forget it,' said Rudi, before I opened my mouth. 'They'd catch you before you crossed the border.'

A week later our whole battalion went on red alert. The spring offensive in Russia had begun and, caught by surprise and by the might of the German army, the Russians were on the run like frightened rabbits. A few days before we climbed aboard the troop train that would take us to the faraway eastern front, we assembled one last time on the parade ground for the fortnightly Schwanzparade. What a spectacle we must have presented for any pervert who had a chance of spying on us from a vantage point nearby. There we stood at attention, side by side, row upon row, with our flies wide open for the usual doctor's examination. Drooping doodles acceptable; dripping doodles fall out to the right! There we were, the whole battalion at its most vulnerable moment! A pull here, a squeeze there, a few anxious moments for some, and it was all over and done with. Dismissed!

6

Hey, Papa, watch me. Your only son is on his way to experience all of those fascinating stories you told him so many years ago!

Forgotten is the stringent training in Danzig; forgotten is the drudgery of Cracow.

Hey, Helga, my sweetheart, watch me. Your husband-to-be is bravely marching on the winding path to glory. I'm adrift in an ocean of pride and ambition and adoration for the Leader who is going to make a real man out of a boy.

Heil Hitler, mein Führer. I salute you. Sieg Heil to Germany and the Thousand Year Reich!

The goods train is on the roll again. And this time it is moving in the right direction. The fight for Lebensraum — space to live — is well and truly on now. The East was German and the East shall be German again. That's what we had been taught in school in those days when we studied the English language and read the *London Times*.

My dreams are coming true. The Russians are running, Papa. Soon I'll be in hot pursuit. Surely they won't surrender before I have a chance to prove that I am a brave warrior. How I wish that you were here with me right now. You'd be so proud of your son, so bloody proud.

My heart is dancing pirouettes, my brain is doing somersaults. I am bursting with pride and excitement. All of us are positively jubilant. The Russians are in full flight, the result a foregone conclusion. The war is almost won. Helga, beloved future mother of my future son, it won't be long now. Not long before the final battle is won.

The straw that was spread across the floor of our rattling, clattering wagon turned blood-red as the sun rose. I filled my lungs with fresh air, and I rejoiced and sang together with my comrades an old cavalry song, 'Morgenrot': 'Red sunrise, red sunrise, you shine for my imminent death. Today I shall hear the sound of trumpets, and I shall die, I and many of my comrades . . . ' An old army song, fit for the occasion. Bullshit! Who is insane enough to think about dying? I wasn't, that was for sure. As long as my water flask was refilled with brandy, I felt alive and vibrant and exquisitely euphoric. I failed to notice that my heart beat faster with every kilometre we travelled.

Not all of us were as eager as I was to get involved in the ultimate fight for the freedom of Germany. My old pal Rudi was one of those who showed a complete lack of enthusiasm. He sat in a quiet corner and wrote to his wife, page after page after page. Some of the 'oldies' did not show any emotions at all. They stared into thin air and kept their thoughts to themselves. But most of us had an absolute ball from one liquor ration to the next.

For the first three days and nights we were ecstatic.

During the early hours of the fourth night we could hear a faint, rumbling sound above the noise of our train, a noise like continuously rolling thunder. Sliding the doors of our 'roving hotel' open, we could see flashes of light shoot up from the horizon, illuminating the distant sky in a pattern of chaotic irregularity. Sleep didn't come easily that night. The incessant rumbling continued. It grew louder by the hour, louder and louder until it made me tremble with fear. Before the sun rose again, the rhapsody of war sounded more like a funeral march than a comforting cradlesong. The lightning that wasn't lightning at all looked both bizarre and fascinating at the same time. For a brief moment I had the distinct feeling that I was riding on the wrong train, for the wrong reasons, at the wrong time.

Our slow journey to hell continued, interrupted only by short breaks to collect our daily rations. Even in the very middle of nowhere the next meal was never far away. As the clamour of war moved closer and closer, I felt less and less hungry. Our laughs weren't laughs any more and our eyes lost the lustre of enthusiasm. Our throats dried up and so did our cheerful singing.

Somebody suggested that we should forget about the war and play a game of poker instead, just to chase the worries away, so to speak. I didn't need a second invitation. I was quite sure that I wouldn't need any money at all where I was going. 'Count me in,' I said, reaching for my wallet.

I had an ace dealt for the first card. But, alas, before I could make a bet, all hell broke loose. Angrily screaming bullets ripped through the heavy timber walls of our wagon, tearing gaping holes in our mobile home. All of a sudden the air was filled with the ack-ack of guns and the howling, whistling sound of aircraft engines. I sat frozen to the floor, waiting either for death or for the dealer to turn up another card for me. I sat there like a damned zombie, until somebody yelled out: 'Air-raid! Air-raid! Let's get the hell out of here. Air-raid! Stop the bloody train, you stupid bastards!'

And the train stopped. We ripped both of our doors open. We could have ripped the whole blasted carriage apart. We spilled into the fields. Trees, where are you? Ditch, where are you? Courage, where are you?!

Damn it, I thought, I've got to get out of here. Away from the easy target on the rails. Away from a certain massacre. I hadn't had time to turn into a hero yet! Give me a break, you Bolshevik murderers. Gimme a break.

Oh my God, is this for real? Run, run, run, Ollie Weiss. Trees are not very far away. Run, Ollie, run. Another fifty metres. Stop shooting at me, you stupid idiots. Run, Ollie, run!

I ran faster than a hare running from a fox, zigzagging across whatever my fleeting feet came to touch. Planes droning like angry hornets. Coming for me. Gunning for me. Trees, damn you, why are you so far away?

Another ten metres. Will I make it? I do! And I hug the tree like nobody on this whole crazy world of ours has hugged anything ever. I hear the bullets smash into the tree, and a sudden rush of insanity makes me laugh like crazy. My bladder empties in a sudden rush, and I don't give a damn. I go on hugging that tree as if it is my long-lost grandmother. I'm shaking and praying and cursing, all at the same time. My whole system is completely out of control until the droning noise of

Russian aircraft engines dissipates in the distance.

The shrill whistle of the locomotive brought me back to reality — or I should say *from* reality.

'All aboard! All aboard!'

Our wagon was an absolute mess. Holes in the walls, holes in the roof, holes in the floorboards. And a hole as large as a Ferris wheel shot right through the centre of my inflated ego.

When the shock wore off a little, and I was capable of controlling my thoughts again, I recalled the days of my early childhood. I saw myself sitting next to my father, listening to his fascinating stories about *his* Great War, as I watched the smoke drift from his cigar towards the window.

Perhaps Papa's war had been more glamorous than mine. Because, boy oh boy, the war I was getting myself into was most certainly nothing to write home about.

A few hours later our train reached the end of the journey. We couldn't get out of the wagons fast enough. Loud voices pierced the air. 'Raus! Raus! Schnell! Schnell!'

We spilled into an emptiness that was alive with the sounds of death. A single rifle shot now, then a burst of machine-gun fire; here the soft thuds as mortar shells left the barrels, there the screaming screech of artillery shells, splitting the air in search of victims and exploding somewhere in the distance.

A convoy of trucks, their canvas canopies aflutter in the breeze, now came towards us, spreading a cloud of dust into the air. They came at breakneck speed from the direction of the front line, bumping and jumping and swerving like fugitives from hell.

'Welcome to paradise,' said a grimy-looking corporal, inviting a small group of us to join him for the ride of our life — or death, or worse. He stood facing us, his back braced against the truck's cabin. The white in his eyes was accentuated by the crusted dirt that covered his face. I have forgotten a lot of things in my life, but I can see his face and hear his words as clearly today as many years ago.

'Welcome aboard,' he grinned, after telling the driver to get going. 'I'm Corporal Schmidt. If you survive the first two weeks out here feel free to call me Oskar. Most of you won't live that long. Hitler might have sent you here to die as heroes, but dead heroes ain't no good to us. So try to stay alive. Stick to the ground, the closer the better. It's the safest place to be. Whatever you do, don't forget that the fellows on the other side use live ammunition too. They'd rather kill you today than tomorrow. If you're in a foxhole and you have to shit during the day, don't forget that the enemy is only three hundred metres away. A Russian sniper can shoot your balls off at twice that distance. Shit on your spade instead. You might live long enough to get the hang of it.'

His speech was suddenly interrupted by a series of loud explosions. All of us, whether standing, sitting or crouching, dived to the floor for shelter. The only one still on his feet was a very amused Corporal Schmidt. The corners of his mouth almost reached his ears.

'I was just about to tell you that we are getting close to our own artillery positions. You can get up again if you like. The big guns are just giving us a bit of support. Relax, we're almost at home.'

Relax? My fears and anxieties were playing Russian roulette with my brain, my bowels, my bladder and God only knows what else. And here was a man with a dirty face telling me to relax? I was scared stiff. It certainly wouldn't be easy to live up to my Papa's standards.

The rest of the trucks had gone off in different directions. We were on our own now. The driver slowed the engine down to just above idling speed. A few minutes later we stopped in a little hamlet — if you could call it that. Just half a dozen cottages built with mud bricks, none with a roof, none with a single pane of glass left in the gaping windows.

Corporal Schmidt put his finger to his lips. 'Quiet,' he whispered. 'As quiet as you can. The Russkies have good ears. You don't want to die with an empty stomach, do you?'

The air was getting damp. Dusk settled around us, giving us a false sense of safety. But it wasn't too dark to see the cook wave his ladle. There was no entree, no sweets, no fruit and finger bowls. Just cabbage soup with big chunks of meat and too many caraway seeds, plus rations for the following day. All I needed was a tummy full of brandy.

Huddled together like a mob of frightened sheep in the corner of a mustering yard, with a wayward artillery shell exploding too close for comfort from time to time, I tried to concentrate on Helga and lilac blossoms and the new life that was growing inside her womb, but I couldn't concentrate at all. How could I? The only music in the air came from lethal shrapnel. I didn't sleep well at all.

Under the cover of dawn, we moved tentatively and cautiously towards the strung-out line of foxholes just below the crest of a gently rising slope. The Russians must have still been fast asleep. My heart beat so loudly,

I was worried that I'd wake them up.

While the lull lasted, the new and the old were shuffled and blended together; one experienced warrior and one apprentice hero to each grave-like foxhole.

Two hours later, the first angry bullet whistled past my ear. I flinched. I didn't like the sound one little bit.

'Don't worry, Kamerad,' said the warrior I shared my new lodgings with. 'If you hear them they've missed you already. And if you don't hear them you don't worry about them. You got a name?'

'Ja, I've got a name. My friends call me . . . '

A shell exploded close to us with one hell of a bang, showering us in our foxhole with half the Russian landscape. It took me a full five minutes before I remembered my name and then I said, 'I'm Ollie Weiss, I think.'

During the following three days of being stuck in a foxhole, and three nights of sneaking back to headquarters to fetch food and ammunition, I didn't know whether I was coming or going. What had happened to the much talked about spring offensive? If the Russians were in full flight, they were certainly not fleeing from us. They'd dug in, and they weren't thinking of budging. Was someone not telling us the truth?

I guess I did learn a lot in those first days of my personal war effort. I found out how valuable every minute of life really is, how to enjoy each draw on a cigarette as if it were my last, and how delightful it was to just take one single breath. I learnt about sleeping in the middle of hell and, waking up, thinking I was dead when I wasn't. In just three miserable, tense and horrible days I grew ten years older. And I hadn't even killed one single man.

At noon on the fourth day a message was passed from foxhole to foxhole: 'Get ready for attack at 1500 hours.' The Russkies had given us hell with some very deadly and accurate Stalin-organ fire from those multi-barrelled mortars of theirs. Our officers in charge decided that we had been sitting ducks for long enough. The time for action had come.

Fritz, my foxhole partner, was an old hand at the game of war. He knew all there was to know. I suppose that without his unbelievable calmness and his encouragement I wouldn't have had the guts to leave the confines of our small shelter.

Fritz hardly said more than one small sentence at a time. I didn't know his family name. I didn't know whether he was married or single. And yet his guidance stopped me from going mad during the first days of my war. Fritz became my friend, though I didn't know him at all.

1245. A little more than two hours before we had to leap out of our shelters. Time slips by so quickly when it is most needed — so quickly and yet so excruciatingly slow.

Fritz reached for his canteen, his Feldflasche, and unscrewed the top. He sipped his drink slowly. 'What's in your bottle?' he asked quietly. 'Coffee, water or brandy?'

'Brandy,' I answered. 'Want a mouthful?'

'No,' he said with a smile of wisdom. 'You drink it. You'll need every drop of it for yourself.'

I was too scared to get drunk and much too frightened to remain sober. 'I'll be drunk before I finish it all, Kamerad. I think I'll settle for a mouthful every now and then.'

Fritz disagreed with me. 'Drink it, damn you, drink it! You'll go round the bend in the next two hours if you don't.'

The neat brandy scorched my inside.

'That's the boy,' Fritz encouraged me. 'It's only the first few gulps that burn. The rest will go down easy. Just make sure you've got one good mouthful left at 1500.'

By 1330 I was fairly tipsy. There was still a lot left in my flask.

'Drink it,' said my comrade.

'I'll be sick!'

'That's better than being dead.'

1400. The dial of my watch played nasty tricks with me. What is time anyway? How long does an hour last? One puff on a cigarette?

1445. Fritz began to curse softly. He delivered the longest speech I'd heard him make. 'That mad major is doing it again,' he said, agitated and very irate. 'The fuckin' bastard just can't help himself, can he? We should have artillery and air support by now. The Russkies are going to slaughter us. The rotter Schweinehund doesn't give a shit about us. Herr Major wants the Knight's Cross, come hell or high water. I can just hear him bragging: 'My soldiers don't need any support! We can do it all by ourselves!' I'm telling you, Ollie, if I live long enough to draw a bead on that bastard, I'll put a bullet right between his eyes, and that's a promise.'

1455. My hands were shaking so much, I had trouble fixing my bayonet to the barrel of my rifle. The longest five minutes of my life began. I drank the brandy to the very last drop, and craved more.

The dreaded 'Auf! Marsch! Marsch! Hurrah! Hurrah!' reverberated from foxhole to foxhole. I couldn't move my legs. I wanted nothing more than to crawl all the way back into my mother's womb. I wished

I'd never been born.

'Come on, Kamerad,' said Fritz, 'I've been in worse shit than this and come out alive. Stay with me, I've got nine lives like a cat. Let's go. You'll be all right.'

But I wasn't all right at all. Far from it. I was frightened and confused. Shouldn't I be running? Shouldn't everybody be running? Why didn't they? Why wasn't Fritz shouting 'hurrah'? Why wasn't I? This was nothing like our basic training in Danzig, when we'd stormed towards a few bales of hay, screaming like nitwits.

We moved stealthily and ever so painfully slowly towards the top of the ridge, hoping for miracles and expecting hell. I looked at my gleaming bayonet. What would it be like to kill a man? What would it be like to die? Would my soul go to heaven or to hell? I was supposed to be drunk, wasn't I? How come I was stone cold sober? Jesus Christ! Blonde hair, blue eyes and lilac blossom, where are you? I must have been crazy to volunteer. I don't belong here. I should be sitting behind the calculator at the council office in Prenzlau, totalling dog taxes. I want to go home!

We made it to the top of the ridge. The Russians knew we were coming. They were waiting for us. If I'd thought that I'd been in hell for the previous few days, then this was hell a hundred times over. Their machine-guns opened up first. Then shrapnel from Stalin-organ, mortar and artillery shells came screaming and whistling at us all at once.

'Hit the deck! Get down!'

I flattened my body against the ground. I scratched a little hole into the hard, crusted soil — a dent hardly big enough to bury my face in. I let go of my rifle and stuck my thumbs into my ears. I didn't want to hear anything. I didn't want to see anything. Was I dead already? This was total insanity. Explosion after explosion sent tremors through the earth and shook my body. Time and again I was lifted off the ground. Goodbye, Helga! Goodbye, world!

It lasted for two hours, two endless hours of sheer hell; one hundred and twenty minutes of dying every second.

Papa, oh my Papa, why didn't you tell me the truth?

Was I still alive when our Stukas finally came in, dive-bombing, their engines howling like a thousand sirens, swooping and diving again? With the Stukas came the Messer-schmitts, flying low, buzzards with keen eyes, ready to claim their prey, firing from all barrels. In a matter of minutes all the Russian guns fell silent, one after another, until there was nothing but the droning noise of our Messerschmitts.

'Are you all right, Ollie?' Fritz's voice was faint. It seemed to come from far, far away. 'Are you all right?'

I was dead, wasn't I? We were all dead, all dead.

'Hey, Ollie!' The same voice again. Were both of us in heaven or in hell? I tried to speak and I couldn't at first. Dead people don't talk, do they? I tried again, and my lips moved. 'What did you say? Is that you, Fritz? I can barely hear you, speak up!' Thank God, I still had a voice.

'If you take your thumbs out of your ears your hearing might improve,' said Fritz. 'You aren't dead yet, Ollie. Did you get hurt?'

Still in a daze, I felt myself all over. My hands came up clean. No blood oozing out of strange places. Obviously I still had both my arms and legs. I got to my feet slowly. I was shaking terribly. My vision was blurred. My eyes were full of dirt.

Fritz stood close to me, brushing the dust from his uniform. 'Hey, Kamerad,' he said cheerfully. 'Relax, you're not dead and neither am I. I told you I was lucky.'

'I think I shat myself,' I mumbled, embarrassed, expecting Fritz to laugh at me.

He didn't. He simply said: 'Don't worry about it. You're not the first one it's happened to and you certainly won't be the last either.'

An armoured personnel carrier came towards us from the direction of our headquarters. As it got closer I could see an officer standing up, waving his machine-pistol in the air, bellowing at us: 'Charge, you cowards! Charge!'

I turned reluctantly, following orders automatically, just like the zombie I was supposed to be.

'Don't you dare,' said Fritz, grabbing me by the elbow and turning me round again. 'Ignore the bastard. We've had enough for one day. He'll soon get sick of shooting his mouth off.'

The mad major ought to have realised by then that the Knight's Cross had gone begging for yet another time, but he wasn't ready to give up easily. He aimed his gun at the sky, fired a few rounds and yelled: 'I am ordering you to attack! This is an order from your commanding officer!'

Perhaps he didn't use exactly those words, but he certainly meant what he said. And just to show us that he meant what he said, he lowered his weapon and sprayed our position with bullets.

It took me a fraction of a second to drop to

the ground. A few rifle shots rang out, followed by a short burst from a machine-gun. This was crazy. We were supposed to kill the Russians and not each other. The shooting stopped. I got up on my feet again. The personnel carrier had already turned and disappeared in a cloud of dust, carrying an over-ambitious and very dead major back towards headquarters, to a cosy and quiet spot, where they would dig a nice comfortable grave for him and have the chaplain give him a true hero's funeral.

And I used my Feldspaten for the first time. The small but useful spade was meant to dig foxholes. Now I used it to dig shallow graves for our fallen comrades, who'd died for nothing but the appalling vanity of an aspiring officer who deserved a wooden cross more than the medal he craved.

Our dead comrades got no crosses at all. All they got was their rifles pushed upside down into the ground with their helmets on top.

At dawn the next morning, our Panzer Corps arrived with their Tiger tanks. This time we crossed the ridge without a single shot being fired. All we found of the Russians was wreckage and the dead they'd left behind.

I guess that from that day on I turned into

a soldier in some way. After burying so many of my own comrades it got a lot easier to pull the trigger in revenge for those who hadn't survived to see another day. Perhaps being a soldier has nothing at all to do with saying 'Yes sir!', obeying orders, or even fighting for the Führer and the Third Reich, as I pretended to do. Maybe the politicians all over the world have known it all along. 'An eye for an eye. A tooth for a tooth.' So says the Bible.

'Slay my friend and I shall slay ten of your ilk,' says the lamb as it turns into a lion.

And so, humanity turns against itself, trying to root out the evil among us. We destroy each other, not for high ideals and principles but for the simple fact that a friend has had his head blown off.

But of course Private Ollie Weiss, unlikely hero-to-be, didn't have a rational thought inside his thoroughly brainwashed and indoctrinated head. My bayonet was still as clean as a whistle and, if I'd killed somebody already, it would have only been a Russian son of a bitch, who didn't deserve to live anyway.

Our war turned into a game of 'catch as catch can'. Now we really had the Russkies on the run. They ran so fast, we couldn't keep up with them. Heil Hitler to you, you bastards! We'll catch up with you, sooner or later.

Every now and then the enemy would make some haphazard effort to resist our advances. It wasn't only outright nasty of them to hit us with a well-aimed volley of Stalin-organ fire just after we'd collected a special serving of meatballs and mashed potatoes — sending the meatballs into space as if they were unguided missiles. I could have forgiven them for that. But to spice Fritz's legs with a more than ample serving of shrapnel was something unforgivable. He was still too much in shock when we lifted him carefully onto a stretcher. He managed a wry smile. 'Don't save any meatballs for me,' he said. 'Take care of yourself, Ollie. Don't try to be a hero, it doesn't suit you at all. I'll see you after the war, ja?'

'Sure, Fritz, don't worry about me. Have a safe trip home.' There were lots of things I wanted to tell him, things like how I'd appreciated his guidance, how I'd valued his friendship. But I couldn't spit the words out.

I shook his hand and turned to one of the stretcher bearers. 'Look after him,' I said, trying to keep the tears from flowing. 'Look after him. He's my friend!' And I watched them take him away.

* * *

Without Fritz I felt more vulnerable than ever before. I was cranky with the world and I was cranky with myself. I was downright furious with the Feldpost, because there hadn't been a letter from Helga for weeks. Well, no news is good news, so people say. Perhaps we were just advancing too quickly and the mail service couldn't keep up with us.

Most nights we camped on or beneath the trucks that carried us further and further away from home. If we were lucky, we could sleep with a roof over our heads in cosily heated mud houses. Most of the Ukrainian village people didn't seem to mind sharing their humble abodes with us. They would bed down where they normally slept in cold weather — on top of their huge ovens, which were used for cooking and for heating as well. We would sleep on the mud floors. We made a rule of paying for their hospitality with chocolates, cigarettes and cans of food. In return they gave us more lice than we could cope with. Some of the older folk spoke a little German. None of them were happy with the regime that had been forced on them. And most of them loathed the loudspeakers that were installed in every home; loudspeakers without buttons to turn them off, lower the volume or change the station; loudspeakers, untouchable, bringing the gospel of Communism into each home against their wishes. I met many old Ukrainians who told me in heavily accented German: 'Hitler good man. Stalin niet good. You go kill Stalin. Heil Hitler!'

On some occasions the Ukrainians, who treated us well, were not so well treated by their own compatriots. Early one morning we were roused from our sleep before dawn. Our reconnaissance patrol had returned with bad news. The Russkies had brought in massive reinforcements during the night, and a lot of T-34 tanks had been shifted close to the front line. That would spell trouble with a capital T.

Avoiding even a cough or a sneeze, we moved stealthily out from the little hamlet and away from its friendly people. Our trucks had to stay behind for the time being. We'd only moved a hundred metres when the Russian orchestra struck up with the overture. We responded instantly by turning the lights on. Our flares dangled from the firmament like huge candles on a giant Christmas tree, turning dawn into daylight.

Nobody had to tell me what to do next. I started digging feverishly. I dug as if my life depended on a shallow hole in the ground — and most likely it did. I swear that I would have won a gold medal at the Olympics if they'd included hole-digging as a competitive sport.

Tanks, artillery, Stalin-organs and mortars all opened up together. The shells zoomed in on the hamlet behind us, razing it from the face of the earth, sparing no one. Despite all the shooting, my spade never missed a beat. I'd be the first man in history to dig his own way to the centre of the earth! I could have dug holes standing on my head.

The sun rose from the horizon in vivid red, competing against the silvery glow of our flares. Sunrise bright, sunrise red, shine for me until I'm dead . . .

Out of the sun they came. Hundreds of them; thousands of them. Their tanks up front — steel monsters with fruit boxes for seats and with lethal guns poking out from the turrets.

They came like a giant steamroller. Wave after wave, running over their dead comrades. Still coming, like a king tide. No stopping them with a few hand-grenades. Reload, shoot, reload, shoot. Somebody help me, please!

The first T-34 blows up in a ball of flame and thunder. Then another. Our own Tiger tanks are coming up fast, firing over the top of us. Hey, that was too short!

From somewhere behind us twenty-milli-metre double-barrelled anti-aircraft guns start barking. We are caught in the crossfire. Einundzwanzig, zweiundzwanzig, kill, kill, kill.

The Lord giveth and the Lord taketh away. What a load of balderdash that is. What a heap of crap. The Lord doth nothing but taketh away, damn it all.

What the hell do You giveth us, Lord? Give us life so we can die? What kind of a cruel game are you playing with us, Lord? With us and with the Russkies? Look at them all, dying in droves. You are their God too, aren't You? Well, aren't You? Some day someone will hold You responsible for all this. Pray and peace shall enter your heart? Like hell it will, God. Like hell it will!

My right hand was covered with blood. The back of the hand looked like a cauliflower gone to seed. A piece of shrapnel had ripped across it and I hadn't felt a thing. But now, after seeing the damage, my nerves reacted and I winced.

My hand was bleeding a lot when I got out of the ambulance at the field hospital. But I was lucky. I could still walk into the large tent, where doctors worked feverishly, trying to stop casualties from turning into corpses. I stood in line and waited. I had all the time in the world. I was not among the emergencies.

Two doctors stood looking at one of the stretcher cases. One said to the other: 'If we can push his guts back into his belly and sew him up, the poor bugger might have a fifty-fifty chance. What do you say?'

'I say let's give it a go.'

Rubber-gloved hands struggled to push the quivering, slithering mess back into the cavity where it belonged. Catgut and needle did the rest.

'Who's next?'

My face turned green. I felt violently ill, and the pain in my hand was very tolerable all of a sudden.

My injury wasn't half as bad as it looked. 'You are very lucky,' said the doctor who examined my hand. 'You'll get two or three weeks holiday out of that.'

My heart jumped into my throat. Prenzlau, here we come! Helga, get the wedding dress ready. 'I'm going home?' I stuttered. I couldn't believe my luck.

The medic shook his head. 'Not quite,' he chuckled. 'We'll send you a bit further back to a proper hospital, where they've got pretty nurses, plenty of hot water and white sheets on the beds. That's not too bad for now, is it?'

'I guess it isn't,' I replied, not trying to hide

my disappointment. 'Maybe I'll be luckier next time.'

'Don't get too lucky,' advised the doctor, as he turned to the next patient and left me pondering my fate.

7

Swept along inside a huge tidal wave of destruction, death and fear, which devastated almost all of the Ukrainian territory, I'd been reduced to little more than a dirty field-grey streak that connected a steel helmet with a pair of filthy, smelly jackboots. I had almost forgotten what it was like to live like a human being. Suddenly and unexpectedly, I found myself showered and clean-shaven, deloused and disinfected inside the sterile environs of a hospital at least eighty kilometres behind the front line. My wounded hand was resting peacefully inside a plaster cast but I twisted and turned restlessly between the crisp white sheets of my bed. Hadn't I always dreamed of a bedroom with windows? I was living like a king. So were the twenty-something wounded, maimed and mutilated comrades who shared the ward with me. There was even glass in the window frames to keep the cold autumn winds out and the warm gastric winds in.

I poked my clean feet out from under the sheet and wriggled my toes, and I was so happy to see that all those digits of mine were still coordinating with the rest of me, for I hadn't laid eyes on them for perhaps a month or longer.

The thumbnail on my left hand was still stained with dried blood after the purging process I'd been subjected to. My right thumb languished under the plaster cast. I panicked a little. After months of practice I'd become an expert louse-killer. I'd come to enjoy that crisp, crackling noise of revenge when I squashed their lives and my blood out of their creepy-crawly bodies, time permitting of course. Could I become a one-handed louse-killer? Or would I have to keep a brick or a piece of four-by-two under my bed?

Maybe I should have kept a piece of timber handy for other reasons as well. I can't have been mortally wounded, because each time a nurse bent over me to put a thermometer under my tongue, my very own and embarrassingly independent thermometer rose higher than the snow-capped peaks of Mount Everest. You want to ask me if those nurses were shaped like sirens with faces like angels and a figure like Jane Russell's? Well, my friend, when you are eighteen innocent years old, and you've been living in holes like a rabbit, eaten by lice, shot at by unknowns, stinking like death warmed up and waiting desperately from day to day for a letter from the girl you love — a letter that never comes — you'd have sex with the sister of the hunchback of Notre Dame, if she'd let you indulge.

Such are the trials and tribulations of war.

You never know how much all the little things in life matter until you have to do without. Little things like turning on a tap and drinking clean water instead of scooping it with dirty hands from a muddy creek and discovering dead and bloated cadavers of horses and their handlers just fifty metres upstream — after you've slaked your thirst.

Things like sitting on a proper toilet seat, reading fifteen-centimetre by fifteen-centimetre squares of newspaper which dangle from a wire hook for your convenience, and, when the time comes, carefully choosing squares that don't depict the Führer, Feldmarschall Göring, Josef Göbbels or sundry other German demigods. And being able to flush the stuff down the sewer by simply pulling a chain.

Things like brushing your teeth and having a shave with clean water instead of lukewarm and, sometimes, fortified coffee.

Things like socks on your feet instead of putrid rags.

Things like feeling human again — well, almost.

146

But, alas, with every high there comes a low. Some low-life lice had survived the delousing process and found a gap between my skin and the plaster cast. They used my hand as a blood bank. I went outside and gathered a few sticks from the hibernating trees. But all my attempts to stab the bloodsuckers that used me as a free meal were hardly worth the effort.

However, my own suffering paled into insignificance when I found out that blowflies had been put intentionally on the gaping wounds of some of my comrades. I knew that I would never forget the first time I saw maggots gnawing away at the wild flesh, doing naturally what medical science wasn't able to do artificially in those days.

'Your hand is healing well,' said the doctor when he removed the plaster three weeks later and replaced it with an ordinary bandage. 'I'm afraid your holiday is over. Enjoy your last night in a clean bed. The Führer needs you. Good luck, soldier.'

Well, that was it. One day I was a spoiled patient who needed a nurse, and the next I was a soldier who needed a lift back to the front line. Still making use of the hospital's hospitality, I had to wait another two days before a supply convoy rolled into town. I used the spare hours to make friends with the corporal who was in charge of the nearby Quartermaster store. I conned him into supplying me with a whole new issue of winter clothes, including a home-knitted jumper and woollen socks, even earmuffs and thick gloves that had tufts of lambs wool knitted into them, all of them proudly collected and provided by the benevolent Winterhilfe organisation in faraway Germany.

The supply convoy that would take me back to my unit, wherever it was now, carried nothing but fuel and ammunition. I still don't know to this very day why I chose to take a ride on one of the fuel trucks rather than one that carried explosives. Perhaps my brain was in too much disarray to make rational decisions. Maybe I preferred incineration to disintegration. Who knows? If I had had the faintest idea of what I was getting myself into, I would have buried my patriotism together with my admiration for the Führer and my urgent need to emulate my father. I would have told my mother to go to hell and revelled in the thought of being the blackest sheep in anybody's family.

If only I had known!

But I didn't. Although America had taken sides with our enemies and its sophisticated aircraft had come to the aid of Russia and to the detriment of our army, dropping phosphor bombs which exploded way up in the air, spraying all and sundry with liquefied burning death, I still believed that I was fighting for the freedom of my Vaterland and for the safekeeping of my beloved Helga and our child.

With enough food to see me through a week, enough cigarettes to give me lung cancer and enough brandy to keep me lubricated for whatever journey I was going to have, I was adequately prepared for the trip. Well, that's what I thought, anyway. I knew what living hell was like. Nothing could possibly be any worse.

* * *

The road that led eastward was full of shell and bomb craters. Our convoy travelled in a straight line across rough fields, rough enough to make me realise that, once more, I'd had no real choice. With an ammunition truck in front of me and one following behind, I'd end up strewn across the fields in bits and pieces anyway, if either of them were to blow up.

As things were, I had an extremely uncomfortable ride atop a cargo of crazily bouncing fuel drums clanging and banging during the madcap cross-country rally. It took all my athletic abilities as well as instant reflex action to keep my fingers out of harm's way. But my struggle with those treacherous fuel drums was nothing compared to the reception our convoy got after we crossed the Don River and entered a corridor which, as I was to find out later, led all the way to the Volga and to Stalingrad. The rather unsafe supply road wasn't very wide either. I could see our Tiger tanks and artillery — firing from all barrels to protect our valuable, much needed cargo — quite clearly to the north and to the south of us. It was good to know that we were deserving of special treatment.

It was not so good to discover that the Russians seemed to think the same thing. That's why they hit us with everything at their disposal from either side of the corridor.

Winter was now knocking at the door, but despite the freezing air I sweated like a pig. I knew from experience that the Russian artillery could shoot the apple from William Tell's head with the same accuracy as that shown by the bombardiers in those slow, heavily armoured aircraft, who could drop a hand bomb straight into your foxhole at night if you were foolish enough to light a cigarette.

I couldn't have lit a cigarette if I'd wanted to. I was shaking so much that my arms almost jumped out of their sockets and I swore that for the rest of my living days — if there were any days left for me to live — I would never ever volunteer for anything, not ever again.

Whistling, howling chunks of shrapnel tore holes in the fluttering canvas canopy and bounced off the dancing fuel drums which were ready to burst into flames.

'No! No! No!' I screamed into the hellish inferno. All my curses and pleas and obscenities, all my fears and all my anger against the whole world, went unnoticed and died, buried by the insane clamour of fury and madness. Hey, you clever God. What's the matter with You? You left Jesus to perish on the Cross. Is it my turn now? Stop it, damn You, stop it!

As if my prayers had been taken notice of for once, Hermann Göring's Stukas saved the day. They dive-bombed the hell out of the Russkies, and at the end of it all I couldn't believe that I was still alive. But I was.

Fate or God, foe or friend or whoever else had spared me to let me live for another day, another hour, another night, should I curse you or should I be grateful?

Our convoy slowed down as soon as the shelling ceased. In the fading light our drivers found their way around craters and bits of wreckage that lay strewn all over the place.

With engines throttled right back, we proceeded at little faster than walking speed in the shelter of a railway embankment that led straight to the east and towards Stalingrad. But long before I could catch a glimpse of that city and see the reflection of stars shimmering in the icy waters of the mighty Volga River, I was dumped in the vicinity of my old unit.

Shaken and bruised, I stood in uneasy silence like a piece of lost property waiting to be claimed. The strong and awful odour of cabbage soup came drifting across the field. And the lingering acrid stench of gunpowder and death did nothing to raise my spirits.

Nearby a small group of soldiers stood in line, eating utensils in their hands, queuing silently for their daily quota of rations. I walked towards the queue. 'Hey, Kameraden,' I whispered, not daring to speak up. 'Could somebody please tell me where I am?'

'In hell,' came a voice from the shadows. 'In hell, that's where you are.'

I would have recognised that voice among a thousand others. It belonged to Rudi Krüger, my chess partner who'd accompanied me on my one and only excursion into the red-light district of Danzig. 'You crazy bastard,' I said. 'You certainly have a nice way of making an old buddy feel welcome.

152

Out of sight, out of mind, I guess.'

It didn't take Rudi long to put a face to my voice. 'Strike me dead,' he said, walking up to me, reaching for my hand. 'I'll be damned. You're supposed to be on the way back to the Vaterland. Rumour had it that you lost a hand. What the hell are you doing back here?'

'You tell me,' I replied, squeezing his rough hand. 'Maybe I've just dropped in for a game of chess.'

My old comrade took me to a culvert underneath the railway tracks, where I reported to a young lieutenant who didn't know what to do with me. Rudi suggested that I should share his foxhole. He'd been on his own since his partner collected a free pass to the graveyard. 'I can't go without sleep forever,' said Rudi.

'Neither can I, Krüger.' The CO glanced at my bandaged hand. 'Can you handle a machine-gun with that hand of yours?'

I nodded. 'Yes, sir.'

'Take him if you want him, Krüger. He's all yours.'

We went to collect our rations of food and ammunition, then crossed the railway tracks and moved stealthily towards a hole the size of a grave, which would be my new home until God or the devil or the Russkies had other plans for me.

Rudi had changed a lot since I'd last shared a meal with him. It was hard to understand how a cheerful and optimistic man, who seemed to have the world at his feet only twelve months ago, had turned into a hapless shadow of himself. He opened the dinner conversation with: 'Cabbage soup is good for you, Ollie. It makes you fart. And there's nothing nicer than a hot fart to keep you warm during these cold nights.'

Up until now I hadn't thought that a crude word like 'fart' would ever slip from his lips. 'What's the matter with you, Rudi?' I asked him. 'What happened to the funny and optimistic bloke I used to know? What's bugging you?'

'I'll tell you, Ollie,' he muttered. 'I'm gonna tell you exactly what's bugging me.'

A couple of flares went hissing up into the sky, then dangled from their tiny parachutes. They transformed night into day and gave me my first real chance of having a good look at Rudi's grim, stubble-covered face. He looked like death warmed up, without a glimmer of hope left in his once so confident face.

He was convinced that Hitler had made a huge mistake in driving a spearhead into Stalingrad in order to get control of the shipping on the Volga — especially at the onset of winter. 'Napoleon wasn't beaten by the Russians,' he said. 'It was the winter that cost him victory. Does your precious Führer think he is smarter than Napoleon? Well, let me tell you, my friend, he isn't. The Russians have set a trap for us and we've run right into it. A huge mousetrap with Stalingrad for the bait. How far is it from the Don to the Volga? Eighty, ninety, a hundred kilometres? It's a long way for a mouse to get a piece of cheese, don't you think? The Russkies could have stopped us if they'd wanted to. How long do you think we can defend that huge corridor on either side before they shut it down?' Rudi looked at me and went on: 'Every Russian we kill is replaced with a hundred others. They kill a hundred of us and we're lucky to get five recruits to fill the gaps. Every second foxhole of ours is empty by now, and the Russians know it. The bastards are teasing us, thinning us out. When the time is right they can walk straight through our lines, anytime and anywhere they want to. And let me tell you, Ollie, when the trap shuts behind us there won't be any chance for any of us to get out. If we don't collect a bullet we'll freeze to death or we'll end up in Siberia. None of the options impress me very much. I don't know how you feel, Kamerad, but I'm convinced that Hitler has just about lost himself the war.'

'Bullshit,' I said. In my opinion Hitler was still God, still my hero and saviour who couldn't possibly put a foot wrong. As much as I disliked being a soldier and saying 'Yes, sir' to any Tom, Dick or Harry, and as shit-scared as I was, I'd never have the audacity to question the wisdom of my beloved Adolf Hitler. I didn't think that Rudi would understand me, but I was smart enough to keep my mouth shut. He'd learn the truth soon enough.

But Rudi hadn't finished yet. 'This place is giving me the creeps,' he complained. 'It gives me claustrophobia. I want to get out of here alive. I've got a wife and two children waiting for me at home. I guess it's all right for you to die for a crazy man's dream of a Thousand Year Reich. You volunteered. I didn't, and I don't want to die for nothing. And that's what we're doing here, Ollie. Think about it. Maybe if you live long enough you'll agree with me one day.'

'Never, Rudi, not if I live to be a hundred,' I vowed. I didn't know how wrong I was.

Rudi gave up on me. 'I'd hate to see you eat your own words one day,' he muttered, wrapping himself into his blanket and ground sheet. Five minutes later he was sound asleep.

★ ★ ★

In the early hours of the morning, when a grey haze still covered no-man's land, the war started all over again. It went on day after terrifying day. Attack and counter attack, attack and counter attack, on and on and on. Artillery pounding us from north and south. Three rows of foxholes, one line for us, one for the Russians and one halfway between us, occupied in turn by them and us. Was that what we were fighting for? A row of empty bloody holes? Kill, kill, kill or be killed. We had no choice, no place to run to, no shoulder to cry on and no way out. We were stuck. We were lost. We were written off as a sacrifice that had to be made to keep the corridor open and the supplies rolling. We were dispensable. We were shelled and we were battered and I was so cold that I had icicles hanging from my dripping nose and hoar-frost in my eyebrows.

Soon two out of every three foxholes were empty. While Rudi slipped into a trance-like trauma and dreamed impossible dreams of his wife and his children, almost removing himself from reality, I sold my soul to the devil — lock, stock and barrel. Helga hadn't sent me a single letter since we'd left Cracow, and I stopped blaming the Feldpost. I had no one to fight for but myself. Timid little Ollie Weiss became what the army had wanted him to be in the first place — a bullet-spitting, hand-grenade-throwing, brainless dickhead. My sanity took leave of absence. I was no coward, no hero, no nothing. I wasn't a human being any more.

Torn between indescribable fear and frenetic furore, with my back to the wall, I stopped fighting a war for anybody but myself. Sure, I'd volunteered to fight for my Führer, for a new and wonderful Germany, for my beloved Helga and for a bright future, for the defence of our freedom and even, perhaps, for that cold-hearted mother of mine to prove to her that I wasn't quite as bad as she made me out to be.

Now all the sugar-coating, all the glamour, had crumbled; all my high aspirations and good intentions lay tattered and torn on the bottom of the foxhole, trampled to death by my filthy, rotting jackboots, together with the shredded remnants of my father's boastful tales of courage and glory. Disillusioned and ravaged by anger, I went through the motions like a robot.

I was absolutely riddled with lice and I learnt to live with them. The stench of my half-dead body made a fart smell like a bed of roses. And yet, when there was time to sleep, I slept like a new-born baby and hoped that an artillery shell would explode right there in the foxhole to put me out of my misery once and for all. I doubt very much that in those horrible weeks I remembered my own name. I didn't care, and nobody else gave a damn anyway.

There were not enough of us left to bury our own dead. The snow fell and in unbiased mercifulness covered the corpses of friend and foe alike with a soft white blanket of innocence.

Somewhere to the west of us the Russians broke through our corridor defence lines and cut us off from the rest of the world. Rudi didn't bother saying to me 'I told you so'. He knew that I knew that both of us were ratshit now. It hardly mattered any more.

But our High Command, whoever they were, still had plans for us. They knew that we wouldn't be of any further use to them once we headed for the Siberian salt mines.

So what? If they couldn't get road transport to get through to us with ammunition and food — lots of ammunition, with food taking second priority — then the Heinkel bombers could still find enough space to land and provide for us.

So the Heinkels became our only link with the outside world. God forgot that we existed, and so did everybody but the lice. Space for wounded comrades was at a premium aboard the few planes that managed to take off after unloading their cargo. Only the serious casualties got a flight home. Others with lesser injuries had to stay. They smeared their bandages with dirt to blend in with their uniforms and kept on defending the dreams of the Führer.

A member of one of the flight crews from the Heinkels still had a sense of humour. 'The Führer sends you his regards,' he told us. 'And he orders you not to get killed. Anyone who doesn't obey that order shall be shot immediately!'

Our food was strictly rationed and so was our ammunition. The only thing that wasn't rationed was the weaponry. With all the losses we'd suffered, we had two machine-guns in each foxhole and there were still some left over for reinforcements which would never reach us.

My old pal Rudi, who'd hardly spoken a word for days on end, kept looking longingly at the aircraft that took off from behind the railway line, and dreamed his own dreams. Until one day he said, out of the blue: 'I've got to get out of here, Ollie, before it's too late. And I need your help, Kamerad.'

Life does play funny tricks on you. When you are up to your neck in deep trouble, even if you go brain-dead for days on end and your memory refuses to absorb what your eyes see, what your heart feels and what your body does, some things keep on flashing up from unwanted and terrible times of your past. And Rudi's exit from the war is something I wish I had forgotten the moment after it happened.

He kept on telling me that he had to get out. I repeated over and over: 'It's too late for that, Rudi. We'll never get out of here alive. If we're unlucky enough to survive, you and I both know that we'll spend the rest of our lives in Siberia. And I for one would much rather be dead, than alive in Siberia.'

But Rudi had it all worked out already. 'I'll give up my right hand to see my kids again,' he said. 'I want to get out on one of those Heinkels while there's still a runway left for them to take off. I've thought about it long and hard. I'd shoot my own hand off if I had a chance of getting away with it. But it's too dangerous. I can't get my hand far enough away from the muzzle. And before you know it you face a firing squad for self-mutilation. I can't do it myself, Ollie. You've got to help me. You are my friend. You . . . '

'Are you out of your flamin' mind?' I was so shocked that even the damned lice stopped crawling for a moment. After catching my breath I told him straight out that he could go to hell all by himself. 'Leave me out of it! Don't expect me to do your dirty work for you. Who the hell do you think I am? I don't care about the fuckin' Russians any more, but what kind of person would I be if I drew a bead on a good friend? Shit no, Rudi, I'd do anything for you, but not that.'

It took him two days and half a night to change my mind. He knew all my weak spots and he exploited every one of them. All the time I kept on telling him he was crazy, he knew that he'd win out in the long run.

'I hope the Russkies kill you before I have a chance to pull the trigger,' I told him when he crawled out of the foxhole just before sunrise, ignoring the rifle fire from the snipers. Somehow he'd got hold of a snow jacket which made him almost invisible to the enemy.

From about thirty metres away he raised his gloved hand and teased me. 'Shoot, you damned Hitlerjugend bastard! Shoot, you shithead! Haven't got the guts, have you?'

I didn't even realise I pulled the trigger. My bullet found the target, and there was nothing more I could have done about it. The deed was done and I felt terribly guilty. I knew that, even if God would forgive me, I'd never be able to forgive myself. I thought that I should put the muzzle of my rifle into my mouth right there and then and put myself out of my own misery. But I couldn't do that. Well, I pondered, maybe I'd kill myself tomorrow, unless the Russians get to me first.

Rudi came crawling back into our foxhole and said: 'Thanks a million, Kamerad. Thanks for the ticket home.'

I'll never ever forget that very special, grateful smile on his face. 'God bless you, Ollie,' he said, and I watched him crawl on elbows and knees towards the railway line and headquarters. He left a trail of blood in the white snow, but he mightn't have even noticed it.

The Heinkel that got him out passed safely through the ground fire. Rudi was on his way home. My insane laughter reverberated all the way over no-man's land and the Russians tried to shoot it out of the sky and they missed, missed and missed again. I broke down, fell into a little heap of utter misery, and cried my heart out — for myself, for Rudi, for his wife and his children who would be stuck with a crippled father for the rest of his life. I cried for God, because He didn't know what He was doing to all of us either.

I went on crying because I suddenly saw before me the face of a young Russian soldier, his huge, fear-filled eyes staring at me as if at the devil himself. He is propped up against the wall of one of the foxholes between the two lines. He is wounded in the chest. His uniform is blood-red. His eyes plead with me, wanting me to put a bullet into his head to put him out of his own misery. Jesus Christ, he is younger than I am and he is so scared! I know how to say 'Hands up' and 'Come here' in Russian. He mumbles something I can't understand. I want to help him. I stretch out a helping hand. 'Idi soo dah,' I say, smiling. One of his hands comes up with a hand-grenade. Suddenly he is not afraid any more. He smiles at me. Maybe they shoot horses after they break a leg but I couldn't shoot my very own adversary. He doesn't throw the hand-grenade at me. He holds it under his chin and pulls the pin. He is still smiling as I jump for cover. The grenade explodes, sending shrapnel screaming through the air. A few seconds later I look at the mangled and bloody remains of a young man who perhaps believed in Stalin's propaganda even more than I believed in the rhetoric of my icon, Adolf Hitler.

★ ★ ★

Today I know for certain that war is death, war is evil, war is horror and degradation. All those who have been there know very well how inhuman it is. Yet hardly anyone who has suffered has spoken up and told the truth. Most of us are just too afraid to speak up. Too many heroes are doing unto their own children what my cherished father did unto me. Even before their own scars vanish they send their flesh and blood out to fight yet another stupid and unnecessary war. Be proud, young man! Stand up and fight for your country! Be a hero, son, so your Papa can be proud of you or put a wreath on your grave in the war cemetery, where most heroes rest forever. Go on, son, spill your blood for the ambitions of a handful of crazed and power-hungry politicians who promise you freedom and send you to die in hell. Are we not the only specimen of God's creations that uses its God-given intelligence to manufacture weapons to destroy its own kind?

Will we ever learn?

But now, for the time being, let me tell you how I survived the carnage of Stalingrad, the carnage that turned the tide of the war. I guess my father would have risen from his grave with pride if I'd died a hero's death. But I wasn't that much of a chip off the old block. My departure came in much less spectacular circumstances. Unlike Rudi, I did not give my right hand to get out of hell, not for Hitler, not for Germany, not for anybody and especially not for my stepfather, Frederik Schuster, much as he might have liked to have me right out of the picture.

I don't even know how I happened to get into the plane. I wish I could remember. If I didn't make it under my own steam I would like to shake the hand of the Samaritan who most definitely saved my life.

One of the few things I do recall vividly is lying face down in the convex glass dome that protruded from the belly of a Heinkel bomber, pushing my nose against the thick, transparent glass, watching the ground slide away from under me. I should have been high-spirited and happy. But I was beyond caring. I was dazed and befuddled, and flashes of memory played hopscotch inside my brain. I couldn't remember being hit by anything. I'd lost the feeling in both legs and I panicked until I assured myself that they were still where they should be. I was frozen stiff. The railway line to Stalingrad disappeared in the distance. Well, I thought to myself, in time to come I'll remember what happened during those last days of mine in hell. Meanwhile it seemed that I was on my way home, and that was all that mattered at the time. Home, sweet home.

I can't recall how I got there. I think I

might have slipped into something of a coma from sheer physical and psychological exhaustion while I was being transported from Russia to a military hospital in Hannover. Somebody in a doctor's white coat told me that I was lucky not to have lost both legs. At the time I was much too insensible and phlegmatic to acknowledge my good fortune. My head sank back into the soft pillow, and I guess I relished being in limbo halfway between life and death for as long as I needed to. For once I was at peace with myself and the whole world. On my slow path to recovery I couldn't help wondering if Rudi could have made it too, without my shoddy help. I should have never given in to his crazy request. Perhaps he could live without a hand, but I was sure I'd have a guilty conscience for the rest of my life.

Some days later the bandages were removed from my legs and the medic arrived to have a good look at the damage. My legs were full of holes from the knees down, ugly and nasty pus-oozing holes, bad enough to frighten the hell out of me.

The harder I concentrated on recalling the events preceding my departure from Russia, the less I could remember. Like an alcoholic sobering up after drinking himself into oblivion, I grappled with the void in my brain and couldn't come up with any answers.

Eventually I turned to the friendly-faced man with the stethoscope and asked timidly: 'What's wrong with me, Doc? What's happened to my legs? I can't remember getting hit.'

'You didn't,' he told me, his smile deepening. 'You didn't get hit by anything at all. You were eaten alive by an army of hungry lice and you got infections in the legs. You were quite a mess when they brought you in. You're over the worst now. You'll survive, and you'll still have a pair of legs to stand on. Just thank your lucky stars.'

He gave me an encouraging, well-meaning pat on the head, put my chart back where he'd taken it from and left me to cope with my own strange and turbulent emotions. My brain refused to accept that I was safely and securely tucked into a hospital bed. I was a nervous wreck. Startled by each and every noise, I spent most of the time with the sheet pulled over my head, living in nightmares, walking a tightrope that stretched from sanity to madness.

The doctors must have known that my mental wellbeing was in a worse state than my legs. As soon as they had full control of the infection, I was sent to a sanitarium in the sprawling heath of Lüneburg, a health resort run by the army for people like me — people who were still young enough and stupid enough to have another go at making the ultimate sacrifice for the freedom of the German people and the glory of the Thousand Year Reich.

The sanitarium was very much like the Garden of Eden must have been at the time when Adam and Eve decided there was a much nicer and more exciting way to create their offspring than sculpturing them from wet and messy clay.

There were perhaps a hundred young soldiers recuperating from mental stress; all of them had family and friends visiting all the time. In our dormitory we had picture windows from one corner of the room to the other. There were tables and chairs all along the wall of glass, and everybody had someone to put his arm around, to smile at and to hug and cherish.

I had myself. Despite the letters I had written to Mutti, my sister and, of course, my sweetheart Helga, I sat alone at the window and talked to the trees, waiting desperately for someone to call out: 'Ollie Weiss. There's someone here to see you.' I was so lonely and so desperate, I'm sure I would even have put my arms around Frederik Schuster and hugged him to death, if he'd made the effort to come and shake my hand. Helga, for heaven's sake, what are you doing to me? Where are you? I am the father of your child. Have you turned your back on me? I love you, damn you, I love you with all my heart!

I don't think that the constant flow of visitors, the many embraces and all the cuddles and kisses I witnessed did one bit of good to me. I was convinced that I was the loneliest man on God's earth, and my nightmares went on and on and on. Lost among all those flashing images of horror, images that just wouldn't leave me alone, I felt myself battling a rising feeling of shame. How could I face my friends at home and explain to them how I had come to get out of Stalingrad? I was supposed to be their hero.

Wouldn't I have been better off losing an arm or a leg? Then I could have returned home to Prenzlau under a halo of glory. I could boast and brag to my friends and, for just once in my life, my mother and my sister and my whole damn tribe would feel sorry for me. Maybe they'd even be somewhat proud of the runt of the litter they called the 'black sheep'.

8

Feeling desperately lonely and alienated in a crowd of revellers who joyfully celebrate the homecoming of their sons and fathers, as if it were a miracle, must be the worst kind of loneliness there is.

To say the least I was deeply confused about the role I was destined to play in the drama of my life as it unfolded from day to day. I even hesitated for a while when, at the end of my so-called 'psychological rehabilitation', I had to stipulate where I wanted to spend the four weeks of furlough that were due to me. I nominated Prenzlau only for one reason. I had to find Helga. I knew that she loved me. I knew that, unless she'd died, she would have moved mountains to let me know that we'd created a new life.

It seemed as though light years had passed by since I'd sung songs of victory and lighthearted ditties together with my comrades on the troop train that took us to the Russian front. So eager to prove myself to my Papa and my Führer, I had fantasised then about my homecoming as a hero, with medals on my chest and pride written all over my face. Neither the stationmaster nor anyone else at the railway station of Prenzlau took any notice of my arrival. My once-harboured delusions of greatness certainly flew right out of the window when not a single soul said 'Heil Hitler' or 'Good day' to me. I felt as if I was persona non grata in my own home town.

Anyway, I was in no mental condition to weather endless speeches and celebrations and all the other nonsense I had dreamed of only twelve months ago. I'd never been quite conceited enough to anticipate a civic reception in the town hall. So I wasn't disappointed when it didn't come to be.

But I was almost shocked out of my jackboots, brand new and spit-polished as they were, when I rang the bell at Helga's parents' apartment after racing past the front door of our own, and a strange woman answered the door.

'I'm looking for Helga Schneider,' I stuttered. 'Helga Schneider. You know her, don't you? She lives here.'

'Never heard of her,' said the woman. 'You must have got the house numbers mixed up. Nobody by that name's living here.'

'But she must . . . '

'Well, she doesn't. Heil Hitler to you,

young man.' She slammed the door in my face.

I didn't get a much better reception from my mother. She didn't even take the time to ask me how I was and how I'd been hurt. 'How could you bring such shame on our well-respected name?' she whined. 'I tried so hard to bring you up properly. Now look what you've done to our family, to yourself and the poor girl you got pregnant. They kicked her out of school, they kicked her out of the League of German Girls, they treated her like a trollop.'

The tirade went on and on. To cut a long and distressing story short, Helga and her mother had gone missing. They couldn't have taken more than a suitcase of personal belongings with them when they disappeared without leaving a forwarding address and without saying goodbye.

'Who knows?' Mother said. 'Rumour has it that her father was picked up by the Gestapo. Maybe they came to take the rest of the family away as well.'

I had to stay at home. I had no other place to go to. The spare bedroom with its large windows had been unused since Frederik the Great claimed Papa's half of my parents' double bed. Dust sheets were once again protecting the furniture from the sun and

173

from terrible fellows like me.

Having been to hell and back again, I expected my status at home to be raised somewhat, but my bed was made up in the hated narrow, dark corridor as always, and, as always, Mother took control of my life. The little bit of self-esteem I'd built up while I was away from home went begging once more. I considered myself to be nothing but a piece of lost baggage that was long forgotten and never missed. And there wasn't a thing I could do about it.

My Papa was still waiting for me under the ivy-covered grave. I wished I'd known if he was glad to see me. After all, he must have been dismally disappointed with the meek and humble son he had sired. 'Sorry, Papa,' I told him. 'Maybe you could have made me into a hero if you hadn't died too soon. Telling me all those lies about your Great War didn't make things any easier for me either.'

After two hectic weeks of searching for Helga and talking to my long-departed father I'd achieved absolutely nothing. I felt so sorry for myself, I ran out of excuses for my sullen, morose behaviour. I'd dug myself into a hole so deep that if I didn't climb out of it soon I might be stupid enough to kill myself.

So far I'd hardly bothered saying as much as hello to the few boys in my age group who hadn't been called up for active duty yet. Now, all of a sudden, I saw the envy in their faces. Gossip runs wild in a small country town like Prenzlau. Everybody seemed to know that I'd come home from Stalingrad. When I made up my mind to enjoy the rest of my leave and to treat my mother with the big ignore that she deserved, I couldn't handle all the invitations to parties and celebrations.

'When in Rome do as the Romans do,' Mutti lectured me. 'As long as you live under my roof you abide by my rules. I want you home and in bed before midnight. And that's an order. Is that understood?'

I clicked my heels, saluted and said, sharper than necessary: 'Jawohl, Frau General!' After what I'd learnt and read about Caesar and his flamboyant lifestyle, I couldn't believe that *he* would have put a midnight curfew on his house guests. At first I wanted to enlighten my strict mother with a few facts of life. But then I thought that I'd only be wasting my time. She'd just have to die incredibly ignorant.

I tried to adhere to my mother's rules for the simple reason that I had no other place to stay at, and I didn't intend cutting my wellearned furlough short.

I didn't break the ridiculous curfew until the night I ran into my former dancing partner, Brigitte, at yet another drinking party. Suddenly the devil reached out for me and I was all too ready to yield to temptation.

She still looked like a million dollars. I searched through a stack of records, found what I was looking for, wound up the record player and put the needle down on the rim.

'I dance with you into heaven, the seventh heaven of love . . . ' The sultry, deep voice wafted through the room and the memories gave me a flush of goose pimples all over. I asked Brigitte for a dance.

'Long time no see,' she smiled, coming into my shivering arms. 'Tell me, what is it like to be a hero?'

'I don't know, Brigitte,' I said, my voice shaking a little. 'I never was a hero and I never will be. Let's talk about nicer things than heroes and war. Anything spectacular happening in your life?'

'I got married,' she said, swaying with the beat of the music.

'You are here with your husband then?' I found it difficult to hide my disappointment.

'I wish I was,' she sighed. 'I wish I was, but I'm not.' I didn't ask any further questions. It was nice to hold a pretty girl in my arms, and the more I became aware of Brigitte's femininity the more I prayed and begged for a miracle to happen. Brigitte put her cheek against mine and her arms around me, and I closed my eyes and promised myself that I would remain faithful to Helga for as long as I lived. I would rather die than betray Helga's trust.

The music stopped. We kept on dancing for a while, each of us following our own thoughts, our own dreams.

Later on, we got drunk together and cried on each other's shoulder, and we discovered that the two of us had all the reason in the world to cry our hearts out. I was terribly frustrated and angry because Helga had gone missing. Brigitte was frustrated and angry because she had married a soldier who, after a short honeymoon, decided to go missing somewhere in Russia, where they don't know anything at all about the conjugal rights of a love-hungry partner in marriage.

The clock struck midnight. My curfew ran out without my being aware of it. We got absolutely rotten drunk without knowing we had. We went home in the wee hours of the morning, shaking hands and suppressing all other human feelings and urges. We were nice and respectable people.

'You'll have to come for dinner one day,' said Brigitte, turning one way as we stepped out into the dark street.

'I'd like that very much,' I told her before I

turned away from her. 'Are you sure you don't want me to see you home safely?'

'It'll be safer for both of us if I go home by myself, Ollie. Hang on a moment. I'll give you my address, just in case, you know, just in case.'

It would have been well past two o'clock in the morning when I took my shoes off and tiptoed up the staircase, hoping that none of the wooden steps would squeak and herald my belated arrival. The keyhole was one of those awfully evasive ones that dodge the key with dogged determination. But in the end I made such a perfect and noiseless entry that even the Almighty would have congratulated me.

My mother had other intentions. She came out into the corridor to wake me up for breakfast. The tone of her voice betrayed her anger. She sat herself down at the far end of our oval, shiny kitchen table like a judge facing a panel of jurors. She was gracious enough to let me finish my bowl of hot porridge. By the time I was ready to butter my bread roll she ran out of self-control.

'When did you come home last night?' she asked quietly. Much too quietly, as a matter of fact. I admit that I should have known better than to tell a fib to my mother. But I looked into her blazing eyes and simply couldn't tell the truth. 'Must have been about midnight,' I whispered, choking on the Ersatz coffee.

To tell you the truth, I still don't know how she did it. We had the whole length of the table separating us. Yet she reached out with an arm that must have stretched like you stretch a piece of elastic. Her hand shot out like a rocket. Her fingers lodged in a vice-like grip between the second and third shiny buttons of my army coat. With immense, animalistic strength, she lifted me straight out of my chair, held me suspended in the air and slapped me across the face — not just once, but again and again. There was helpless me, the frightened little man and would-be hero, who'd tried so hard to be a real man and a valiant soldier, crumbling once more under the wrath of my unyielding Mutti.

Since Papa died, this was the first time my mother saw tears running from my eyes. Tears of embarrassment, tears of shame, but most of all tears of hate. 'If there is a God, how can He create a mother like you?' I said, trying to stop the tears from flowing.

★ ★ ★

Twenty minutes later I walked away from my mother, my past and my childhood. I didn't

179

notice the little boy who walked beside me and tried to keep in step with me until I heard his voice. 'Heil Hitler, Herr Soldat,' he said. 'Are you a hero?'

His question forced a smile to my face. 'No, young man. I am not a hero. I'm just a plain soldier.'

'If you're a soldier you must be a hero,' the little boy insisted. 'When I grow up I shall be a hero too. My Papa is a hero. He is in the SS because he hates the Jews. Have you killed many Jews, sir?'

I stopped to look at the boy. He was nine or ten years old and dressed in the regulation uniform of the Jungvolk brown shirt and black shorts. His kerchief was gathered around his neck and threaded through a ring of woven leather. His little cap nestled in a crop of corn-yellow locks.

Holy mackerel, I thought, he is me all over again — a cocky, cheeky little bastard shouting 'Heil Hitler' for all the wrong reasons. Would he live long enough to become a hero? Would he grow up to call his father a liar?

I quickened my stride and walked away from him.

'Heil Hitler,' he shouted belligerently.

'Heil Hitler, you little creep,' I responded, sad and downcast. Oh, dead Papa. Can I change places with you?

When I came towards the market square, I stopped to look back all the way down the tree-lined avenue. Lindenstrasse, shall I ever see you again? Memories eddied through my confused mind like the sails of a windmill. How many years had passed since a new invention called a 'zipper' had found its way onto the shelves of the local drapery store? I recalled how I'd burst with jealousy when Mutti sewed one of those modern contraptions into Lieselotte's Sunday dress. As always, I was second cab off the rank. But after pestering and badgering Mother persistently, and receiving a few crisp backhanders into the bargain, she finally relented. She cut the buttons off the fly of my best shorts and replaced them with a shiny new zipper.

Well, you should have seen me! I ripped my old pants off, put the new ones on, and I was off like a rocket, down the stairs and out into the street. Running up and down the whole length of busy Lindenstrasse, I pulled my treasured zipper up and down, up and down for everybody to see. I shouted at the top of my voice: 'Look what I've got! Look what I've got!' I was the proudest boy in Prenzlau, and I couldn't understand why people were laughing at me. 'Look what I've got! Look what I've got!'

But now nobody laughed at me.

Perhaps it wasn't one of my brightest ideas to go and knock on Brigitte's front door. 'I'm sort of desperate,' I told her. 'I have no other place to go. Can I stay here for a few days? I'll sleep on the floor if I have to.'

'You won't have to do that. Come in. You can camp on the couch. Have you had breakfast yet?'

It was Brigitte, instead of Helga, who accompanied me to the railway station when my leave came to an end. She didn't wait for the train to arrive. 'Take good care,' she said.

'You too,' I replied. A short embrace and she was gone.

'Thanks for all you've done for me, Brigitte!' She kept on walking without turning her head.

The train arrived on time. The locomotive belched black smoke. The shrill sound of a whistle signalled readiness for departure. Yesterday was gone once and for all. Would there be a tomorrow?

Well, mein Führer, I thought, all that's left for me to do now is to deliver myself to you, to your army and to your war. At least you won't reject me like my mother does. I'm sure you'll welcome me with open arms.

My travel documents told me that my reserve unit had been shifted to Elbing, a town some fifty kilometres to the southeast of Danzig. After changing trains in Stettin I found myself in a crowded compartment packed with young civilians who were on their way to taste the first nasty bite of army discipline. I felt like an old veteran among the highspirited youngsters, who got themselves carried away, riding an exciting wave of enthusiasm and bullshit.

I had no reason to rejoice. My reveries of conquering the world had died halfway between the Don River and the Volga. My carefree days of the Hitlerjugend, when I marched through the streets of Prenzlau on the Führer's birthday, my chest swelling with pride, were no longer of importance, although I would never forget strutting past the cheering crowds shouting 'Sieg Heil' and 'Heil Hitler', past houses which had Hakenkreuz flags fluttering in the breeze from almost every window as a token of freedom and pride and joy.

Now my ideas were tainted with the real smell and the real devastation of war. Somehow I knew now that the indestructible might of the greatest army on earth was not so invincible after all.

Well, Ollie Weiss, in for a penny, in for a pound. Caught together, hanged together.

I caught a streetcar to the barracks that

would be my new home for a while. My arrival was a non-event. I was no stranger to life in barracks. So it was once again back to the straw-filled mattress, the double-decker bunk, the steel lockers and the haunting nightmares.

But man is not meant to be an island. I was lucky to have a nice guy like Kurt Reinhard choose me for a friend. We became a winning combination in the many games of cards we played in a constant fight against boredom.

Kurt, in my eyes, was what a proper German soldier should be like. He wore three Panzer-stripes on the sleeve of his coat, one stripe for each T-34 tank he'd destroyed singlehandedly. Kurt picked me out to be his friend, and I made him into my hero. He wore his Iron Cross medal with distinguished pride and he could drink me under the table any time he wanted to. He never once complained about a hangover and I admired him for all the attributes I was lacking. I liked the blond-haired, blue-eyed giant of a man very much. I never ever gave it a thought that I might have used him as a substitute figure for my father, my dead hero.

One day our bugler got his marching orders and the army was in dire straits. A garrison without a bugler is like a farmyard without a rooster. Thanks to my experience in

Left: With my mother, Elise Holz, and sister, Lieselotte, about 1926.

Below: Playing in the backyard with Lieselotte.

Above: This picture was taken just before my father died, in 1930. My mother knitted black stockings which itched so much I used to take them off at school and put them back on when I returned home.

Right: I finally made it into the German Army in 1941. I was known as 'matchstick' by my colleagues.

Left: This was taken after the horrors of war, in 1946. I had become a mature and reflective adult by age twenty-two.

Below: Me in 1999.

My home town Prenzlau.

our Hitlerjugend marching band, I had some limited knowledge. For once I broke my solemn vow not to volunteer for anything as long as I wore a grey uniform. I didn't have to go through any audition; I was the only applicant. I walked out of the office with a bugle, a bottle of brass polish, a soft rag and a happy face.

My services were required for a few minutes five times a day, seven days a week. I had all the time in the world to practise, because I was naturally excluded from all other duties. Within a week my bugle was shiny enough to use as a shaving mirror.

With a large dose of spare time on my hands, I began to write letters to Helga again, but I never posted them. I waited impatiently for my name to be mentioned at mail call. I longed for the impossible to happen. It didn't.

Helga didn't write and I didn't turn into a soldier. I was still a misfit, an outsider, a young tree with all its roots cut off. What had happened to the ever so exuberant and confident boy from the Hitler Youth?

Hitler did not come to Elbing. He did not stand by my side when I stood in the middle of the quadrangle night after night, sounding the Zapfenstreich at 2200 hours, lost and lonely, watching the narrow strips of soft light

185

disappear from the edges of the blackout blinds.

The world was at war. Ollie Weiss was at war with Ollie Weiss. With my eyes tightly closed, I could see my father sitting next to me on the lounge, smoking his Sunday cigar and reciting his autobiography of courage and heroism. But now I could hear all his pretentious derring-do clatter, crumble and fall away into nothingness.

I swore to myself that I would never hide the bitter truth from my own children, nor would I glorify war the way my father did — if I was lucky enough to survive.

'We'll have a fog tomorrow,' I said to Kurt, when we returned to our quarters after indulging in a few drinks at the canteen. The full moon had broken through the clouds. Beyond the perimeter of our barracks the trees moved gently in the moist breeze that caressed my face. It would be summer soon and the world was still at war.

9

All things come to an end, good and bad. The German army doesn't give you any second choices either. Some wise owl in High Command decided that the living remains of anything that belonged to the Paulus army which was defeated in Stalingrad should be put to good use.

I was bugling no more. Together with Kurt and many others I was declared A1, fully well enough to do some shooting instead of hooting.

Word had it that we would go to France where a new elite unit, the Regiment Feldherrnhalle, would be put together and trained to use the most modern weaponry.

'Sounds like the army is getting sick of being outdone by the Waffen-SS,' said Kurt. 'Anyway, I hope the brothels in France are as good as they're supposed to be. My balls are getting heavier by the day.'

Hitler's army had no sentiment, no compassion and no time to waste on small-time heel-clickers like us. Two days after passing the medical we'd passed through half of Germany in our rattling cattle wagons, heading due west.

If I could ever get hold of the spying bastard who told the British that our troop train would arrive in Cologne at a certain day and a certain time, I'd choke the living daylights out of him. How else could they have known that we were approaching the bridge across the Rhine?

We sat in the open doorways of our rambling carriages, dangling our feet in the air and doing nobody any harm. Not far away on my right I spied the Kölner Dom — the Cathedral of Cologne — rising untouched and unscarred in its majestic beauty amid the ruins of uncountable homes.

'Why does God protect His own house when He doesn't seem to give a shit about the homes His people live in?' I wondered aloud. Nobody even attempted to reply.

Our train slowed to walking speed as it approached the huge bridge. We sang in high spirits: 'Oh, Du wunderschöner deutscher Rhein . . . '

Then the air-raid sirens started howling and we swallowed the lyrics of the song and cursed the pilots of those enemy planes, which were still not more than a few conspicuous dots in the clear sky.

Our train stopped in the damned middle of the damned bridge, halfway across the

188

blasted Rhine, and halfway between heaven above and death far below.

'Holy Moses!'

'Never mind Moses! Let's get out of here!'

I jumped and, unbelievable as it might sound, I did a hundred and eighty-degree turn in midair and landed between the tracks and beneath the protective floorboards of our wagon.

I peered through a gap in the decking of the bridge and looked straight down, very far down, at the peacefully rambling 'Oh, Du wunderschöner Rhein' and for a brief moment I thought I had a little 'wunder-schöner Rhein' running down my trouser legs. But that was sheer imagination.

The bombs came hurtling down and my throat was much too dry to utter the first words of the Lord's Prayer. And, dammit, I shook twice as much as the bridge did. Let me assure you, most of us were not very cool, calm and collected when we remounted our carriages and continued on our way.

'It would be nice to see Paris,' said Kurt. 'I'd love to walk the whole length of the Champs Elysée, climb up the Eiffel Tower and cheat on my missus with a gorgeous redhead.'

'I'd like to send a dirty postcard to my mother,' I replied, imagining the effect it would have on her.

'You wouldn't, would you, Ollie?'

'Try me, my friend. You want to make a bet?'

Luckily for my middle class, God-fearing mother we never made it to Paris. We skirted the city and kept on going south, and two days later, about five o'clock in the morning, we arrived in the city of Nimes.

We jackbooted our way through the centre of town, waking all and sundry with our marching songs. Oh, if only the French had known that, bristling with weaponry of all descriptions as we were, we didn't have a single round of ammunition to defend the honour of the Third Reich. But the French didn't know how vulnerable we were and not a single angry bullet buzzed through the crisp, early morning air.

Nor were we accosted by busty and lusty French belles with hot lips and accommodating loins as we had anticipated in sweet reveries. When things settled down we were still in barracks, still in Hitler's army and still eating rolled oats for breakfast. Being part of the first German troops to occupy the so far untouched south of France, we were met by animosity and deeply rooted prejudice.

Isn't it strange how we are fascinated by everything that's new to us? We want to crawl back into childhood, into those precious days when we experienced something new all the time; when every second of living brought a new discovery into our perceptive minds. We hear things, we believe things and we imagine things. Everything we know is not half as exciting as all those things we know nothing about. We need to explore. We need to reach for the stars.

Being in France was a whole new experience to me. I for one wanted to know what it would be like to 'acheter saucisse' from the 'boucherie' instead of buying sausage from the butcher.

I have never considered myself to be a sex maniac, but the mere thought of being in France certainly did strange things to my repressed libido. By the time I had my first breakfast in France I could ask, 'Voulez vous couchez avec moi?' without breaking my tongue. The French letters I had in my mind weren't the ones people put postage stamps on.

On Sunday the bullfights were on in the amphitheatre, the 'Colosseum' of Nimes, in the centre of the ancient city. We didn't have to buy tickets. No, we were not presented with the Key to the City, we just took it. And no one was game enough to object.

I don't like amphitheatres and I abhor

bullfights. This huge oval in the south of France reminded me of the era of gladiators who fought for their lives to please deviants like Caesar, Nero and others, who were empowered to condemn a man to death by turning down a fat thumb.

I was the only one in the large crowd to cheer an enraged bull when it picked up a matador with its horns and tossed him across the wooden barrier into the gawking crowd.

'You talked me into coming to watch this disgusting spectacle,' I said to Kurt. 'I want to get away from here. Come on.' Army rules did not permit me to walk through the streets of Nimes on my own. 'Are you coming, Kurt?'

'Where do you want to go?'

'I don't care, as long as I haven't got to watch another bull slaughtered for the sake of human vanity.'

'All right, then,' said Kurt. 'I'm not keen on it either.'

We forced our way to the exit. The streets were almost deserted. Every able body was watching the bullfights.

A couple of young kids played hopscotch on the footpath. Approaching them, I put my hand out in a friendly gesture. 'Bonjour, mes amis,' I greeted them, having my first go at saying something in French. 'Comment ça va?'

One of the kids lashed out at me with his tiny hand and slapped my wrist. Then he spun around and ran a few paces to where he felt safe. He faced me once more. The big eyes in his little face were alight with hatred. He kept yelling at me and he spat at me and screamed at me, and the only words I could understand were 'Boche! Boche! Boche!'

I was flabbergasted as much as Kurt was angry. 'Go get the cheeky little bastard,' he challenged. 'Go get him!'

I almost did, then decided against it. 'Let him go, Kurt,' I said. 'If the French invaded Prenzlau I'd spit in their faces too. Maybe his father got killed in the war. I can't blame him for hating us.'

★   ★   ★

Even the old-fashioned German army realised that sex is an important part of life. That's why it had confiscated a beautiful huge palace in Nimes and made it into a brothel, where every soldier in need could screw his heart out for a small fee with the blessing of the Führer and the Thousand Year Reich, as long as he queued up for treatment by the medic on the way out.

I only went there to satisfy my curiosity. But once inside, I was caught hook, line and upright doodle. If I'd had any sense or self-respect at all I would have turned on my heels right there and then, instead of standing there like a gnome in Mutti's front garden. But I didn't. I simply couldn't move. My eyes sparkled, my bottom lip drooped and I dribbled from the mouth and trembled like nobody's business.

At first I saw nothing but beautiful girls in exquisite gowns, one as pretty as the next. I was in some kind of a ballroom. A small all-girl band was playing romantic music, sensual American stuff that we weren't allowed to listen to in Germany. Lots of couples danced cheek to cheek on the mirrored floor. The tables were crowded, the champagne flowed freely and the heavy-sweet scent of French perfume drove me almost out of my mind.

An apple a day might keep a dentist at bay, but it certainly does nothing about frustrations. Here I was in a Garden of Eden, where a hundred delectable, sexy Eves offered much nicer things than a bite of the apple. *My* apple turned out to be an impossible dream come true. Her name was Yvette. She had almond-shaped eyes, full, sensuous lips and a million tantalising flavours all blended together with perfection.

I didn't just take a bite. No, sir. I swallowed the whole apple and enjoyed every morsel of it, pips and all.

We stayed in Nimes for another two weeks. I wished we could have stayed forever. I saw as much of Yvette as time permitted. She sent me stony broke and made me deliriously happy. She made me forget all about Helga and gave me a whole new outlook on life. It was Yvette who explained to me that a bidet was not a hand-basin.

Yvette taunted me into being myself and she dared me to lose myself within a world that must have been the closest thing to heaven. She was a whore to others, but not to me. I would have married her if she'd said yes to my proposal, but she didn't.

Yvette had been a student at the Sorbonne in Paris when France lost the war. She'd been rounded up with many others by the SS, who gave her a choice between working in an army brothel in France or a munitions factory in Germany. She opted for what she deemed to be the lesser evil.

In time to come the French would tell Yvette that she was the scum of the earth. Once the war was over, her own people would crucify her. They would spit on her and call her a collaborator. They would shave her head or drown her in a river of the country she loved and called her own.

* * *

'Charmant' is not the real name of the small township that was next on our itinerary. I choose the name because it does justice to the town, its surrounds and its people better than any other name. Even a whole company of brash and alien soldiers from the Feldherrnhalle couldn't destroy the obvious tranquillity that held the whole district in firm embrace.

I don't know if we were an exception to the rule. We did not rape the women and loot their homes. We did not destroy their churches.

Our CO had put down strict rules for us to follow. If we broke them we had to cope with the punishment.

When a farmer complained that he'd seen one of us walk out of his vineyard with a bucketful of grapes, we were ordered to assemble outside headquarters. Our CO and the Frenchman walked along our lines. The farmer identified the thief. 'C'est lui,' he said, pointing at one of the young rookies. 'C'est lui.'

The culprit was not to be seen anywhere

for the following three days. He got no trial, no sympathy and nothing but bread and water. When he got out of his dungeon he'd lost his appetite for grapes.

But a few of us were invited to trample the grapes that were picked in the vineyards and heaped into huge wooden vats which took in most of the market square at the end of the harvest. All of us, French and German alike, celebrated the end of a great grape season. Nineteen forty-three was not a bad year!

Yet, if fate hadn't been on our side, our whole lively company could have been turned into corpses right there on the outskirts of Charmant. We were out in the field to hone our military skills. We used wooden dummy bullets, dummy hand-grenades and the most recently invented weapon of the Führer's infantry: rifle-grenades.

Our exercises were like playing kids' games until real bullets kicked up dust around us and buzzed past our ears. We dived for cover and filled the whole space between us and the partisans with a lot of noise and a mass of purple wooden fragments with our practice ammunition. From that day on all of us had to carry a strip of five real rounds in one of cartridge pouches. With our officers assuming that we were stupid enough to use the live ammo instead of the dummies during practice shooting, we had to wrap the strip of real bullets in a piece of newspaper, just in case.

A young boy had now come into our lives. Pierre was a kid of about fourteen. He was our middleman for wheeling and dealing. For a few packets of cigarettes or a couple of tins of beef you could buy almost anything from him, even nylon stockings which weren't known then in Germany. Pierre introduced me to his grandfather, M. Dubois, who in due course became the only Frenchman I ever had reason to hate. M. Dubois had his own vineyard. He made his own wine and matured it, stored it and blended it in the large cellar under his house.

I had done Pierre some little favours and he promised to let me have a look at his grandfather's winery. And he kept his promise.

I remember following Pierre down the damp steps. I even remember the wrinkled, weather-beaten face of his grandfather smiling at me, saying 'Bonjour, Monsieur', and I can still see the do-it-yourself cigarette sticking to his bottom lip, dancing up and down and defying gravity. In my mind I can still, even today, see the rows of wooden barrels of maturing and aging wine. I have a slight memory of walking from cask to cask with the old gentleman, who obligingly proffered a sample from each barrel as we went along. God only knows how often he said 'A votre santé', and how often I responded with 'Merci beaucoup' and, after a while, 'Berci meaucoup' and even a few very screwed-up 'Schankedöns' or something like that.

I felt lightheaded and wonderfully pleasant when I attempted to scale the steps that would lead me away from further vinous trials and tribulations. What I wasn't to know at that moment was that, as soon as I reached the fresh air, something would hit me with the force of a well-aimed length of four-by-two and knock me out cold. Partisans, I thought, bloody Partisans! Should have been more careful. Shouldn't have trusted the French. Should have killed the bastards. Now they'd killed me.

Just before I lost consciousness I saw the smirking face of my mother. I whispered into a kaleidoscope of sparkling colours: 'Hey, Mutti, are you happy now? I'm dead! I'm a hero! You can be proud of your son now.'

The following morning I had the worst hangover I'd ever had the displeasure to suffer.

It was 'au revoir Charmant' as well as 'vive la France' before I had time to catch up with

Pierre or his grandfather.

Armed to the teeth and now provided with lots of live ammunition, we sat on our rumbling trucks and prayed that the talk of an impending invasion in our area would not become reality.

'The enemy is going to drop paratroopers in the Rhone Delta,' was the rumour that circulated through the ranks.

The transformation from human being into brainless robot was oh so frighteningly easy.

Die for the Vaterland. Heil Hitler, you bastards. Fight for freedom! Fight for Germany! Fight for the Thousand Year Reich!

Foxholes hastily dug into soft soil. I hate this war! War makes no sense at all. Doesn't anybody care? Doesn't anybody want to know?

Two hours watch, two hours off, two hours on, two hours off. Eyes stabbing at the sky day and night, hoping to see nothing unusual. No noise from approaching aircraft, no parachutes, nothing. Nothing but pregnant silence screaming at me. Where are you? I'm ready to kill you before you kill me. Why the hell can't we stop fighting and be friends?

Our CO visits our foxholes, one by one, making his presence felt day and night, giving his orders over and over again. 'Shoot as many of the bastards as you can as soon as they open their parachutes. Remember they can't shoot back at you while they are dangling in the air. You are the Regiment Feldherrnhalle! The Führer depends on you!'

The CO comes to Kurt and me in our musty little hideaway. 'Hey, Weiss,' he says to me. 'Are you ready to die for your country?'

'Yes, Captain, sir,' I lie unashamedly, shaking from top to toe. 'Yes, Captain, sir.'

'Thou shalt not kill', says the Bible.

'Love your enemies and pray for those who persecute you.'

'Blessed are the meek for they shall inherit the earth.'

Well, you mysterious God up there, You didn't create us as perfect as you'd wanted to, did You? I'm pretty sure that I won't inherit anything at all. Maybe I'll end up with a hole in my head, rotting away in one of these boggy shitholes.

'Love your enemies.' What the hell are You talking about? This is not a game of killing each other with kindness. Nobody is using heartshaped bullets in a bloody war, nobody!

I was not one little bit upset when the invasion of France did not eventuate in the Rhone Delta.

After a week of red alert, we abandoned our positions. Tired, filthy and aching all over, we loaded our weapons and equipment onto the trucks and made our way back to the friendly village we had left in such a hurry.

Sure, we didn't get anything like the welcome accolades our garrison troops of Prenzlau enjoyed on their return from routing Poland. But the friendly people of Charmant didn't pelt us with rotten eggs and tomatoes either. They stood in their doorways or leaned out from their windows and waved to us, obviously quite happy to see us back. Many of the children ran, laughing and shouting, alongside the trucks and followed us into the school yard, where Pierre waited for us, already prepared to do business with us once more.

We had a big party that evening. Our army cook prepared enough meals to feed us and half the population of Charmant. We supplied the calories and they reciprocated with the alcohol needed to turn an informal gathering into a humdinger fiesta. And while some grimfaced, dyed-in-the-wool Boche-haters hid their disgusted souls behind heavy drawn curtains and cursed such frank display of fraternisation, the rest of us had ourselves a ball. We drank together, we ate together, we danced together and we rejoiced together. And, strange as it may sound, we had the same reasons to celebrate. We celebrated peace together, the peace that was still well alive in a little township in the deep south of France, a peace that would have been shattered if a British or American invasion had eventuated.

Françoise, the local school teacher who had a German mother and spoke German fluently, told me why she had reasons to celebrate. 'We don't want to have the war on our very own doorstep,' she explained. 'We are happy because there was no invasion. We don't want Charmant and its people destroyed, neither by you nor by the English or the Americans. We didn't ask to be occupied and we need no liberators to destroy our village. All we want is to live our own lives in peace and harmony.'

★　★　★

But army life is so damned unpredictable. We had only just settled back into the daily routine of field exercises, of brainwashing, of demolishing the odd bottle of vin blanc or vin rouge, when the army decided to shift us from the little village where I for one would have loved to spend the rest of the war, perhaps even the rest of my life.

We said adieu to Charmant and to the friends we'd made. Pierre made me promise that I would come and visit after the war. We boarded our trucks and headed off into the unknown again, uncertain of what the future held for us.

A couple of hours later we were on top of the world. I'd never seen waters bigger than dear old Uckersee in all my living days. Now I feasted my eyes on the breathtaking vastness of an ocean, as our convoy followed the coast road along the shores of the Mediterranean Sea. Suddenly the glum and pessimistic mood gave way to joyful jubilation. To convey our total exhilaration to all and sundry, we sang ditties of utter misery, dirges of death and of river barges crashing into the Lorelei; and even the young man who broke his neck climbing a mountain in search of an Edelweiss as a token of his love got a fair go in our joyful medley of woeful songs of unrequited love and despair.

Yes, we'd reached the pinnacle of happiness.

The road we followed took us along the coastline all the way from Nice to Monte Carlo. I kept on glancing at my jackboots, waiting for them to turn into glass slippers and for our coach to revert to a pumpkin again. But it wasn't a fairytale ride at all.

This time, however, we did move into private quarters. As a matter of fact my group was assigned to a palatial mansion that nestled into the mountains rising gently from the sea. A corporal from the Quartermaster staff took twelve of us through the building. He opened the curtains in a huge living room and pointed at the magnificent view across half of Monaco, the harbour and the sea.

'Cop an eyeful of that,' he said. 'No Jew, no matter how rich he is, deserves a view like that, ja?'

'A Jew owns all this?'

'Sure did, but not any more. Lucky for him he got away before the Gestapo got hold of him. God only knows where he's hiding. Anyway, make yourselves at home. You aren't averse to sleeping under damask bed sheets, are you?'

It's a crying shame, but we even used expensive white damask sheets for camouflage when we were assigned to ocean watch at the slender lighthouse on the end of the narrow pier that reached a long way out into the tranquil blue ocean. The white walls of the lighthouse were alive, reflecting a gently moving pattern of sun and light and waves. We were in paradise and I hoped we could stay there until the war was won.

'Or lost,' said Kurt, my wise Kamerad and friend.

Then, with conditions as perfect as they could possibly have been for me and my comrades, the blasted Italians had to come along and spoil it all. One day they were our friends — a friendship we looked upon rather doubtfully — and the next day they turned against their government and joined forces with the opposition. Well, what the heck, history has proved that it's to one's advantage to have Italy for an enemy rather than an ally anyway.

While it wasn't a comfortable feeling suddenly to have the front line almost at the doorstep of our mansions, we took the news lightheartedly. It would be a lot easier to thrash the Italians than to defend the beach of Monaco against an invading armada of British and American warships.

'Red sunrise in the morning, glow for us, for we shall soon die' — that's what we sang at the break of day, when we mounted our trucks in full battle gear, more than ready to punish the traitors.

It took about half an hour before we crossed the border and entered enemy territory.

The streets of Menton were deserted. Not a single shot was fired. Were we driving straight into an ambush? We waited tensely for something to happen. We had one round in the barrel and five in the magazine. A machine-gun, mounted on the cabin roof of our truck, was sweeping apprehensively from side to side, the gunner's finger on the trigger. With adrenalin surging through our tensed bodies, sweat dripping from our armpits, our convoy of 'braves' crawled slowly and ever so cautiously towards an empty sentry box and the open gate to an army barracks complex that housed hundreds of Mussolini's Carabinieris — spaghetti eaters we called them.

Really, we should have known better. We should have thrown caution to the wind. But we didn't. With our nerves almost reaching flashpoint, we were disappointed and relieved at the same time when our disbelieving eyes fell upon rows and rows of Italian warriors standing neatly assembled outside their barracks with their hands raised high in surrender. Their weapons were stacked tidily in pyramid fashion at their feet. The whole damn lot of the 'new enemy' grinned at us as if they'd already won the war and we were losing it quickly. Maybe they were right!

Very unprepared to imprison or take care of a whole battalion of retiring former allies, and definitely unwilling to share the luxury of our mansions with them, we ensured that all their weaponry was safely locked away and told them to go home to their families.

My Papa must have had his wires crossed

when he kept on telling me how much he hated the French. If he was really serious about disliking anybody at all, shouldn't he have despised the Italians rather than the amicable French?

Kurt had a letter from home waiting for him when we got back to our palace in Monte Carlo. He read it a few times, then sat on his bed and shook his head. 'I don't believe it,' he mumbled.

'Bad news, Kurt?' I asked him.

'Yeah, pretty lousy news,' he replied, crumbling the letter in his hands. 'It doesn't make sense, Ollie, no sense at all.'

'Something wrong with your family at home?'

Kurt reached for a cigarette, found one and lit it. The hand that held the match was shaking. He took a couple of deep draws, looked once more at the crushed letter and said: 'My wife writes that they're carpet-bombing Berlin. She and Christina spend almost every night in the air-raid shelter.'

'That's terrible! That's awful news.'

'It's gonna get worse, Kamerad,' mused Kurt. 'And worst of all is that everybody will say afterwards: 'It wasn't my fault.' I ask you, Ollie, what the hell are we doing here in Monte Carlo? Shouldn't we be at home, blasting the Tommies out of the sky instead of screwing French prostitutes?'

Maybe I shouldn't have mentioned to Kurt that our Luftwaffe was bombing shit out of London as well. For a brief moment I thought he'd knock me out. But he kept his temper and muttered: 'Two wrongs never make a right.'

I could have argued with him about that all day. If two wrongs never made a right, how come it was right for human beings to kill each other? But I was wise enough to keep my thoughts to myself. Perhaps if I'd had Helga and our child sheltering in air-raid bunkers every night, I would have felt more compassion for my angry friend. Maybe I was lucky that I had no one to worry about but myself.

10

'Achtung!'

Our company stood assembled in front of headquarters. All the sentries had been recalled from their outposts and vantage points along the rocky foreshore some hundred metres to the west of the lighthouse, where I'd spent many wonderful hours on coastwatch duty, perching in the lofty cliffs like a mutton bird, gazing through binoculars and dreaming of a distant paradise where the words 'Schnell!' and 'Jawohl!' and 'Achtung!' had never been heard of.

Now there was something more in the air than a gentle autumn breeze. Even if the army had turned you into a complete jackass, and you had convinced yourself that the penis was the one and only friendly weapon at a soldier's disposal, you were still quite receptive to premonitions. I knew, before another word was spoken, that I would never stand guard outside the Monte Carlo Casino again, where, in spite of the war, the roulette wheels still spun twenty-four hours a day; where fortunes were made and lost faster than lives on the Russian front.

'Die Augen . . . rechts!'

Our heads jerked to the right, eyes fixed in a glassy stare. Right hands holding the rifles. Middle fingers of our left hands lined up along the seam of the trouser leg. Motionless we stood, like remote-controlled zombies, like play-dough in the palm of fate. We watched without seeing and listened without hearing as the senior sergeant reported to the CO that the whole company was assembled, ready to hear the good news. Good news in the *army*?

'Germany needs you,' proclaimed our CO, as if we didn't know that already. 'Our Führer depends on your fighting spirit. The Russian front needs brave soldiers like you. It needs soldiers who know how to fight and destroy Stalin and his degenerate hordes of Bolsheviks. All Stalingrad veterans step forward.'

My boots were glued to the ground for a few seconds. My heart was beating so fast, I was afraid it would shatter my rib cage. Not Russia again! Holy hell, not bloody Russia again! Haven't I had my fair share of blood and mud and lice and fanatic Russkies?

I honestly felt like jumping off the cliff into the sea and swimming all the way to wherever the tide would carry me. If I drowned, it would still be a better choice to drown in the ocean rather than die for something I found harder to believe in as time went by.

211

Together with all my old comrades, I stepped forward nevertheless. I glanced back. All the young rookies, who had yet to find out what an angry shot sounded like, had not moved from their spots. All of them were openly displaying bitter disappointment and envy. All of them were bursting with the same eagerness to fight and to die for the Führer, the Volk and the Vaterland, that I had experienced before I discovered there was no glamorous side to a war.

'Damn You, God,' I muttered through clenched teeth, and I looked up into the sky to catch a glimpse of the One who was supposed to watch over us. 'It's not fair, God,' I said. 'You've done it again, haven't You? Don't You know that You've got Your priorities all wrong. Why do You have to pick on me again? Haven't You punished me enough for whatever I've done wrong in the past? Why can't You send the rookies to Russia? Do You hate me that much?'

Our CO wasn't through with us yet. He must have felt uneasy about sending us off and him staying behind with his luscious concubine, living the good life. 'I really wish that I could go with you and lead you into the first charge when you get to the front,' he lied. 'But I can't. I have to follow my orders just as you have to obey yours. Go with God,

Kameraden. God is on our side. Good luck! Heil Hitler!'

'Heil Hitler,' we shouted obediently. But our voices lacked the old enthusiasm. Silently, we cursed Hitler and the army and the Russians and the whole damned war.

Our guest role in the Regiment Feldherrn-halle had come to an unexpected and sudden end. With the removal from our coat sleeves of the strip that spelt 'Feldherrnhalle', the transformation was complete. Our stint in the army elite was over. It didn't take the waving of a magic wand to turn us back into what we were supposed to be: valuable but expendable cannon fodder.

Kurt and I got drunk together on our last evening in Monte Carlo. Actually, we wanted nothing more than a few drinks to rid ourselves of inhibitions, so we could go out and screw every prostitute who was willing and desperate enough to take us on. But our plan misfired. Our consciences got in the way. Kurt started talking about his family, and how much he loved his wife and his daughter, and I started crying out for my beloved though vanished Helga, and we didn't put a foot outside the door.

Before the night was out, Kurt was dancing with a broomstick and singing: 'Heute blau, und morgen blau, und übermorgen wieder.'

Yes, drunk today, drunk tomorrow, and drunk again the next day. Oh, what the hell, wasn't it better to get rotten drunk rather than to put the muzzle of your rifle into your mouth and pull the trigger?

The following morning, nursing an almost unbearable hangover, we sat on a thick layer of straw and let our legs dangle from the open door of a cattle wagon.

I used to love trains when I was a kid. I didn't love this one. Now the clickety-click of iron wheels grinding along the steel tracks got on my nerves. We were going in the wrong direction. Our journey would take us from the crisp white sheets, soft beds and pretty girls to a hole in the ground somewhere, some-bloody-where; a hole a metre and a half deep, only a bit shallower than a regulation grave, and just the right width for a coffin.

The carefree and proud days of the Hitlerjugend had gone, once and for all. Fighting for the Führer and dying for the Vaterland were no more the greatest honours bestowed on an aspiring German youngster like myself.

All too soon, Mother Russia opened her arms wide in embrace. Welcome to the war. Welcome to the mud. Welcome to the lice. Welcome to hell on earth.

Once we got off the troop train, we did

what infantrymen are trained to do. We walked and we walked. Some wayward artillery shells exploded uncomfortably close. We didn't know where we were, but we certainly knew where we were going to.

It must have been around midday when we marched into the deserted remnants of a city. What an eerie place! It was hard to imagine that, not long ago, happy children had played hopscotch in the now rubble-covered streets. 'Go away,' warned the chimneys that sprouted from the desolate ruins. 'This city is for the dead. Go away and leave us in peace.'

Most likely, the Russians knew of our arrival. Their heavy guns were zooming in on us, and shells were exploding all over the place. We jumped for our lives long before we were told to take cover. I spotted a cellar window at street level, about three metres away to my left. I dived for it — rifle, gas mask, backpack and all. I never even came close to touching the window frame as I flew through the opening into the cellar, like Superman on a special mission. When the barrage stopped I had a hell of a job to get out of the window back onto the street. I had to take all my gear off first, and it was still a tight squeeze. So how did I get into the cellar in the first place? Perhaps it was what they called shrinking in awe of the enemy.

It took me a while to put all my goods and chattels back where they belonged. By the time I'd caught up with the tail end of our procession we were well clear of the ruined city. We were out in the open field, and I couldn't see my pal Kurt anywhere. If ever I needed a friend I needed him now.

The shelling, which had eased up for a moment, started once more. The Russian gunners had adjusted the range and we walked in the middle of hell again. Oops, that was close! Backside up in the air, nose close to the ground. Hurrah! Didn't get me this time, did you?

'Kurt, Kurt! Where are you?'

'Pick up your rifle, soldier! Get up and bloody walk.'

'Yes, sir.' I followed orders blindly.

The world around me had gone stark-raving mad. I screamed into the inferno: 'Kurt! Where the hell are you?'

'Keep walking, soldier!'

'Hey, Russki. Hit me on the head with one of those damned shells. I don't want to be a cripple for the rest of my life. Hit me on the head or don't hit me at all, you bastards. Kurrrrt!'

'Keep your voice down, you stupid idiot. If you shout any louder Stalin will hear you in the Kremlin.' Kurt's voice. Thank God he was still alive. 'Come on, you big hero,' he teased me.

I felt like I was half dead. 'I don't want to be a hero,' I moaned. 'Heroes don't live long enough. I'd rather be a coward and stay alive.'

Honestly, I didn't know whether I was shivering from the cold or from sheer terror. What did it matter? One was as bad as the other. There wasn't much difference between freezing to death and being blown to pieces. The end result would inevitably be the same.

I don't think I would have survived another day without the support and strength of my friend. All the nightmares from Stalingrad started to haunt me again. Kurt was my Rock of Gibraltar. I knew I could weather any storm with him by my side. He was walking next to me now, carrying a wooden box of hand-grenades by one handle. Kurt was my crutch and my brace. If I had to die, I'd much rather die before he did.

'You look tired,' he said, still mocking me. 'Why don't you hang onto the other handle of this box and have a rest?'

'I'm not a pack mule,' I protested. But I reached for the rope handle just the same and kept on walking next to him. Walking, stumbling, taking cover next to him and rising again by his side like a shadow. Finally, the order came to dig in for the night.

★   ★   ★

At dawn the Russkies opened up with everything they had. They had plenty of it, every round falling about five hundred metres short of our position. There were plenty of Russian tanks out yonder as well. Long before we could hear the noise of clanging tracks, the T-34s betrayed their presence with the spine-chilling bang-boom of their cannon.

I couldn't understand why we hadn't been shifted into the front line during the night. Kurt was smarter than me. He thought that our Big Brass had expected this morning's attack. 'Take my word,' he said angrily. 'They're sacrificing the poor bastards up front, and we've been brought in to stop the stampede.'

Now it made sense that, some fifty metres behind us, hushed work had been carried out right through the night. Mounds of earth had been pushed up. And it was now light enough for us to see the multibarrelled twenty-millimetre anti-aircraft guns behind each mound.

We received strict orders. 'Do not open fire until the ack-acks open up.'

It was freezing cold and yet sweat was running down my brow from under the helmet, stinging my eyes and staining the

218

lenses of my spectacles. I trembled from head to toe.

Then they came running towards us, weaving, stumbling, shouting, screaming with panic-stricken voices. 'Don't shoot, Kameraden! Don't shoot!'

Men in the proud uniforms of the Third Reich, running for their lives. German soldiers in chaotic retreat. God Almighty, this can't be true! Germans — men just like Kurt and myself — dropping their rifles, running, running for their lives.

The first fleeing comrades are crossing our lines, continuing their run towards safety. I can see their ashen faces, their eyes wide open, filled with dirt and fear. Some die before they reach us. Jesus Christ. German soldiers shot in the back! What the hell is going on?

Towering shadows of T-34 tanks are breaking through the murky mist that forms the horizon, spreading death, spitting fire and brimstone like ferocious dragons. The first outlines of Russian soldiers emerge through the haze.

They come at us, hundreds of them, thousands of them. Sweat is still running down my face, sweat as cold as ice. I still tremble.

And without warning, fear turns into rage,

into fury, into madness. Man turns into robot without soul, without conscience. The flak starts firing from behind us. Bang, you're dead. Bang, you're dead. Bang, you're dead.

What is it that turns me into a murderer? The devil within? The devil without? No! It is raw and unadulterated fear that makes me pull that trigger, that makes me scream: 'Kill the bastards! Kill them all!'

'For Christ's sake, Ollie, fix that bayonet on your rifle.' Kurt is furious with me. 'Damn you! The bayonet! Can't you hear me, you stupid bastard? The bayonet!'

I hear what he tells me. I scream back at him. 'I can't, Kurt. I bloody well can't!'

'Go to hell, you good for nothing bastard.'

'I'm there already,' I yell. And I put my rifle down and reach for the hand-grenades. Too many Russians out there. Can't kill enough of them with a rifle. I pull the first pin. Jesus, three seconds seem longer than a lifetime. Einundzwanzig, zweiundzwanzig, dreiundzwanig and throw. And again, and again.

Our multi-barrelled anti-aircraft guns are mowing them down like a million scythes cutting the stalks of golden rye at harvest time. Yet the T-34s are breaking through our lines. Kurt and I are in momentary darkness as one of the steel monsters straddles our foxhole with its tracks. We brace ourselves in the corners of the hole. I bury my head between my legs and cover my face with clammy hands. I want to pray to God but the words won't come out. My heart stops beating. I wait for the steel tracks to twist and bury me alive. But they don't. God only knows why they don't. Light floods back into our refuge. We are still alive. For how much longer will we breathe?

Bang-boom. Bang-boom. Our Tiger tanks finally come to the party. They come racing towards our lines, firing as fast as they can. And the guns of the Russian T-34s can't penetrate their armour.

The Russian attack folds and turns into defeat. Burning T-34s are scattered all over the battlefield, together with rows and rows, waves and waves, of Russian soldiers who died for Mother Russia because they had no other choice.

In hot pursuit of the enemy our tanks grind their way across the battlefield, their blood-stained tracks smashing prone and not so prone bodies into pulp, friend and foe alike. Above all the battle noise I can hear shrill voices calling out for help. 'Hilfe! Hilfe! Sanitäter!'

Death knows no prejudice. Death does not discriminate between friend and foe. Death has no friends. It has victims, nothing but victims.

I got out of our foxhole not because I wanted to; I crawled out of the safe shelter because Kurt did, and so did all of my comrades. Follow orders, you shitheads! And that's what we did, no matter how reluctantly.

Thus we began our counter attack. My feet stumbled over dead bodies. I didn't dare look down too often. Whenever I did look, to stop myself from falling over something, I had dead eyes looking at me — dead eyes, terrified eyes, irreversibly dead eyes.

We kept on running forward, kept on shooting at anything that moved, until we reached the foxholes of our original front line. We had regained approximately a kilometre, a lousy kilometre of land that wasn't even our own, land that never belonged to us and never should. And every square metre of the recaptured soil was drenched with Russian and German blood. Heroes and cowards, friends and enemies lay side by side, very dead and blessed with eternal peace.

Time was nothing, and time was everything. Time gave us another sunrise to look at. Time gave us another ration of brandy or schnapps to dull our sense. Time gave us a chance to smoke another cigarette. Time was God and God was time; that is, if there was a

God at all. And time was the devil as well. All of us believed in the powers of the devil, because before the sun set again there would be more agonised voices calling out loudly, wailing voices, desperate voices, dying voices. 'Sanitäter! Medic! Help!'

Time does not stand still for anybody. It just goes on like an endless chain, making you a day older with every sunrise, if you are lucky enough to survive. I lost track of time. Each night, when the protective mantle of darkness descended over friend and enemy alike, it was the Russian aircraft that had full control of the airspace above us. Hermann Göring didn't just renege on his promise to protect the skies above Germany with his beloved Luftwaffe; he obviously had neither Heinkels nor Messerschmitts or Junkers left to make our situation a little more tolerable.

We called the Russian bombers 'sewing machines'. From the distance, they sounded very much like the old treadle machines our parents were proud to own. The heavy, clumsy bombers could fly at incredibly low speed without falling out of the sky. Their undersides were fortified with armour. Unless one could draw a bead on the pilot, it was almost impossible to shoot them down with a rifle or machine-gun.

We had a tremendous respect for their

hawk-eyed bombardiers, who could see the end of a cigarette glow in the dark. It seemed that they waited for you to take just one careless puff. Then they'd pick up one of their hand-thrown bombs and drop it fair and square right into your very lap. And, bingo, you were cured of your addiction to nicotine!

Sundays and weekdays were all the same, passing by unnoticed and rather uncherished. The coming day, the tomorrow, was the one and only thing that mattered. Each time I watched the sun rise, I thanked God for letting me survive. No, I don't think I thanked Him because I believed in Him. I simply thanked Him because I had nobody else to say thank you to.

My infatuation with Yvette, I suddenly realised, had turned back into what it was in the first place. Though it had had everything to do with sexual drive and expertise and unbearable frustrations, it had had nothing at all in common with true love. There was only one girl I loved, really loved. And I pleaded with God to take good care of her until the day we could be reunited. To me, Helga was the only thing in my life worth dying for, worth fighting for. I sure didn't want to die for nothing at all. Nobody wants to die for nothing.

We soon got used to the term 'tactical

withdrawal', which sounded a hell of a lot better than 'running away from the enemy', which happened almost every day. Once in flight, the fighting spirit flagged. On most occasions we offered only token resistance. The war was lost. Why did we have to go on killing each other? Why didn't our Führer just cut his losses, salvage what was left to be salvaged, surrender, and stop spilling the blood of those who believed in him?

Like so many times before, the Russians came at us again. This time they attacked in broad daylight. They really meant business. We had no ack-acks to reinforce our lines, no tanks to increase our firepower. It was us against them. And neither the most fervent nor the most desperate could have turned the enemy back.

They came and they conquered. They were just as insane as we were. They came like a huge steamroller, destroying all in their path, closer and closer, unstoppable and indestructible, outnumbering us perhaps ten or a hundred to one. You could shoot ten, and twenty others would fill the void. Our situation was despairingly hopeless.

I considered my options. No, I reflected, I was not scared of dying. I was much more frightened of losing an arm or ending up as a prisoner of war somewhere in God-forsaken

Siberia, where I'd suffer a slow and horrible death. Never!

I fell to my knees inside our foxhole. I recalled my encounter with the young Russian soldier who'd put a hand-grenade under his chin and blown his head off. I wouldn't have the guts to do that. How about pushing a grenade down the pants, where I couldn't see it, and blow the crap out of myself? 'Oh, God,' I mumbled. 'Give me the strength, will you, please give me the strength.'

I don't know if Kurt knew what I was up to. His voice interfered with my plans. 'Come on, Ollie. We'll be dead meat if we don't get out and run. Come on!'

I didn't budge. I cowered in the corner of our hole, trying to hide from reality for as long as possible. 'Leave me alone,' I grunted. 'Mind your own business. I'm sick of running.'

Kurt grabbed me by the collar of my coat and started to drag me out of my shelter. I screamed at him: 'Get your dirty hands off me, you big hero!' But he wouldn't let go.

'You stupid, spineless heap of shit!' he yelled. 'I'm not gonna let you die, do you hear? I'm not gonna let you. Be a man just for once, for Helga's sake, for your own sake. Come on. We've run many times before and we've survived. Come on!'

He dragged me all the way out of the foxhole. 'Run for it, you gutless bastard! Run!'

'I don't want to run, Kurt,' I wailed. But I did run. Once out from cover I had no choice but to run. After a few strides I threw my rifle away. I unbuckled my belt and dropped all the ballast that slowed me down. For a fleeting moment I visualised the inscription on the belt buckle: 'God with us.' God had changed sides now, hadn't He? Well, it was no real surprise to me that I couldn't rely on Him when I needed Him most. It was just as well that I could run faster than anyone else. Maybe I could outrun my fate.

We ran towards a cluster of apparently abandoned trucks. I thought to myself, wheels are faster than feet, and I shouted at Kurt: 'Can you drive?'

He said he couldn't.

'Doesn't matter, Kurt. I'll get us out of this.' I suddenly thought, if I can fly through a cellar window that's too small to crawl out of, I can do anything.

Kurt told me I was crazy.

'That's what my mother kept on telling me. Come on!'

Suddenly I had no time to be frightened any more. I was in command, I was the boss.

I was the driver. We claimed the first truck we came to. Somehow we got the engine to start. The gearbox sounded as if it would disintegrate but it didn't, and we were on our way. I couldn't change gears. I pushed the accelerator all the way to the floor and got us out of trouble, though I had a hell of a job trying to stop the vehicle until the engine stalled.

'Well Kurt, how about it! I told you I could drive a bloody truck, didn't I?'

Kurt didn't answer. I nudged him in the rib cage with my elbow. He sat slumped in the corner and pretended not to hear me. I laughed at him. 'Hey, stupid, stop fooling around. We've made it. It's time to celebrate.'

Kurt was still playing dead. I nudged him again. He slid off the seat. His head was screwed around in a ridiculous angle. And then I saw the blood and the torn flesh of his neck. I lifted his head and turned it, and looked into the eyes of a dead soldier.

I guess I screamed with rage as I dragged him carefully out of the truck cabin. I put him on the ground gently, sat down and placed his head in my lap. I closed his eyes — I didn't want him to see me cry. I cursed the army, the war, the Führer and the Man in Heaven who'd let it all happen.

Later in the day, when the sun set and

painted the sky with the colour of Kurt's blood, I chased everybody away who wanted to help me dig his grave. He and I had dug so many holes together. This one was my job, and only mine! I emptied his pockets and put the contents in a neat little pile. I removed the dog-tag from his bloody neck and lifted him a little, so I could slip his belt, together with the Feldflasche and Brotbeutel, out from under him. I found his wallet in his back pocket and discovered a photo of his wife and daughter. Then I pulled him carefully into his resting place, put the family snapshot on his chest, and cried and cried as I covered his body with soil. Erde zu Erde — dust to dust. Somehow, as I sat there and grieved for my friend, I found it difficult to believe in life after death.

Kurt was dead, very very dead. And nothing would raise him up again, nothing. I wished that I could have died instead of him. He had so much to live for, and I had so little to lose.

To hell with you, Adolf Hitler! To hell with your war and your promise of a Thousand Year Reich. You are no better than Stalin and Churchill and all the others. Why the hell can't you all go out there and fight your own battles? It's not fair, do you hear? It's not fair at all.

I handed Kurt's effects over to our platoon leader, keeping the belt and the attachments that went with it for myself to replace those I'd thrown away. I felt proud and honoured to wear part of my friend's equipment. Then I pushed his rifle upside down into the ground and put his helmet on top. Goodbye, soldier. Goodbye, my friend.

The newsreaders in radio stations all over Germany would tell their listeners that another 'tactical withdrawal' on the Eastern Front had gone as planned, with no significant loss of life.

* * *

When the Russkies came for us again a couple of days later, I was more than ready for them. Perhaps it takes the loss of one's best comrade and friend to make a soldier out of a frightened youngster. I had a lot of avenging to do, and I had no scruples whatsoever. Up to now I'd only aimed my rifle at faceless shapes and shadows in uniform. Not any more! The Russkies were bastards. They had murdered my friend. They deserved to die.

Rain is not as particular as God. Rain takes no sides. It is impartial and, as was the case with us, it brought our series of 'tactical withdrawals' to a tactical impasse. Things got kind of bogged down between us; the no-man's land turned into a quagmire where no man would want to go. And when the steadily falling rain turned into sleet, everybody on either side pulled down the hatches and tried to make life somehow bearable.

Since Kurt parted company with me I'd turned into a hermit. I stayed by myself and minded my own business. I didn't want to get attached to somebody else again, only to end up burying him. Anyway, I was on the warpath with war, with God, with Hitler and with myself, because I was lousy company, even to myself.

I had fifteen centimetres of water in my foxhole and my boots were too soggy to take off to check if I'd grown webbing between the toes. I'd covered my 'home' with my ground sheet to keep the water out, but it was a hopeless battle. Water had come trickling in from everywhere, turning the foxhole into a duck pond.

And there I was one day, feeling as low and rotten as humanly possible, when a strange voice called out: 'Hey, you, soldier! Are you down there?'

I would have lifted the ground sheet very quickly if the words had been spoken in

Russian. But lucky for me they weren't. 'Whoever you are,' I yelled, 'go away. I don't like having visitors in weather like this.'

The caller must have been an idiot or a sadist or both. He grabbed the corner of my 'roof' and pulled. I protested angrily: 'Hey, man, what the hell do you think you're doing? It's raining out there, in case you don't know.'

The sleet was coming down quite heavily. I couldn't see too well with a whitish, watery mess sliding down my spectacles. One day I'm gonna invent windscreen wipers for glasses, I thought to myself. I'll make a fortune.

But, alas, Lady Fortune did not smile at me at that very moment. The voice barked: 'Stand to attention, soldier!'

I got all confused and panicky and failed to react.

'Achtung! And I mean Achtung! Aaaaa-aaachtung!'

Struggling to my feet, I tried to click my heels like any good German soldier when he's told to stand to attention. But my boots didn't want to click. They just went slosh, splash, slosh in the muddy water. Then I saw the caller's boots. I froze. A beautiful pair of longsided boots — covered in mud but beautiful. Only officers wore boots like that. I looked further up and the face that looked angrily down at me seemed to be vaguely familiar. Then the penny dropped. How unlucky can a man get? The officer commanding our battalion had come to pay me a visit. Why me, for heavens sake? I had enough trouble with army life as things were. Why did he have to pick me out of the crowd?

'Attention!'

As ridiculous as this may sound, it actually happened. Our battalion commander stood outside my foxhole in pouring rain and gave me seven days detention for failing to make a proper response to an officer.

The whole scene was unbelievably comical. I found it very difficult not to laugh out loud. But I couldn't stop a smile from creeping into my face as I said: 'Much obliged, sir. Thank you very much, sir.'

The man with the expensive boots and expansive waistline did not smile back at me. He said instead: 'Make that another seven days for insubordination.'

I was still smiling. I couldn't help myself. I wondered if he'd kick me out of the army and send me home to Prenzlau if I gave him a bit more cheek.

He saw nothing funny in the situation at all. 'Get out of that hole right now, soldier. Report to your CO on the double. Move!'

I was quite certain that he'd be happy to

shoot me if I decided to disobey his order. It took me a while to scale the slippery sides of my foxhole. Then, after taking a few stumbles in what I hoped was the right direction, I turned to have another glance at the crazy officer, to ensure that my bearings were right. He had vanished into thin air. As I moved on, I saw nothing around me but the grey, opaque mess of sleet. The only noises I could hear came from raindrops splashing into puddles, and from the thump, thump of my fast-beating heart. Believe me, I was not a happy warrior.

There is a lesson to be learnt from everything that happens. I knew now exactly how a blind man must feel when his guide dog runs away from him. What if I should stray away from our own lines and end up on the Russian side?

Not wanting to be heard by the Russkies but wanting to be heard by my comrades in the next foxhole, I kept on whispering, almost inaudibly, 'Hallo, Zweiter Zug.' Hello, Second Platoon. And guided by the responses of my comrades I tumbled and slithered along our defence line. All went well until I fell into a mud hole. When I got to my feet again I'd lost all sense of direction. With neither moon nor sun nor stars for guidance, I was hopelessly lost.

I counted my paces. I knew that our foxholes were approximately forty paces apart. But not all of them were occupied. 'Hello, Second Platoon. Hello, Second Platoon.' Thirty, forty, fifty, sixty paces without an answer to my calls. Dear God, help me. I froze and listened in the leaden silence. I sneaked into the unknown for another ten frightened steps. I called out ever so softly, and heard no reply. What was I going to do? Sit down right there and wait for the weather to clear? The thought alone made my skin shrivel with fear.

'Our flag is fluttering up front . . . ' I'd sung that song a hundred if not a thousand times. Holy hell, did I need a flag now to show me the way! I forced myself to put one foot in front of the other, every step driving me closer to a well-deserved nervous breakdown.

Where, for goodness sake, were our lines? Anybody out there, say something to me! Say something, as long as it's not 'Idi suh dah' in Russian.

I scolded myself for my stupidity. If only I'd moved back into my own foxhole after I first turned and lost sight of the High Chief, I would have been safe. I guess the thought that I might be able to spend a whole beautiful fortnight in a dry and cozy lockup somewhere way behind our lines had been too tempting to ignore.

Now I'd got myself into one hell of a jam. I knew that the first words I'd hear would determine my fate. I didn't like the odds.

'Zweiter Zug,' I whispered with baited breath.

'Halt! Wer da!'

Jesus Christ, who says that the German language is ugly, guttural and harsh? 'Halt! Wer da!' was like music to my ears.

'Don't shoot, Kamerad! Don't shoot,' I said in a shaky voice. 'It's me, Ollie Weiss from Second Platoon!'

I was indeed a lucky man. The German words came from right in front of me. Somehow I'd walked in a circle instead of a straight line. If the circle had been a bit wider, I'd have been on my way to the Siberian saltmines or else I'd have been dead by now.

I only had another hundred metres to go to the bunker of Company Headquarters and I got there without getting lost again. Fate once more intervened in my life. I was just about to tell my CO that the battalion commander had sentenced me to two weeks detention when I slipped, hit something hard and lost consciousness. My nose was bleeding profusely when I came to. My spectacles lay broken in the mud, and the CO grinned at me and said drily, 'Don't you think you take dropping in for a visit a mite too literally?'

In spite of everything imaginable going wrong on this most remarkable day, the cards were stacked in my favour. My CO was himself myopic. Without his spectacles he couldn't see the sights of a rifle any better than I could. He said to me: 'You aren't much of an asset to us even with your glasses, Weiss. And without them you'll be a straight-out pain in the arse; the army will be better off without you. Hitch a ride back to the field hospital — if you can find someone mad enough to drive in this weather. And don't come back here in a hurry!'

'Thank you, sir,' I grinned.

'Hang on a second, Weiss. I'd better give you a note to verify that you broke your spectacles by accident when you crashed into my helmet. Without official verification you might find yourself flirting with a firing squad instead of a pretty nurse.'

He extracted a small writing pad from a waterproof container, found a pencil, wrote a short note and handed it to me. 'Put it in a safe place,' he told me. 'Don't lose it or you'll be in more trouble than you can handle. Keep in mind that malingerers are shot nowadays.' And for a final goodbye he added: 'Take all the time you want, Weiss. Don't come back before the war is finished. We won't miss you.'

On the day Kurt was killed I'd thrown all ballast away, but I had kept the tin that was meant to hold the gas mask. Most of us discarded the mask as soon as we got to the front. Sturdy and weatherproof, the tin kept our cigarettes, matches and writing materials from getting wet. Before my CO had a chance to change his mind, the treasured note was safely tucked away in my waterproof 'treasure chest'.

'Just one last question, sir.' I was already digging my hands and toes into the slippery clay to make a speedy departure. 'Which way do I have to go?'

Maybe the Russians heard my question. Perhaps they were looking for me or for the battalion commander. Anyway, stupid as it was to shoot flares into the air in lousy weather like this, they did. I could only just see the glow in the sky. It didn't tell me where to go but it certainly told me where not to. I took off like a rocket. I slipped and slithered but didn't fall once.

★   ★   ★

When I told the interviewing doctor at the field hospital that I needed nothing more than a pair of glasses, he muttered something about handing me over to the military police. But he changed his mind after he read the note from my company commander. 'I guess there is a first for everything,' he said, still confused. 'But this is utterly ridiculous. Why come to see me? I can sew your guts back into your stomach. But spectacles? I'm a surgeon, not a bloody optometrist.'

He must have read that note from my CO twenty times before he filled out a cardboard tag and put it around my neck. 'It's your lucky day, soldier,' he told me. 'I'll have to put you on the next train. I still can't believe this is actually happening.'

'Neither can I, Doc,' I grinned, somewhat embarrassed.

I made myself useful on the hospital train that took us from the Eastern Front all the way to a proper hospital in Cracow, the Polish city where I'd guarded the motor-pool two years earlier, when I still had my brain full of slogans and bullshit along with ambitions to sacrifice my life for my Führer and the Thousand Year Reich.

Perhaps I was a coward among heroes on that train. Yet I didn't feel like a coward at all. To be helpful to people was a lot easier for me than killing them. Even the slightest hint of a smile I could bring to the face of a badly injured comrade was more valuable to me than the death of a hundred Russians. I felt as if I'd missed my vocation. For once in my life I seemed to be doing the right thing — not only for myself but also for those who could do with a helping hand and a kind word. Funny, isn't it? I'd broken my last pair of glasses, but I could see much more clearly now.

They were used to doing first things first in the army hospital in Cracow. They deloused me. They stripped me naked and sent me into a tiled cubicle to indulge myself in a hot and heavenly shower. For the first time in months my thumbnails were not stained with the blood of the myriad lice I'd squeezed to death.

They gave me an army-style haircut. They put me into new underwear and a brand new uniform. They replaced the mouldy and sodden rags I'd wrapped around my feet with a pair of warm woollen socks. They gave me a packet of smokes, a clean bed and a three-course dinner. They even gave me back a little bit of long-lost self-esteem.

The only thing they could not provide for me was a pair of glasses. None of the flabbergasted doctors had ever come across a case like mine. They really didn't like the idea of me sleeping in one of their white and comfortable hospital beds. They scrutinised my CO's note and agreed that it wasn't a forgery. Before I made myself feel too much at home in the pacifying realms of their hospice, they concluded that it was best to wash their hands of me.

They finally told me: 'If your CO states that you would be a burden and a nuisance to the whole army unless you were fitted with replacement spectacles — which of course we can't supply here — we have no option but to send you back to some place where they have damned optometrists and spectacle makers.'

As the army had apparently never considered that a shortsighted soldier might be in need of replacement spectacles, be it through misfortune or an act of God, my lucky streak continued.

Perhaps the Creator of all mankind had good reasons to stop me from dying. Perhaps He simply couldn't make up His mind whether He should send me to hell or to heaven, or to let me self-destruct without going anywhere at all.

11

I knew him only by his first name — Klaus. He was just eighteen years old. I adopted him as soon as our hospital train left Cracow and headed towards the borders of the Vaterland. At every scheduled stop we made, smiling ladies from the Red Cross supplied us with much appreciated refreshments, and trained nursing staff transported their allotted consignment of wounded soldiers to the ambulances that waited on the platforms.

Klaus never once looked out of the window, despite all the commotion and clamour that went on each time our train pulled up at a station. He just sat in his corner and waited for me to put him in the picture. I put the coffee cups into his hands, lit his cigarettes, helped him to eat his meals, walked him to the toilet and provided him with a travelogue as we crossed Germany from east to west.

It wasn't that Klaus didn't want to see with his own eyes what went on around him. Klaus had no eyes left to see anything at all. 'I would have been all right if I hadn't put my head out of a foxhole at the wrong time,' he told me when we first met on the train. 'All I can remember is a big bang, and then the lights went out. The doctors say I collected a face full of shrapnel from a hand-grenade. I guess the good news is that I won't be able to look at myself in a mirror.'

It was way beyond my range of comprehension that an eighteen-year-old boy, who had nothing but his mouth showing from a head covered with bandages, still had the gumption to hang on to his sense of humour.

I told Klaus what had happened to me and why I was a passenger on the hospital train. He laughed and said, 'Wouldn't it be a lot easier to send a pair of glasses to the front rather than sending you all the way home?'

As the train rattled along I described all the nice things I saw from the window of our carriage, but I never said a word about the sad and horrid things that brought tears to my myopic eyes, like the many ruins in and around each city we passed through. I recalled the day when I'd listened to one of Josef Göbbels' speeches on the radio: 'Do you want a total and radical war? Do you want bread or cannon?' I felt ashamed now that I had been one of those who'd said a fervent yes to an all-out war. Had I really been stupid enough to prefer cannon to a stomach full of food? I must have been out of my mind!

Now I could see the dire consequences of total warfare. Whole blocks of tenement buildings lay in ruins. The front line wasn't in Russia any more. It was right here, all over Germany, killing the very people the soldiers were meant to protect. It would take Adolf Hitler 999 years to rebuild his Thousand Year Reich. It was high time to throw in the towel, to put an end to a war that had got completely out of control.

Klaus and I and a handful of others had to change trains in the Hauptbahnhof of Frankfurt am Main. I helped Klaus to move across the platform to another train with only three or four carriages.

'I got you a window seat,' I said to my blind comrade, as soon as we settled down in a first class compartment.

'Thanks for nothing,' he replied promptly.

I'd done it again! Offering him a window seat was like buying a pair of shoes for a man without legs. Why didn't I put my foot in my mouth and keep it there?

I fumbled with my cigarettes, lit two and put one between his lips. My hands were shaking, yet his were as steady as a rock. I kept looking at the bandages that covered his face and wondered how many times he'd begged God to let him die. How would his family come to terms with his injuries and his handicap?

Even though my mother and my sister hated me, and my stepfather treated me as if I had a contagious disease, I was still a hell of a lot better off than Klaus. I still had eyes in my head to search for Helga and to look for a future for the three of us. Klaus had nothing but darkness for an unshakeable and constant companion. I couldn't help thinking that being blind might perhaps be worse than being dead twice over.

'Endstation! Alle aussteigen,' said the stationmaster, as soon as our train reached its final destination, Königstein.

I helped Klaus off the train. 'We're in the middle of the Taunus mountains,' I said. 'There's still plenty of snow about. I might take you for a sleigh ride one day, ja?'

'That would be nice, Ollie.'

★　★　★

For the life of me, I can't remember the name of the specialist who was in charge when I arrived at the eye clinic. I would love to meet him again, just for long enough to shake his hand and thank him for his kindness. You see, my life was really in his hands. Yet, when he found that I'd come all the way from the

245

Ukraine for nothing but the issue of new spectacles, he did not put me on the next train to get me back to Russia in a hurry.

As a matter of fact, he half killed himself laughing. Tears ran down his cheeks when he said, between fits of laughter: 'I can't believe this! I'm sure you've set a record of some kind, Weiss. But I don't know what to do with you either, you see. You're in the wrong place again. I can fix you up with a pair of glass eyes if you like, but we neither fit nor supply spectacles to any of our patients. We are eye surgeons, not optometrists.'

For a fleeting moment I had alarm bells ringing inside my head. 'You are not sending me back to Russia, are you?'

'No,' he said, wiping the tears from his face. 'I couldn't do that to my worst enemy. We are extremely short of staff here, and you'll come in very handy for odd jobs around the place. Tell you what, I'll make an appointment for you with an optometrist in Frankfurt, as long as you promise to work for your board and lodging. Are you any good at emptying bedpans?'

'Am I what, sir!' I said, all too eager to please. 'I'm the best damn bedpan cleaner in the world, sir. Trust me.' I slept like a baby on my first night as a 'patient' in the eye clinic. I woke up when one of my room-mates pulled up the blackout blind. 'Looks like we'll have a nice and sunny day today,' he said, opening the window. He stuck his head out and sniffed the crisp mountain air. 'Yeah,' he assured himself, 'no snow today. I might go for a long walk after breakfast.'

Much surprised, I took a few sharp breaths. He closed the window again, turned and walked towards the door of our ward. His steady hand found the handle without fumbling. He twisted the knob and stepped out into the corridor. Before he closed the door he turned his head. The two holes where his eyes were supposed to be stared straight at me. 'Sorry, Kamerad,' said the man without eyes, 'I didn't mean to wake you up.'

'How did you know I was awake?' I gasped. 'I didn't even stir. I just opened my eyes. How the hell did you . . . ?'

'Same way I know that it won't snow today,' he replied, smiling with his lips. 'Don't worry, I *know*.'

And he was right. It didn't snow for the whole day. But fluffy white snowflakes came tumbling down the following morning when I caught the early train into the city to keep my date with the optometrist. I had plenty of time to spare when I arrived in Frankfurt. I walked past the tramway stops across the railway square into the large city's main street, the Kaiserstrasse. I was stunned and speechless at seeing so many houses either destroyed or badly scarred by air-raids. But the ruins didn't affect me half as much as the sombre messages that were scrawled all over the remaining facades of bombed-out and burned-out business and tenement houses — messages which told a dreadful story all by themselves.

'Rudolf, we are alive. Staying with Anna.'

'Family Baumann. Have been evacuated. Contact Erna.'

'Max, where are you? We are safe.'

On and on it went: message after message; greetings from heaven and postcards from hell. Families searching for the rest of their kin; sisters looking for brothers; desperate, innocent people praying and hoping for miracles.

And whores looking for clients at nine o'clock in the morning, lurking in the shadows of ruins, flaunting their tattered and sleazy merchandise, hiding their tired and worn-out faces behind thick layers of powder and paint.

'Hallo, Liebling,' they cooed as I walked the gauntlet. 'Willst du ficken?'

Almighty Father in Heaven, what was this world coming to? Heart-rending, hastily scribbled scraps of information on battered

248

walls. Battered prostitutes in tawdry, dirty, skin-hugging dresses trying to drum up business.

I quickened my stride. My roving eyes fell upon one slogan that stood out from all the others. It was scrawled in red paint and asked in huge letters: 'Mein Führer! Can you sleep tonight?' I couldn't take my eyes off the blunt message. Whoever had written it must have been a very courageous person. I felt as if I was committing a crime against the Third Reich just by reading the candid words.

I almost missed the optometrist's premises. His shop was on the ground floor of a multi-storey apartment block that had had every pane of glass blown out from the many wooden frames. The shop window was boarded up. On a large piece of cardboard, tacked to the splintered door, was a sign which read:

E. PICKERT, OPTOMETRIST.
STILL OPEN FOR BUSINESS.
PLEASE ENTER CAREFULLY!

I pushed the creaking door open. An elderly man with an unruly mane of grey hair was busy sweeping bits of glass and rubble into a corner. He looked at me from behind his thick, horn-rimmed spectacles. 'Can I help you?'

I handed him my requisition form from the eye clinic. 'I need two pairs of glasses, sir. And I'm not in a desperate hurry.'

He smiled, as if he could read my mind. He'd only just finished the examination when the chilling, wailing sound of air-raid sirens glued me to the chair I sat on. I was terrified. Herr Pickert didn't even blink an eyelid, but he saw the fear in my eyes.

'We are used to it by now,' he said, dragging me to my feet. 'No need to worry whether your time is up or not. We have an excellent cellar with a strong, arched ceiling. You'll be safe there unless we score a direct hit. And if we do, well, then both of us won't be needing spectacles any more. Shall we go?'

The engines of approaching aircraft hummed like bees coming to the hive — the proud sons of Mother England homing in on the vulnerable and helpless men, women and children below. Hey, Mr Propaganda Minister Göbbels, if this is the total and radical warfare you had in mind, you can stick it right up your fat arse! If I'd only known what your intent was, I wouldn't have screamed yes . . . or would I?

The bomb bays opened and, as I cursed Josef Göbbels, dear old God forgot all about me. I was supposed to be a brave disciple of the Führer. And yet I shook like a leaf that had gone berserk. I had volunteered to become a hero and to sacrifice my life for my Vaterland, yet I was shit-scared.

The people I came face to face with in the damp cellar hadn't volunteered for anything at all. All of them looked like heroes to me — men, women and children alike.

A single light bulb dangled from the lofty, whitewashed ceiling, illuminating the musty shelter just enough to let me have a good look at the kind of prey the alien bombers pursued. I was startled by the obvious indifference shown in everybody's face. It seemed to me that I was the only person in that cellar who felt angry and intimidated — and I felt utterly useless without a rifle in my hand, without some means of defending myself against the monster that raged outside and threatened my very existence.

In no time at all, the clicking noise of busy knitting needles filled much of the room and tried to block out the dull thuds of exploding flak shells and bursting bombs. A young baby suckled its mother's breast and couldn't care less about war and bombs and sudden death.

The earthen floor trembled under my feet when a bomb exploded nearby. The shock made me choke on my own breath. I tried not to believe that I was sitting inside a sealed coffin. But, just to ease my mind a little, I prayed for death to come swiftly.

The children in the cellar found a piece of chalk with which to draw squares on the dirt floor, and they played hopscotch.

While the bombs came hurtling down like greeting cards from Churchill and the devil, the children fought over whose turn it was to play their game. I wanted to scream out loud at the ghost-like men and women around me — scream at them, scold them and shake them out of their lassitude. 'Do something,' I wanted to yell at them. 'For God's sake, do something! Don't just bloody well sit there!'

It was all over and done with in less than half an hour. Complacency turned into anxiety as people rushed past me towards the exit, eager to find out whether they still had a home to go back to.

By the time I came back up into the street, firefighting crews were already at work, trying to salvage whatever there was to be saved. Dark clouds of billowing smoke and dust blocked out the rays from the sun.

The mother who'd breast-fed her baby during the raid pulled a woollen shawl across her child's face, as if she wanted to say, 'This is not something babies should see.' I offered my help, but Herr Pickert sent me away, saying: 'We don't need you here. You'd better go and find out if the railway station has been hit and put out of action. If the trains still run, come and see me in a fortnight, verstanden?'

'Yes, I understand.' I turned towards the Hauptbahnhof and walked straight into chaos. Burning houses to the left and the right, rubble spilling across the road from footpath to footpath. Shocked men and women turning into statues, just sitting in front of what used to be their homes, covering their faces in disbelief, unable to cry. Oh, my God, can You look upon this macabre spectacle and still be proud of the mankind You created? I am crying, Lord! Are You crying with me?

My burning eyes fastened on a lofty tenement block. The whole facade of the building was gone. All the floors were dangling at an acute angle, ready to collapse and yet hanging there, not wanting to let go.

Some time after I smashed my glasses on the CO's helmet, I'd discovered that, if I clenched my fist and peered through the tiny hole at the end, I could see quite clearly, as if I was gazing through a makeshift telescope. Now I saw, way up high, a shiny white door which swung gently to and fro from a papered wall that depicted shapes of clowns and circus animals. On the floor, slanting as it was, a child's cradle tried to defy the laws of gravity. And inside the cradle, leaning against the wooden drop-side, sat a huge brown teddy bear. As I watched, with emotions running wild inside me, the timbers creaked as if in protest. The floor, the child's cot and the teddy bear slid away from the wall and tumbled downwards to join the rubble below.

My hands reached out in a futile gesture. There was nothing I could have done. I started walking again. I cried. I didn't know if it was anger, sorrow or frustration that made my tears flow freely. I cursed my mother for bringing me into a world I couldn't understand. No one took any notice of me, the little meek nobody who, clad in drab field-grey army clothes, stumbled and slithered through the rubble that lay strewn across the street.

The alien bombers had missed the railway station. The trains were running on schedule. The counters and ticket boxes were open for business, and life went on as if nothing at all had happened only a few hundred metres away. On the wall of the refreshment room a brightly painted slogan proclaimed brashly: 'Strength Through Pleasure! Book Your Cruise Now!'

My eyes roamed from traveller to traveller. What I saw all around me was pretty hard to believe. Most of the people wore clothes they wouldn't have wanted to be seen dead in a couple of years before. Even the luggage wasn't what it used to be. Cardboard boxes instead of pig-leather suitcases. Tokens of 'Armut,' of poverty, everywhere; it seemed to have come back into vogue. What was happening to the prosperity of the Third Reich?

Not far from where I stood, a sergeant from the infantry scanned the milling crowd with anxiety-filled eyes. His uniform could have done with a good wash, and his jackboots were begging for a spit-and-polish. He had 'Russian Front' written all over him. A pretty, young woman came rushing up to him, carrying a girl, perhaps three years old, in her arms. The little child yelled at the top of her voice: 'Are you my Papa? Are you really and truly my Papa?'

The woman and the sergeant laughed and cried and hugged each other. Their little daughter was still yelling excitedly: 'Papa! Papa! Mein Papa!'

The soldier took her into his arms and assured her: 'Ja, natürlich, mein Liebling, of course I am your father. And let me tell you that you are much more beautiful in real life than in the snapshots your mother sent to me.'

The little girl kept on hugging her daddy over and over again. She said, ever so proudly: 'I do have a Papa, Mutti. I really do! I'm the luckiest girl in the world.'

★ ★ ★

I found little time to think about rights and wrongs and problems in the days that followed. I didn't even have the time to feel sorry for myself. For once in my life I was doing something positive and worthwhile, even if the chores included emptying dozens of bedpans each day. I became an expert in rolling and lighting cigarettes. I rolled up hundreds and hundreds of metres of washed bandages across my knees, and I read innumerable newspaper articles to Klaus and anybody else in the same situation.

I washed and polished the floors, and learnt how to put a smile on a blind man's face. I taught some of them how to eat and how to find the toilet without a guiding hand. I guess, by doing something worthwhile, I learnt to like myself just a little. Perhaps Mother was wrong, and there was a bit of good in me after all.

On the eve of my second visit to the

optometrist, I stood at the dormitory window and watched the awesome fireworks in the distant skies over Frankfurt during yet another air-raid.

In the morning, when I went to pick up my glasses, thick smoke was hovering above the whole city, but the optometrist could still muster a grave smile. 'How are your blind friends?' he asked.

'Most of them are doing surprisingly well,' I replied. 'They have more courage than I'll ever have. I'd really hate to be in their shoes.'

'So would I, my friend, so would I.'

The shop door had fallen off its hinges. It was blocking half the entrance. I offered my help: 'Want me to fix the door before I leave?'

'No, don't worry about it, son,' said the optometrist. 'Who needs a door in this mess anyway? Your lenses have arrived and your spectacles are ready. Come and let's try them on.'

The glasses fitted. I could see all the misery around me much more clearly now. What a treat!

Herr Pickert handed me the second pair, the one that had straps instead of arms to fit over the ears and was meant to be worn under a gas mask. 'Hope you don't have to wear these before the war is over.'

He walked out with me. Pointing from one

end of the street to the other, he said mournfully: 'Look at what they're doing to us. What have we done to deserve this? Our street used to be the showpiece of Frankfurt. Now it looks like the despondent smile of a prizefighter who's lost half his teeth. Go with God, son, if there is a God, which I begin to doubt.'

I bought the daily paper at a makeshift stand on the way to the station and scanned the headlines.

'One hundred enemy bombers shot down over Berlin.'

'Knight's Cross for German air ace.'

'Tactical withdrawal on Eastern Front great success.'

'No planes lost in massive air-raid on London.'

'Germany another step closer to final victory.'

I browsed through the locally produced newspaper from cover to cover. Was it bad journalism or good politics that there wasn't as much as a mention of the previous night's air-raid on Frankfurt? I did find columns and columns of funeral notices, though, and just as many advertisements under the heading Missing Persons. Those endless columns did not need any headlines in large print to tell the horrid truth about the all-embracing tragedy of this war, a war that knew neither pity nor respect for any living soul.

On my return to the eye clinic in Königstein I expected to receive my marching orders before the end of the day. An old adage says that one must lie in the bed he has made. Well, I slept in mine for another two weeks. Somebody must have been happy with the job I'd done in the clinic. I didn't find out, until the day I was handed my travel papers, why they'd let me stay at the clinic for longer than necessary. It was that a soldier who'd returned from the front to a hospital in Germany for a term of four weeks or more was entitled to a minimum of two weeks convalescence leave before being sent back.

'That's the least we can do for you,' said the eye doctor whose name I still can't remember. 'You've been a great help. We'll miss you, Weiss. Good luck.'

I was reluctant to say goodbye to the people with no eyes, who had enriched my vision a great deal. I would have liked to stay with them and care for them until at least the end of the war. But the army did not give me a choice, though I was convinced that I'd be a much better nurse than a soldier.

When I said goodbye to Klaus, he squeezed my hand and gave me a piece of advice. 'Whatever you do, Ollie, don't come back here as a proper patient. Promise?' I told him it was good advice.

On arrival in Frankfurt I had two hours to spare before catching another train to Reutlingen. The reserve unit of 92 Infantry Regiment had been shifted from Elbing in the east of the country to Reutlingen in the west.

Rather than spending two hours in a crowded waiting room in the station, I decided to go for a walk and pay Herr Pickert a visit.

He hadn't waited for me to come and say goodbye. He had gone, and so had the whole block of apartments — no windows, no walls, no house, not a bloody thing.

Ashes to ashes. Dust to dust. Hell no, it wasn't fair. It wasn't right! All that was left was a heap of rubble. I wondered if the children in the debris-covered cellar were still playing hopscotch.

★　★　★

The CO of the Genesungskompanie, the convalescence company of the 92nd, to whom I had to report, welcomed me with unexpected cordiality. He wanted to know when and how and where I'd been wounded. When I told him the truth, he made me repeat my report three times, and even then

260

he didn't believe me for a while. I just stood there and watched the expression on his face change gradually, and I knew that I couldn't expect any favours from the old warhorse. When he asked me very quietly and very politely, 'Are you any good at peeling potatoes, Weiss?', I knew what I could expect. If I said yes, he would tell me: 'Very good. We need your expertise in the kitchen.' If I chose to answer no, he'd reply: 'Very good. You'll be an expert in no time at all. Thanks for volunteering.'

I didn't have to be Einstein to figure out that I was in a no-win situation. I didn't ask him why. I simply asked, 'For how long, sir?'

'For as long as it pleases me,' replied the captain.

'You win, sir,' I muttered in resignation. 'You win.'

'I always do,' came the swift reply. 'That's why I'm an officer and you're a good for nothing private.'

I peeled potatoes for a whole week — round ones, oval ones, square ones, and ones that didn't fit any description at all. I cut their eyes out with a vengeance. I denuded them; I circumcised them; I mutilated them; I violated them and desecrated them in any way I could think of.

It wasn't until a massive air-raid took place

that my services were urgently required elsewhere. A few days prior to the bombing, thousands and thousands of leaflets had been dropped over Stuttgart. With Reutlingen less than eighty kilometres away, many of the airborne handbills found their way into the quadrangle of our barracks.

'Stuttgart im Loch, wir finden Dich doch!' promised the boldly printed headlines on the leaflets. Stuttgart in the hollow, we'll find you anyway!

The message spread by the allies was dismissed by all and sundry as a futile and laughable attempt to create panic among Stuttgart's population. We used the handy-sized paper as heaven-sent, ready-cut toilet paper.

Up to that time, Stuttgart had escaped any full scale assault from the air. The city was surrounded by rolling mountains, which apparently provided a natural defence against attacks from the air. Rumour had it that half the anti-aircraft guns in Germany were assembled around Stuttgart — enough guns to blast the whole British, Canadian and American air force out of the sky. Surely the Allies wouldn't dare attack this city.

But they did. They came at night, myriads of them. They flew right through the almost impenetrable curtain of exploding flak shells.

They lit up the sky with their unholy Christmas trees — flares suspended from little parachutes, dangling above the city, drifting slowly and marking the targets for the bombardiers, who pushed the buttons at the correct moment to release their deadly cargo.

On their way back, halfway across the English Channel and out of danger, they'd congratulate each other for a job well done. They would thank God for their safe return.

Perhaps, during the same night, only a few kilometres separating foe from friend, our Junkers 88s would be on their way home, crossing the Channel in the opposite direction after a successful raid on London. And, out of immediate danger, those crews would also congratulate each other on a job well done. They would thank the very same God for sparing their lives one more time.

★ ★ ★

'Alle raus! Marsch, Marsch! Get onto the trucks!'

We got out of bed in the middle of the night and dressed in a hurry, then stumbled down the flights of stairs and boarded the trucks which were waiting for us in the quadrangle. After an hour's hasty journey, the first whiff of acrid smoke made me sneeze.

Five minutes later, we saw the first burning buildings and heard the first frantic cries for help. Our vehicles continued on their way and drove straight into hell. Buildings were still collapsing from inside out and outside in, sending dust and smoke and sparks high up into the sky.

Of all the places to choose from, our truck stopped on a children's playground. No frolicking kids on the swings now. Not a single child on the slippery-dips.

Desperate cries of 'Hilfe! Hilfe!' all around us. And a shrill, wailing voice, louder than all the others: 'For God's sake! Please help me, pleeeeease!'

Frenzied people digging frantically in the rubble, clawing at brick after brick with torn and bleeding hands. An old lady pleading, her voice trembling: 'They're all buried down there. Please help. They'll never get out by themselves. Please, please! Oh, dear Lord! Our Father who art in heaven, hallowed be Thy name . . . '

Tonnes of bricks, tonnes of twisted steel. Tonnes of despair.

My soft hands are bleeding already. I touch something soft, softer than brick and mortar. I stare at it in the flickering light. A child's hand reaching out for me. Stay alive, baby, stay alive! Keep on breathing, please. Ollie

Weiss is here to save you. I'll help you. Breathe, baby, hang on. I'll have you out in a minute.

I dig carefully and yet in wild panic. I work myself into a frenzy as I tear brick after brick away from the buried child. Easy now, easy. I have freed the arm all the way to the elbow. Trust me, baby, you'll be all right.

The arm protruding from the rubble stands motionless for a moment or two. Then it topples over, all by itself. Just a child's forearm, nothing else. No body, no child. Just an arm with a hand.

Oh, my God, help us! Help all of us! My stomach turns inside out and I vomit all over the mountain of bricks.

'Hilfe, Hilfe.' A muffled voice coming from somewhere under the rubble. 'Hilfe!'

'Look for sandbags! Where you find sandbags you'll find windows behind them. Carefully now. Take it easy. Slowly, slowly.'

'I can hear voices!'

'Keep on digging. You, get hold of that sandbag.'

'They're alive! Thank God, they're alive.'

A sandbag slips away into the yawning darkness below. Agitated voices from the cellar getting louder and louder. 'Get us out of here! Please, hurry!'

I cuddle a baby girl in my aching arms. I

hug her and comfort her. Her incessant cries for her mother tear me to pieces. 'Mutti, Mutti, I want my Mutti!'

I simply can't take it any more. 'Shut up,' I yell at the poor little mite. 'Shut up! I'll find your bloody mother. Shut up, dammit.'

A woman's hands reach out to take the frantic child from me. 'It's all right now, my baby,' says the mother with a soothing voice. 'It's all right now. No need to cry any more. Your mother is here, don't cry.'

But the frightened little girl can't escape the trauma. She just keeps on crying and crying, seeking her mother who already has her protective arms around her. Seeing nothing, hearing nothing, the baby whimpers, 'Mutti.'

That was only the beginning of five nights of sheer terror. How could I ever forget those horrendous nights when God chose to forget all about the people of Stuttgart? During the following four bloodcurdling nights it was safer for us to shelter in the gutters or even in the middle of the street, away from crumbling cellars, clear of tumbling walls and falling debris.

In the morning after the third raid, we were called to the ruins of a leading hotel, where about fifty people, guests and staff, were presumed to be alive and well in the wine cellar. We smashed and dug our way through the rubble. Between us and the wine cellar was a furnace that provided hot water and central heating for the whole complex. The furnace had collapsed and a whole pile of coal was well alight. The toxic carbon monoxide made us retreat quickly for a breath of fresh air. When we finally made it to the wine cellar, we were much too late. Most of the barrels and kegs and bottles had burst from either heat or impact. The whole floor was covered to a depth of sixty centimetres with hot wine: red and white; Rhein and Mosel; wines with delicate bouquets and expensive labels; Champagne all the way from France. The corks and the empty bottles drifted lazily among the floating, already bloating corpses. I hoped that all of those victims had found enough time to get themselves rotten drunk before the carbon monoxide killed them.

Still, the bombings weren't over and done with. The executioners in their buzzing flying machines returned the following night, like perfectionists who weren't quite satisfied with the job they'd done so far. The bombs kept on coming down, gurgling like a man who's had his throat cut, only much louder. Gurgling, bursting, gurgling.

I flatten myself once more in the gutter of a

convulsing street. I cling to the ground like the ivy clings to my Papa's grave, with my eyes closed and thumbs stuck into the ears as far as they can go. Shockwaves come and go, lifting me, dropping me. No pain, no time for prayers. Nothing but horrendous fear.

I swear, if God were spiteful enough to let me live for two hundred years I wouldn't be able to forget the horror that was Stuttgart for five nights in a row. If I were to live to be three hundred I'd still not know why it had to happen at all.

Not a single bomb had fallen to disturb the peace in Reutlingen. Instant war and instant peace — what a crazy, remarkable and rotten world I was condemned to live in.

★ ★ ★

Before the end of the week I was called into the Schreibstube, the administrative office, to pick up the documents I needed to go on four weeks' furlough. The following day I was on my way. No more potatoes to peel for a whole month. What a blessing!

Prenzlau was the only home I knew, the only home I had. Even if I wasn't welcome, I simply didn't have any other place to go.

What was home? What did it mean to me? Was it the street I lived in? Or the boys I masturbated with under an old chestnut tree? Was it the grave of my father, the man I never really got to know properly? Was it the lilac bushes in Mutti's garden, or the cobblestones I marched so proudly on, wearing my immaculate Hitlerjugend uniform, staring at life with a conceited smile and raising my right arm in an inspiring and proud and defiant Hitler salute?

For a black sheep, is home just a forlorn corner in a paddock? For myself, was home the kitchen corner where Mutti made me stand for hours on end, facing the wall in punishment for something I did or didn't do, telling me a thousand and one times that I was a disgrace to the family name, that I was less than nothing, making me feel intensely ashamed of myself; and forbidding my own sister to speak to me, to ignore me and to treat me like a heap of garbage?

Was that the place where I wanted to spend not only my four weeks' leave but also the rest of my life?

I was still pondering the good and the bad of my childhood and early teens when I stepped out onto the platform of the little railway station at Prenzlau. Nobody knew that I was coming and no one met me at the station. I should have been on top of the world; I guess I would have been if Helga had been there to put her arms around me. But she wasn't.

I certainly wasn't ready to face my mother and that little bedfellow of hers who'd never be able to walk in my father's footsteps — *never*. I paid a visit to my real father's grave first. But instead of telling him how good it was to talk to him, I scolded him for telling me lies, and for leaving me behind in a world I couldn't understand.

Then I took a stroll to the Uckersee. The air was still, the water was calm and the sunlight made the surface of the lake sparkle like an ocean of diamonds. Soon afterwards, as though drawn by a magnet, my feet moved automatically across the cobblestones of the market square and into Lindenstrasse, where every wrought-iron fence, every house and every tree that lined the wide, straight street held very special memories. Hallelujah! Despite a host of bad memories, it still felt good to be home. It would have been a lot nicer if I hadn't been frightened of facing my mother and her beau again. Alas, beggars cannot be choosers.

I wanted so much to be really welcome at home. I wanted so much to love my mother the way I used to love her before everything went haywire. I suppose if Mutti had made up a bed for me in one of the empty bedrooms she would have opened a door for both of us. But she was much too headstrong and too old-fashioned for compromises. She proved that when I got there.

'You've slept most of your life in that corridor,' she declared firmly. 'It's been your room since you were a baby. I really can't think of any reason at all why you shouldn't sleep there now. It's always been your room.'

'It's a corridor,' I said, more to myself than to her. 'It's never been my *bedroom*.' I knew that my stubborn mother would never make any concessions, not to me anyway — maybe to her treasured second husband, but not to me.

If Mutti had only been a little more approachable and not quite as vindictive and unforgiving, perhaps my whole life would have taken a different course. But she said hardly a nice word to me for the duration of my furlough. She couldn't help herself. I was still the black sheep of the family — today, tomorrow and always.

I was much too young to cope with all the horrible things I'd experienced in Russia, in Stuttgart and in Frankfurt. I badly needed a shoulder to cry on, and found none. I needed somebody to tell me that I had changed, that I wasn't the sly and brash Heil Hitler-crying

271

bastard any more. Wasn't there anybody out there who'd take the time to listen?

Stewing in my own misery, I knocked on Brigitte's front door, but she'd moved to another address. All my former school friends and comrades from the Hitlerjugend were out fighting the war or had already become dead heroes.

I ran around like a madman in my quest to locate Helga's whereabouts. She'd vanished just like Dr Rosenbaum, like my gypsy friends, like Helga's preacher father and many more. Those who were still healthy had lost their laughter, their enthusiasm and their hopes of winning the war. They were a scared bunch of people, going about their daily business without a smile, trusting no one, grieving over the past and too frightened to look ahead.

Every night I went to bed in that corridor — in my room without a window — I pledged in the darkness, 'Tomorrow I'll kill myself!' The nightmares made me scream in the stillness of night, and a thousand skeletons appeared from nowhere. Each damn one of them raised a warning index finger, as they all said at once: 'Why did you kill us, Ollie Weiss? Haven't you heard of the Ten Commandments? Thou shalt not kill, not kill, not kill!'

And I pleaded: 'It's not my fault. Don't blame me.'

The skeletons replied: 'Nobody made you pull the trigger, you did it all by yourself. You are a murderer!'

I saw Helga give birth to a thousand babies dressed in army uniform, born without heads, without arms, without legs. I could feel the warmth of Kurt's blood as it oozed from his neck and ran through my fingers.

Besides my dead father who refused to talk to me from his ivy-covered grave, there was absolutely nobody, not a single soul, I could trust and talk to.

At the end of my furlough I stood alone, very much alone, on the platform at the station, waiting anxiously for the train to take me away from my family and my home town. But in reality, I guess, I was trying to run away from myself. Little did I know then that I'd never be able to do that. Well, goodbye, Prenzlau. Thanks for nothing!

12

My eyes opened slowly. The rays of the morning sun came tumbling through the foliage of the forest, dancing from leaf to leaf, prancing from branch to branch in a cascade of glittering gold.

Where was I? What had happened? What was I doing sitting propped up against the rough bark of a huge tree? I lit a cigarette and watched the smoke hitch a ride on the gentle morning breeze. Then I remembered.

On arrival in Stuttgart I'd boarded the right train to take me back to my reserve unit. But I didn't get off in Reutlingen, as I should have. Instead of catching a streetcar to take me back to the barracks of the Ersatz Company, I did the most courageous thing I'd ever done in my life. I continued my journey all the way to the shores of Lake Constance and the Austrian Alps. For the first time, after years of doing what I was told to do, thinking what I was trained to think, believing what my Führer's disciples wanted me to believe and trying so hard to emulate my father, I did what my heart told me to do. So Ollie Weiss, the would-be hero, turned into a despicable deserter and low-down fugitive. My whole world had betrayed me, cheated me, lied to me and deceived me. Now it was my turn to stand up for what I really believed in.

No more Heil Hitlers for me. No more shooting, no more killing, no more pretences, no more trying to be what I wasn't and never would be. I was on my own from now on. My father was dead. Helga, the only person in my life who'd understood me and loved me for what I was, had vanished. I had nothing else to live for but my own life. I saw neither purpose nor reason to die for my mother, my sister and the rest of our clan. Even if Hitler could still fulfil his dreams of a Thousand Year Reich, it would be built on the spilt blood of millions of innocent people. What kind of a Germany would that be? The straw that broke the camel's back was when I saw the child's severed arm reaching out to me from the rubble of a tenement block in Stuttgart. Finally, after many years in the wilderness, my conscience rebelled and I listened.

Much later in the day, when twilight made the shadows fade away, I sneaked out of the woods like a nocturnal animal. At peace with myself, I sat on the shore of beautiful, tranquil Lake Constance. I turned my back on the blacked-out windows of a little Austrian township and feasted my eyes on the twinkling, glittering, lights of Switzerland. The depressing gloom of war met the shimmering splendour of peace somewhere along the middle of the lake. Peace and freedom were so near, and yet so far away.

Later, back in the shelter of the trees, I pondered my future. Did I have a future to think about? I was twenty years old. Within a matter of days my name would be added to the wanted list, here in Austria as well as in Germany. Dead or alive, the authorities would say, dead or alive.

I had reached the crossroads of my life. From now on I would have to make my own decisions and be strong enough to face the consequences. I couldn't leave the thinking to the horses any more. I couldn't blame anyone for the mistakes I would make in days and years to come. Would I be strong enough to shoulder the burden of responsibility?

I was frightened. I could still board a train back to Reutlingen tomorrow. I'd get away with a severe reprimand for returning late from my furlough. Could I live with myself if I backed out now? Or would I hate myself for the rest of my living days?

How many living days would be in store for me if I didn't return to the folds of the

Wehrmacht? I didn't give myself too much of a chance of survival unless Germany lost the war in a hurry. I had no illusions about what my fate would be if I got caught. I would be executed. Would I be strong enough to face a firing squad? The Russians had tried their utmost to send me to an early grave and had made a hash of it. I'd considered suicide at least a hundred times. I obviously lacked the courage to take my own life at the worst of times. Perhaps twelve men, with twelve rifles aimed at me, wouldn't fail to do the job I couldn't do by myself.

'Every man is the architect of his own destiny,' my dear old comrade Kurt had lectured me only a couple of days before I buried him. 'Just remember, every passing day is a building block for your future.'

Like an alcoholic who'd decided to kick the habit, I lived one day at a time. I roamed the surrounding mountains and valleys day after day, like a hungry goat in search of greener pastures. For as long as I could remember, I always wanted to be as free as a bird. But after only a few days of self-inflicted freedom I wasn't so sure any more. Anyway, I hadn't run away to find freedom. I was on a protest mission against war. Well, wasn't I? Maybe I wasn't so convinced any more that I'd done the right thing. What could I possibly achieve while I searched for berries and mushrooms and anything else that was edible? It was too late now to change my mind. I'd made my bed. Somehow I had to find the courage to lie in it, no matter what.

It didn't take me very long to realise that man can't live on berries and freedom alone. Hunger drove me out of the wilderness and into civilisation. I didn't skirt the next village that lay in my path. To hell with the consequences. It was the 'tomorrow' I was afraid of, not the 'today'. I forced myself not to walk stooped and stealthily like a hunted fugitive. The thought that my boldness might bring my short career as a deserter to an abrupt, early end hardly crossed my mind.

Luckily for me, the odds were stacked in my favour that day. I'd only walked past three or four homes when I saw an elderly couple waving to me from their verandah. I waved back at them. Old habits don't die in a hurry. My hand automatically moved up towards my cap and I almost said 'Heil Hitler', forgetting for a brief moment that I'd promised myself never to say Heil bloody Hitler again. I knew that everybody around here was Catholic. I'd walked past dozens of crucifixes and little shrines scattered along the paths and adorned with fresh flowers. Being on my own, I never bothered with removing my hat and singing

Ave Maria or something similar. But now, out in the open, I knew what was best for me. I said 'Grüss Gott', Greetings to the Lord, even before I wished them a jolly good morning. And I reaped the rewards: an instant invitation for a cup of coffee; the real stuff, not the Ersatz coffee I had to be content with in Prenzlau. Best of all, the old lady had baked a cake she called Gugelhupf. She cut off a large chunk and put it in front of me, saying: 'You look like you haven't eaten for a month. Go on, eat it. It won't kill you. Don't be shy.'

Her husband — how could I ever forget the way he twirled the ends of his Kaiser Wilhelm moustache — smiled at me and asked straight out: 'Bischt g'flohe? Bischt fort-g'laufe?'

Though his hard-to-understand dialect baffled me for a moment, I could figure out what he was asking me. And as a straight question always merits a straight answer, I replied: 'Ja. I have fled. I am on the run. I am a deserter. I hate the war and what it does to people. And I am very, very hungry. Can I have another piece of that delicious cake before you turn me over to the police?'

As I said before, this was one of my lucky days. Herr 'Gugelhupf' loved and adored the old Kaiser as much as he hated the new Führer. And, sceptical about trusting any of his neighbours, he was more than happy to talk to somebody he could be honest with. I was invited to stay overnight. When I said 'Auf Wiedersehen' and 'Grüss Gott' to my hosts in the morning, I carried enough bread and cheese with me to see me through a whole week. But most importantly, I was now in possession of a hand-drawn map that would direct me all the way to the Swiss border.

'The sketch is easy to follow,' said Grandpa, as he shook my hand. 'The border is only two, three hours walk from here, depending on your fitness. Be careful though. The guard dogs are pretty vicious, so I've been told. God's blessings and good luck, son.'

I squeezed his hand. 'Why are you doing this for me?'

'I'm doing it for myself,' the old man said quietly. 'I hate Hitler and his good-for-nothing politics. Go now.'

Two hours later I could hear dogs barking in the distance. A sudden rush of adrenalin made me feel lightheaded. My heart was pumping away like crazy. I had to stop myself from running and stop myself from hiding. I craved a smoke and my hands shook so much that I had trouble holding the burning match. The tobacco tickled my throat. I needed to cough. I didn't dare.

I spent twenty-four hours in the crown of a tree, timing the rounds of the guards, who would meet at regular intervals at a certain point and then walk away in opposite directions. If my calculations were reasonably accurate, I'd make it safely into Switzerland before the guard dogs had a chance to sink their fangs into my buttocks.

God alone knows what went wrong with my sprint to freedom. I picked the best possible moment for my dash to liberty. A strip of twenty, perhaps, thirty, metres on either side of the three metre high boundary fence was cleared of trees and undergrowth. The wire mesh fence was topped by three strands of barbed wire. I'd tackled worse than that on the obstacle course, when I was a recruit pretending to be a ferocious, blood-thirsty little bastard with no brain of my own.

I was up and running. I hurled the small bag with my few belongings across the fence. The bag hit the barbed wire, hung in midair for a while, then tumbled back into Vorarlberg, Austria.

What the hell. I didn't need luggage, not where I was going.

I was two-thirds of the way up the fence. Just another two footholds and I'd crawl under the barbed wire and drop into the tranquillity of a beautiful neutral country. Fuck you, mein Führer. And to hell with the Vaterland.

No guards in sight yet. Not a single yapping, vicious dog tearing at my pants. Just the fence and me, and peace forever.

Then, with nothing but a flimsy bit of barbed wire separating me from the freedom I yearned for, with a whole new future reaching out for me, things went terribly wrong. My feet slipped away from the fence. My hands let go. I touched the ground, picked up my bag and raced towards the protective trees, got there, dropped onto the leaf-covered ground and cried and cried and cried.

All the trees nearby had swastika armbands around their massive trunks, and they yelled at me incessantly: 'Heil Hitler! Heil Hitler! Sieg Heil! Shame on you, you scrawny little bastard. Can't you do anything right?'

I told the damned trees to go to hell, but they did not want to move at all. I turned away from the safe haven called Switzerland and went straight back into the uncertainty and misery that seemed to be my destiny for now. I gave up praying for miracles like the surrender of Germany. For most of my waking hours I wanted to get caught, and yet I prayed for survival. I had no plans to follow and no destination to reach. I walked and walked on my pilgrimage to nowhere in particular. Every single step I made seemed to be a sacrifice. Every day I survived did nothing but prolong my suffering.

★　★　★

Perhaps I was meant to be a fugitive, a doubting Thomas. Maybe my mother was right when she told me over and over again that I was a black sheep with nowhere to go. I just kept on walking and waited for the inevitable to happen.

I was almost at the end of my tether when I crossed a mountain pass somewhere between St Anton and Bludenz. I was caught in a terrible snowstorm. The wind was colder than ice. It blew straight through me when I was halfway up the steep, winding road. Road? There was no road. Just snow. Bracing myself, pushing into the raging storm, I kept on walking and prayed for death. I should have succumbed right there and then. God only knows why I didn't. I had icicles on my eyebrows and frozen tears hanging from my burning eyes. Yet I kept on walking into a hostile and almost impenetrable wall of dense, swirling snow. Death would surely have been a gift from heaven. But God didn't let me die. And the devil didn't want me either.

The greater my suffering, the more I screamed out for freedom. I was consumed by this great new passion of mine, a passion called freedom. Dogs nurture the same kind of passion, an obsession that makes them chase every speeding car that comes anywhere near their cold wet noses. What if a dog did catch a car? What could he do with it? He certainly couldn't drive it.

If I could catch freedom, what would I do with it? I didn't even know what it was. Freedom! Freiheit! Liberté! What a glorious word in any man's language. Where is it? Does it exist? Is it within you? Without you? Oh, twinkle, twinkle, little star of freedom. How I wonder what you are!

Two days or a week or a month or an eternity later, dear old God must have thought that I needed a good bath or shower. He opened the floodgates and down came the rain. I was drenched to the bone when I stumbled upon an old hay shed at the edge of a lush green meadow. The door had fallen off its hinges, but the straw-covered roof was an answer to my prayers. It offered shelter, protection and a soft bed to sleep in. I offered a sincere thank you to the Boss of all human beings, who must have realised that I'd suffered enough for the time being.

The musty, smelly hay was dry enough for me to bed down for the night. I took my wet uniform off and draped it across the hay. I put my ever so faithful, putrid-smelling jackboots just inside the door on sentry duty, just in case some unexpected visitor dropped in.

I fell asleep and had the craziest dream. Helga was with me, and those beautiful, blue eyes of hers were glowing with excitement. We were making love, climbing to heaven together. She whispered: 'Make me a baby, Ollie, mein Liebling. Make us a baby.' But before we reached heaven I was blindfolded and my arms were tied behind my back. A clear, crisp voice shouted: 'Raise your rifles! Take aim! Fire!'

Bullets pierced my heart and my body and I didn't feel any pain at all. My knees wanted to buckle but I wouldn't let them. Helga was still with me, holding me, kissing me, crying tears of joy and whispering into my ear: 'It's all right, Ollie, be happy. From now on we'll be together for ever and ever.'

The dream ended rather abruptly. My heart took one giant leap all the way up into my throat when a harsh voice exploded nearby and very much in reality. 'Git off my land! This here is private property. Git off your arse an' git outa here, or else . . . '

I had one quick glance at the giant of a man who stood in the doorway, blocking the only exit. I rubbed my eyes and took a closer look at the unwelcome intruder. He must have been well over two metres tall. The sheer size of him frightened the hell out of me. But it was the army rifle he waved at me menacingly that got me up on to my feet in a hurry and saying 'Sorry, sir' faster than either of us could blink an eyelid.

I didn't like the man one little bit. He had the face of a weirdo, the eyes of a snake and the overall appearance of a manic ratbag. But he was more than twice my size, carried a gun, and his trigger finger was in spasms. I knew what was best for me and started talking, smoothly and soothingly, telling him about losing all of my family in a terrible air-raid and so on and so on. I put up a performance good enough to fool the biggest fool. After all, I had always been a skilled, slick and convincing liar. Just ask my mother. She'd be happy to verify that.

Anyway, the giant's eyes mellowed. He even sat down, put the rifle on the ground and formally introduced himself to me. His name was Gustl. He was living alone in a little log cabin not far from where we were. He'd been on his own, waiting patiently for his mother to come back from heaven for a number of years, ever since they'd taken her away in a wooden casket.

I humoured him, lied to him and pacified him. I'd never come face to face with an oddball like him. I was quite proud of my excellent performance which prompted him to invite me to his little mountain retreat for a cup of coffee and a bite to eat. How could I refuse? I was hungry enough to eat the buttons off my grimy uniform.

The little shack he called his chalet was in a terrible mess. It seemed as though he hadn't swept the floor or done the dishes since his mother passed away. There might have been a few dots of fly shit on the chunk of cheese and mould on the loaf of bread he sliced, but it was precious food. I devoured it as if it was manna from heaven.

Gustl was as mad as any one man could be. But despite his menacing dimensions and shifty eyes, he didn't seem to be a significant threat to me and my liberty. I listened patiently to his whole life story — confusing as it was — and when he invited me to stay for the night I accepted his invitation without any hesitation at all.

I should have heard the alarm bells ring when I detected an old army helmet resting like a trophy on the mantelpiece above the fireplace. It had swastikas all over it, painted in all the colours of the rainbow. But I felt in complete control of the situation. I ate Gustl's food, drank his liquor, smoked his tobacco, and in return I pretended to listen to all the garbage that crossed his lips.

When it was time for him to go to bed, he spread a couple of blankets on the floor for me. 'Ain't much of a bed,' he apologised. 'Still beats sleepin' in a hay shed, don't it?'

Before I went to sleep I wondered if it was still necessary for me to hide from all and sundry. I hadn't spoken to anybody for quite a while. Maybe the war was over already. I promised myself to ask Gustl about that, first thing in the morning.

He woke me just on daybreak. I thought I was having another of my nightmares when I saw the giant Austrian bending over me, wearing his swastika-covered helmet. And I found that I *wasn't* having a bad dream when he poked me in the ribs with the muzzle of his army rifle. 'Hey, Gustl,' I stammered. 'What's got into you? What's all this about? Stop playing stupid games. Somebody might get hurt.'

'I know,' said the man with the gun. 'And it won't be me. Don't try no stupid stuff if'n you wanna live a bit longer. I ain't playin' no games, you hear?'

He pointed the rifle away from me and pulled the trigger. The bullet hit the heavy, wooden table top and ricocheted into the slab wall. I was very frightened.

'I kin shoot a rabbit from five hundred metres,' he said menacingly. 'Don't try nothin' foolish or you'll be deader'n a rabbit.'

Then he asked me quite casually, still waving the gun in front of my face, 'Do ya want eggs or rolled oats for breakfast?'

'Both, thanks,' I replied, thinking that I'd rather die with a full stomach than an empty one.

He shoved a dirty plate in front of me. 'Eat,' he said. 'After breakfast you an'I's goin' for a walk. I ain't half as stupid as you thinks I am. I kin read if'n I wants to.'

I froze when I saw my paybook and travel papers in his big dirty paws. 'I don't like no deserters,' he proclaimed with frightening calmness. 'I's gonna take you for a nice walk into town to say Grüss Gott to the gendarme.'

I soon found out that the madman wasn't joking. He made me walk in front of him all the way along a winding, narrow path that cut through the wilderness. He scared me more than any Russian I'd come face to face with. My brain was working overtime. I didn't fancy my chances once he handed me over to the local constabulary. If I made a dash for freedom my insane captor would kill me without blinking an eyelid, just like he'd kill a rabbit.

I had to make a decision now, while I still had a choice. If I didn't try to get away from Gustl and his single rifle, I'd be facing twelve rifles of an execution squad after a short court martial. I'd be dead, very dead indeed. Maybe just one bullet in the back of the head wasn't such a bad choice after all.

So I made my choice. I ran like a gazelle, waiting at each stride for the thud of the bullet that would blow my brains away and put me out of my misery. But no bullet, no sudden end to my existence yet. Just a frustrated yell from behind, before Gustl caught up with me. His powerful hands got hold of me. He lifted me off my feet and tossed me across his shoulder as if I was a bag of rags. His right arm locked like a vice around my torso and his left paw tightened like a clamp over my scrotum. I yelped with pain as he squeezed the most sensitive particles of my anatomy.

'You move an inch, I squeeze real hard, ja?' said the not so gentle giant. Even my toes stopped wriggling.

True to his word, the fool called Gustl delivered a bigger fool, called Ollie Weiss, into the hands of justice.

When Gustl finally dumped me unceremoniously at the county gendarme's feet, inside the tiny police station of a Tyrolean village with a name I'd rather forget, the surprised constable waved a warning finger at Gustl, shook his head, grabbed my hand and apologised for the inconvenience Gustl had caused me. 'I hope you won't press charges, Kamerad,' he said to me. 'Gustl can be a bit of a handful at times. He is really quite harmless. I'm sorry.'

If the crazy giant hadn't thrown my outdated travel papers into the policeman's face, to prove that he had indeed nabbed a real fugitive, I would have walked out of the cop shop a free man. But for once Lady Luck was not on my side. I spent a horrible and sleepless night inside a tiny lockup, promising myself that I would never ever, for the rest of my entire life, consider myself to be superior to anybody else, including halfwits like a ball-grabbing Austrian giant called Gustl.

* * *

The military police acted promptly and efficiently. They arrived early in the morning, put handcuffs around my wrists and gave me an unexpected shove in the backside that sent me flying across the floor, through the open door and down the few steps. I tripped over my own feet and landed face down on the gravel road. My hurt ego ached ten times as much as the gravel rash on my knees and elbows.

They picked me up and bundled me into the back of their car. The more I protested the harsher they handled me. They slammed the door in my face, hopped into the front and, before I knew it, we were on our way to doom and gloom, to justice and due punishment.

The transfer from the police cell to an army gaol took a fraction of the time I would have liked it to take. But then, what did it matter? I found out soon enough that a cell was a cell, wherever it was.

When the sky turned from blue to black, and the stars lit their bright and sparkling lanterns to show the moon which road to take, I stood and stared at the steel bars of my window, which cut the glittering firmament into even, little rectangles. Steel bars, cold, nasty and horribly hostile.

Somehow I still hoped that someone would come along to open the door for me, to tell me that all this was a terrible nightmare. Nothing happened. I pleaded with God and prayed for his guidance and divine advice.

Nothing happened. He must have been out of town, away for holidays or something. Why didn't He respond to my prayers?

He said nothing at all. Instead of filling my lustreless cell with a golden glow of merciful forgiveness, He sent in the clouds and wrapped me in a mysterious shroud of unforgiving darkness.

I said to myself: 'I was nothing, I am nothing and I shall never be anything. Life is not worth living any more. Tomorrow I'll kill myself.'

At first light the following morning the cell door opened and a young corporal, with an MP's armband halfway up his right sleeve and a set of handcuffs dangling from his hand, told me that it was time to leave. He made me put my hands out in front and the cuffs were locked over my wrists.

'Time to go, Weiss,' he said. 'Don't try anything funny. I'd hate to be the one to shoot you.'

'I don't intend to die today,' I replied morosely. 'Tomorrow yes, but not today.'

Although even the sun might rise and set without being noticed by lots of troubled and preoccupied people, no one is blind enough to ignore a set of handcuffs on a man's wrists. One moment I was just another face in the milling throng of people, and the next moment, when my guardian and I stepped into the crowded compartment of a second-class carriage of the Deutsche Reichsbahn, I turned into the topic of the day.

At first there were a few timid glances and whispered remarks from curious but embarrassed fellow passengers. But once the train pulled out from the station I turned into fair game for all the biddies and buddies and busybodies who had nothing better to do than to argue about the kind of heinous crime I must have committed. I reacted to their speculations and implications with a bland and innocuous smile which infuriated my critics all the more.

Only a few months earlier I had put my life on the line for the very people who were passing sentence upon me now. I couldn't help thinking that I might have killed the wrong enemies in my war. Perhaps the Russian soldier who'd held a hand-grenade under his chin and blown his head to smithereens could have been a better friend to me than a whole trainload of my very own clan.

13

I didn't expect to be greeted with a twenty-one gun salute when I was duly delivered to the watchhouse of the barracks in Reutlingen, which was still headquarters to 92 Infantry Ersatz Regiment. I was promptly bundled into a cell and left to stew in my own misery.

I listened to the strains of the bugle echo across the quadrangle and almost forgotten memories came flooding back. It seemed that decades had come and gone since I stood alone on the parade ground in Elbing, pushing my lips hard against the mouthpiece, hoping that the right notes would come out of my shiny bugle; hoping that the war would be won in a matter of days or weeks; hoping my mother would put her arms around me and hug me to death; hoping there would be a letter from Helga to tell me that she and our child were safe and well; hoping that the Third Reich would indeed become the Thousand Year Reich.

Now all my dreams and aspirations lay splattered and broken on the cold concrete floor of my three-by-two-metre cell. As much as I tried to convince myself that I was still the same Ollie Weiss I used to be, there was nothing I could do now to justify or rectify what I had done. In the eyes of everyone I had committed a horrible and unforgivable crime. Yet in my own mind I only did what all of us should have done at the very beginning of the war. If only each one of us had been courageous enough to stand up for what we really believed in, if only all of us had said NO to war, millions of innocent people would still be walking in peace and laughing at life instead of crying from their untimely graves. I was as scared as anyone could ever be. Would I be strong enough to suffer the consequences. Oh, what the hell! Life wasn't worth living anyway.

Some of the sentries who brought me my rations or took me to the toilet were old comrades who'd shared foxholes with me in Russia. Now they pretended not to know me at all. Even comrades who I thought were old friends treated me with disdain. They supplied me with more cigarettes than I could smoke, yet they refused to acknowledge that we'd gone through tough times together.

I couldn't help thinking that my true comrades were all dead. To most of the people who knew me I was a nuisance, a traitor, a criminal and a pain in the neck, though, come to think of it, some of them had been more than a pain in the arse when they arrived with a new batch of terrified Ersatz men at the front line.

Martin Kuntz was a typical example. He'd come a long way since he'd arrived at our section of the Stalingrad corridor with the last reinforcements that got through to us. He'd climbed up the ranks since then. He was a sergeant now. He brought me my lunch one day. I recognised him instantly. I grabbed his free hand, shook it and said: 'Hey, it's great to see you're still alive, Martin. So you were lucky and made it out of Stalingrad. How are things?'

I could see by the expression on his face that he knew who I was. All of a sudden he was in a hurry to get away from me. He pushed the food tray into my hands and said, just before slamming the door shut: 'You must be mistaking me for somebody else. I'm sure we haven't met before.'

I was never any good at remembering people's names. But when it comes to recalling a face, that's an entirely different kettle of fish. Martin had shared my foxhole only for twenty-four hours. But how could I ever forget him? He'd cried twice as much in a day as I'd wept in six months. When it was time to collect rations from the field kitchen that operated beyond the shelter of the railway embankment, I couldn't make him budge.

'I'm scared,' he'd whimpered, 'I'm scared!'

'You'd be mad if you weren't,' I'd told him. But I'd felt sorry for him, and I went myself to fetch our supplies and ammunition. I got caught up in a very nasty barrage of artillery fire and was very fortunate indeed to survive.

'You bastard,' I now said to myself. 'I risked my life for you and you have the nerve to treat me like shit now!'

What's the name of the apostle who denied three times that he knew Jesus Christ? Was his name Martin bloody Kuntz?

Involuntary solitude became more acceptable to me from day to day, making me more and more introverted. I was certain that nobody out there could understand me, just as I could not understand any of them. Slowly but surely my inhospitable, miserable cell, with its tiny barred window and the peephole in the door, turned into my safe haven and shelter. It protected me from a hostile outside world in which there was no freedom, no compassion, no justice and no verity. Why couldn't I just stop breathing and drop dead? Would there be freedom in death?

Christmas time wasn't very far away. The icy northerly winds blew straight through the open cell window that was set high up in the wall so I couldn't reach up to shut it.

Christmas — there would be no decorated pine trees this year for Ollie Weiss, no lametta, no angels' hair, no flickering yellow flames sprouting from slender white candles. And there would be no 'Silent Night' for me to play on that dreaded violin I'd inherited from my father — the precious violin which was stowed away in a wooden case that looked like a small version of the coffin my father was buried in.

All things, good and bad, must come to an end eventually. When one of the sentries opened the cell door one day and told me that someone was waiting for me in the guard room, my heart jumped with joy. 'My mother or my girlfriend?' I wanted to know. Of course, I'd written to Mutti and told her where I was, hoping that she might come to see her only son. Had she buried the hatchet?

'Neither of them,' said the sentry, Schadenfreude lighting up his pockmarked visage. 'Let's go. It's time to face the music, your trial is coming up shortly. Have a nice trip and a beautiful execution.'

It took less than two hours to transfer me from an inconspicuous little army lockup to the cruel hell of clanging steel walkways, banging steel doors and narrow steel stairways strung crisscross through the maze of an intimidating institution situated behind a thick and very high red brick wall.

I had goosebumps running amok all over my body as soon as I set foot in the complex. I couldn't help feeling that I'd just stepped into my very own coffin. The gate shut behind my back with a harsh sound of finality.

In a matter of seconds I lost my right to be a human being. I lost my name and became a six-digit number. I was now not only a deserter; I was also, instantly, a 'verdammter Schweinehund', a damned pig-dog and a spineless, gutless, good for nothing bastard.

Before the day was over, they took me to have a hot shower. Watched by a couple of warders who joked openly about my involuntarily exposed penis, which had shrivelled into extraordinary insignificance through sheer embarrassment, I saw my last remnants of pride swirl in protest around the plug hole and disappear in an eddy of foam — disappear into nowhere like Dr Rosenbaum, like my Gypsy friends, like Helga's father, and many others who'd done no wrong and no harm to anybody. The only crime they'd committed was simply to be who they were.

Well, compared to Dr Rosenbaum, I was lucky indeed. At least I was in gaol for a reason. I was a deserter. I'd committed an unforgivable crime against society. And, caught up in a predicament like that, neither my vast Aryan lineage nor my impeccable record in the Hitler Youth did me one bit of good.

Night, unwanted as it was, came and went. Sleep, much as it was needed, didn't come to me at all. My breakfast sat untouched on the tiny fold-down table when my cell door opened and a warder told me: 'Time's up. Take your personal belongings and let's go.'

'I haven't even got a toothbrush,' I whispered. 'I have nothing at all.'

'All the better,' said the warder. 'It'll save us the trouble of sending a parcel to your next of kin after your execution. Come on, then. You mustn't be late for your own funeral, ja?'

I followed my keeper like a lamb that's led to the slaughter. They handcuffed me before they shoved me into a van. The massive gate of the Stuttgart Army Gaol screeched on its hinges as it swung open and sent me on my way to the most important rendezvous in my life.

I wasn't too sure what I needed more to see me through this very special day — a roll of toilet paper or a magnum of brandy.

★　★　★

An old army sergeant grabs me by the arm and leads me up two flights of polished, sweeping stairs into a small, cold and hostile room. I sit down because I'm told to sit down. The only thing I do without being told is breathe. I wish that I could stop breathing right here and now — get it all over and done with. I try so damn hard not to breathe, but I keep on gasping for air. Can't I do anything right? Involuntarily, my pores exude rivers of hot sweat and I shiver with cold. Jesus Christ, what's wrong with me? I've gone through worse than this. A man can only die once, can't he?

The sergeant takes me through an open door into the courtroom. I tremble from top to toe. I hate myself for being weak. I am ashamed of being frightened. But there's nothing I can do about the way my body reacts.

The sergeant pushes me onto a wooden chair. 'Get a hold of yourself,' he snarls.

'I want to throw up,' I reply, choking on my own vomit.

'Achtung!' yells the sergeant.

I jump off my straight-backed chair like a jack-in-the-box. My index fingers find the seams that run down the sides of my pants. I freeze. The word 'Achtung' still works on me like a magic spell that transforms me into a statue. I don't even shiver any more.

The judges enter the room. I want to see their faces but I can't move my eyes, which are stubbornly focused on the shiny tips of my jackboots. A huge, highly polished table stands between me and those who are in charge of my destiny.

After the brief preliminaries have been dealt with, I'm told to sit down. Questions are coming at me from nowhere and everywhere. I find myself hopelessly caught in the centre of an unrelenting crossfire. Caught like a fly in a spider's web — the more I struggle to retain my sanity, the less I can comprehend what is going on. Sometimes I contradict myself, sometimes a question makes less sense to me than my reply. I have been set adrift amid the turmoil of a raging ocean, and the shore is nowhere in sight.

'I don't know,' I shout at my inquisitive peers. 'I don't know!'

'But you must know,' says the voice of the law. 'You must know. You carried a mud-map in your pocket, a map that showed you the way to the Swiss border. Isn't that right?'

'Yes, sir.'

'Who gave you that map?'

'I can't remember, sir.' No matter what happens to me, I must never denounce anybody, least of all those good Austrians who treated me so well.

'Lying won't help you, Weiss. We'll get the truth out of you one way or another. Who gave you the map?'

'I don't know, sir.'

'Tell the truth!'

'I'm not lying, sir.'

Fear is replaced by sudden anger. They're just like my mother. Even if I tell the truth and nothing but the truth, they won't believe a word I say. Are they going to pull my pants down and spank me on the bare bottom? Are they going to stand me in a corner to make me feel sorry for myself? Will they invite my mother to my execution?

I take a deep breath. I muster enough courage to raise my head and scrutinise the panel of men who are endowed with the power to destroy me. Their round, flushed faces all look the same to me. They are not even trying to hide their own feelings behind a veneer of indifference. Arrogance, hostility and the contempt they harbour for me are on open display.

I realise that I have no hope in hell. I've been found guilty before my trial began. May God forgive me for hating my critics as much as they hate me, their victim. May God help me to be a man for once in my life.

I sneer at the rows of colourful ribbons

and shiny medals attached to each officer's tailor-made uniform. I despise those manicured fingernails of theirs and those velvet-skinned hands that protrude from braided sleeves. With hands like that none of them could dig a foxhole if their lives depended on it. I bet they have supersoft pink toilet tissues to wipe their aristocratic bottoms with. A handful of leaves or a few blades of grass or sometimes nothing at all were good enough for us. Not for them, though!

I want to ask my decorated judges how many obedient soldiers they have sent to the grave for each of the medals on their bloated chests. I don't ask. I am already in more trouble than I can handle.

The court martial goes on and on. 'You have done the most cowardly thing any soldier can do, Weiss. You deserted your own comrades.'

I can't control my temper any more. 'My comrades are dead, sir! They are all dead! I didn't run out on nobody. No sir, I did not!'

'You did.'

'If I did, I buried them first, sir. Yes, I ran away. How could I refuse to admit that, sir? But I didn't run away from my comrades, and I didn't run away from the enemy. I turned my back on your war, sir. Yes, sir, I wanted to flee into Switzerland. I was halfway up the border fence. But I couldn't turn my back on my country. I love my country, sir. I'm just sick of killing and sick of fighting and sick of hearing mutilated children crying out for help. And if that makes me a coward then I am a coward. But I'm a human being too! I have seen and suffered more than I can bear. I am not cut out to be a soldier, sir; I guess I never was. I offer no excuse for my actions, because I am convinced that I did what I was meant to do. You can hang me, you can shoot me, you can put a rifle in my hand, but neither you nor anybody else can make me pull that trigger ever again. I have nothing else to say.'

I don't know whether it was audacity or utter stupidity on my part that brought a few seconds of hush to the courtroom.

Then, breaking the momentary silence, the unsympathetic prosecutor glared at me with his cold blue Aryan eyes and proclaimed, begrudgingly, I thought: 'We must take into account the previously unblemished record of the accused. Although according to the law the penalty for desertion is execution, the death sentence might be a little too harsh in this case. But, nevertheless, the judgment we are about to pass must be severe enough to destroy the future of the accused.'

Fifteen years gaol with hard labour, that's what the court martial decided was a fitting punishment for a little rat like me. Fifteen years 'Zuchthaus'. I would never survive, never. I was sure of that.

The panel of ordained judges didn't even give me a last glance as they strutted out of the courtroom. They'd done their job and done it well for the sake of the Führer and the troubled, crumbling, mortally wounded Third Reich.

I cried for myself and I cried for my country. I wasn't ashamed of my tears any more.

The old sergeant who was in charge of me tried to cheer me up a little. 'Don't give up hope yet,' he told me as he took me downstairs. 'At least you won't have to face a firing squad tomorrow morning. It'll take some time to have your sentence confirmed. And with a bit of luck the war should be over by then. If we win, you'll lose. But if Germany loses the war you might be a free man much sooner than you could hope for. Think about it. Trust me.'

'Trust you?' I muttered. 'How could I? I can't even trust my own mother.'

★ ★ ★

'I should take you straight up to death row,' said the guard who ushered me up the clanging staircase as soon as I got back to the prison.

I protested. 'You can't take me up there. I only got fifteen years. I'm no target for the firing squad yet!'

'You will be,' said the guard, as he pushed me into a cell on the second floor. 'You will be. Take my word for it. Deserters don't get no second chances, not in our army, they don't. You shoulda thought twice before running away.'

Slumped into a corner of my new abode, legs pulled up, my head resting on shaking knees, I folded my hands in prayer, but the words just wouldn't come past my lips. Anyway, would prayers help a man who had descended to the bottom rung of the ladder? I didn't think so. I was absolutely nothing now, nothing and nobody. The sooner I could get used to the idea, the sooner I'd come to terms with myself.

I knew for certain that I would never survive fifteen years of imprisonment. I did not have the admirable patience of the lonely, long-legged spider who had somehow made a corner of my gloomy cell into his very own home. He'd spun his gossamer web with the kind of obstinate diligence only a spider can muster. Now, since he'd completed his work of art, he sat motionless in a corner, waiting for any insect stupid enough to get itself caught.

Rotting in gaol for fifteen years! I began to look at death as a welcome means of rescue. Yet somehow I was terribly frightened of not being alive any more. Well, perhaps tomorrow I would be strong enough. Tomorrow I would pluck up enough courage to kill myself. Yes, perhaps tomorrow.

For days and days on end I practised thinking of nothing at all. I lay on my bunk and tried to outstare the walls and the ceiling. But even when I closed my eyes the walls wouldn't disappear. They kept on terrorising me, closing in on me a tiny fraction at a time, cursing me and invading my own world and my whole brain inch by dreaded inch.

At night, when the walls covered their white coat of innocence with an infinite mantle of darkness and nobody was spying at me, not even my spider friend, I tried hard to look at myself. Yet I saw nothing but the bottomless blackness of doom.

I remembered my old comrade and friend Rudi, his hand sticking out from the snow; a flare lighting up the sky; Rudi swearing at me, cursing me, pleading with me to turn him into a cripple. All hell breaking loose; I, pulling the damned trigger, maiming my good friend for friendship's sake. Right or wrong? It didn't really matter now. We lived like animals, and we behaved worse than any other living creature on earth.

It didn't matter whether you were a hero or a coward when the grinding steel tracks of a Russian T-34 tank straddled your foxhole and you waited, petrified, for the tracks to turn in opposite directions to bury you alive.

Were you a hero when you died with a 'Heil Hitler' on your lips? Were you a coward if you died crying for help? How many different kinds of heroes and how many different kinds of cowards did it take to make up an army in any man's country?

I turned twenty-one without receiving the key to the front door of a house. But there were fireworks that made the melting snow sparkle on the roofs of the prison complex. Deadly fireworks they were, bringing devastation instead of congratulations.

At first it was the flak firing from all barrels. Wayward shells burst high above and hot shrapnel whistled through the wintry air like telegrams from hell. And then the bombs fell, screaming: 'Twenty-one today. He's twenty-one today. Oh, he's a jolly good German, he's a bloody bad German. Oh, he deserves to be killed today, and so say all of us. Hip, hip, hooray!'

Maybe today was my lucky day. What nicer day to die than your twenty-first birthday?

I jumped on to the cast-iron radiator mounted against the wall beneath the small barred window. I poked my arms through the bars and waved, shouting as loud as I could: 'Come on, you Amis or Tommies or Canadians. Come on, whoever you are up there in the sky. Come on, give me a present for my birthday, you bastards. I want a direct hit, do you hear? Come on, hit me, hit me, hit me!'

But neither God nor the devil nor any one of the alien bombardiers could have heard me. The only bomb that might have had my initials on it didn't whistle or hiss at all. It came gurgling down all the way into the quadrangle below. I'm sure it was meant to be my present. But before I could say thank you it buried itself with a dull thud. No explosion, no shattered windows, no collapsing walls, no victims and no early grave for Ollie Weiss. Nothing.

The next bomb exploded more than 200 metres away. Honestly, how unlucky can a man get?

Even those Spitfires that came diving out from the winter sun, spewing hell and brimstone and bullets, didn't oblige, though they came straight at me. It took me all the strength I could muster not to duck for cover when the bullets slammed into the walls around me. And yet, I seemed to be invincible.

When the raid was over I was still alive. The battered snow kept on melting. The fire engines raced towards crumbling homes. The smell of burning timber mingled with the acrid stench of explosives and phosphor. A cloud of smoke and dust rose quietly to hide the shame and horror of war. And, damn it all, I was still alive.

The next morning, at sunrise, a loud salvo of rifle shots told us that another condemned prisoner had fallen victim to the bullets of a firing squad. What would it be for me? Fifteen years or death at sunrise?

I wished that I could muster the courage to tear the bed sheet into strips, tie it around one of the window bars, put it like a rope around my neck and hang myself. I toyed a long time with that idea.

I was more and more possessed by the fascinating idea of putting an end to my own life. Suicide seemed the only credible way out of my dilemma. Fifteen years in prison at the best. What other option was there for me? I had to find a way of putting myself out of my misery. I really had no choice.

I thought seriously about going on a hunger strike. But then, I'd just recently regained my appetite, and the food wasn't all that bad, once I got used to it.

Couldn't I just lie down on my bunk and stop breathing? I tried and I failed dismally. Every time I was on the brink of blacking out, I gulped for air and continued to live.

Surely there must be an easy way to die. I racked my brain trying to find a solution to my death wish. I considered all sorts of stupid strategies. Although I discarded them all after considering the pros and cons, my new obsession made the days pass a lot quicker.

Then one day I came up with a superb idea. Knowing that I didn't have the guts to hang myself, or cut my throat or wrists or stab myself to death, even if I could get hold of a knife to do it with, my method of doing myself in had to be a lot more subtle and a lot less messy.

Thinking back to my troubled days of childhood, I recalled that my mother used to make me stand in the corner somewhere for hours each time she caught me with a rubber band tied around a finger. 'You'll kill yourself, you silly little idiot!' she'd scream. 'Don't you know that those rubber bands cut off your blood circulation and you'll end up dying from gangrene?'

Well, Mutti, I thought now, taking a good look at my fingers one by one, you told me I'd go blind if I masturbated, but you were wrong. Now let's find out how right you were about this gangrene business.

I pulled strands and strands of cotton from the hem of my blanket, spat on them and spun them into a reasonably strong piece of string. I tested the string for strength and, when I was satisfied, wound it tightly around the index finger of my left hand.

Hoping that, for once, my mother had told me the truth, I considered my exit from life already a fait accompli. I sat smugly in the corner of my bunk and waited for doomsday to happen, just as patiently as my friend, the spider, waited for a victim to stray into his web.

I waited, and waited, and waited. My bloodstarved finger began to throb like hell after a while, but there was no acute pain and, most importantly, no blood.

Throb! Throb! The damn pulsing kept me awake all night. So what! I'd have all the sleep a man could ask for once I'd succeeded with this ingenious suicide of mine. Goodbye, Adolf bloody Hitler!

After twenty-four hours of strangulation my dead-looking finger had turned into a greyish obelisk that stood away from the other healthy digits, as if it was making a statement to me and the world. Grey and ashen and lifeless, it stood like a tombstone. Ashes to ashes. Dust to dust.

I let another day and another sleepless night pass by before I shouted an emphatic 'Sieg Heil' from the cell window. I took a final look at the world and the freedom that lay beyond the iron bars. I steeled myself, said goodbye to myself and, feeling somewhat like a hero, bit through the tight knot. The string fell away and the hot blood pounced on the cold, almost dead and unsuspecting finger. I screamed in agony. I said goodbye to Helga, to our child and to the world. My heart was labouring twice as fast to move the toxic blood from my finger to every part of my body.

I reclined on the bunk and folded my hands under my head. Euphoria swept into every corner of my brain. Memories came and passed, memories of Helga and of lilac blossoms; sweet memories. I love you, Helga. I love you. Bonjour, Yvette, je t'aime. Voulez vous couchez avec moi for one last time?

Hey, Mutti, don't push me. I can do this dying bit all by my own little self. Oh, what a wonderful feeling it is to slip and slide away into merciful and everlasting unconsciousness. Oblivion, here I come.

At that very special brief moment when I felt my soul rising from my earthly remains to hitch a ride to heaven, the bloody warder called out: 'You there! What's the matter with you? Don't you want your breakfast today?'

Damn you, Mutti. I had myself so convinced that you'd told me the truth for once. Oh well, another wishful dream gone down the drain. The grey obelisk on my left hand had turned back into a pink index finger. I was alive — and I was as mad as a rattlesnake can ever get without losing its rattle. Why the hell couldn't I just drop dead like any other human being?

The last slabs of snow moved haltingly from the tiled roofs of the cell blocks, turned into life-giving water and helped to still the thirst of all those seeds that sensed the advent of spring after a long and harsh winter. Before long the sleeping branches of trees woke up and began to grow a new coat of leaves.

★ ★ ★

I was incredibly homesick in spite of all the nasty feelings I harboured towards my family. Blood was still thicker than water. There had been no Christmas greetings and no birthday cards either from any of my ever so respectable and God-fearing clan; not a single message to let me know that somebody somewhere in this world still cared for me. Although I knew that it was the truth, it was not easy to accept that I was, and always would be, the black sheep in the family.

What a crazy life it was! Only fifteen or eighteen months ago I had broken all speed records in full flight from the Russian hordes. If only one single stray bullet could have wiped me out instead of killing my best friend. Even if it had been a bullet in the back, I would have died a hero's death. My whole clan would have gathered in the quaint ancient church that stood opposite my former school. They would have lamented and grieved over me. They would have cried for me and prayed for me, and they would have said to each other: 'Poor Ollie. What a shame he died so young. Maybe we treated him a bit harshly, but we loved him nevertheless. May God have mercy on the soul of a true hero.'

My dear old mother, being a hypocrite by birth and by nature, would have worn black for a whole year of mourning in memory of me. Everybody in town would have felt sorry for the poor woman.

But, since I'd run away from the war as well as fleeing from the Russians, I was a curse to all and sundry. And, unless whispered very, very quietly, my name was

317

never mentioned within the hallowed folds of the family that spawned me. Once a black sheep, always a blemish on the otherwise clean-as-a-whistle family tree.

Ironically, it was only my death wish that kept me alive and kicking and smiling at my keepers. Meekly and willingly, I let all of them treat me the way they chose to, without raising a single word of protest. My meek behaviour brought privileges for me. I was eventually permitted to clean the shower room on our floor every day and, depending on the generosity of the warder on duty, more often than not I ended up with a few cigarettes — which were the most treasured possession in gaol — or even an extra half ladle of soup.

Without the granted privileges I would never have discovered the old rusty razor blade that had been secreted by a fellow inmate, some time ago, behind the shaving mirror fixed to the wall in the shower room. Being a 'trusted inmate', I had no problems with bringing the blade back into my cell. The thin piece of steel became my pièce de résistance. I treasured it like a true gift from God. If I had been a Catholic, I would have gone down on my knees and prayed my heart out. Instead of praying, I speculated on what to do with this present from heaven.

I handled the rusty razor blade with great care. After all, I didn't want to cut my fingers and watch the blood ooze out. No matter how much I wanted to die, watching myself bleed to death would be the very last of my options.

I had all the time in the world to plot and scheme and plan. But I couldn't come up with anything satisfactory for some days. Then a heaven-sent brainwave provided me with the perfect solution to all my worries. Taking utmost care, I broke the 'gift from heaven' into small pieces. After I finished my breakfast of rolled oats — I didn't want to die hungry, of course — I gathered every piece of the shattered blade in the palm of my right hand, pushed them into a heap and placed them carefully on the tip of my tongue. Then I picked up my mug of Ersatz coffee and drank until it was empty. I searched every cavity in my mouth. Finding no leftovers anywhere, I sat back and relaxed, ecstatically pleased with the fact that I'd finally done myself in. I would bleed to death, yet there wouldn't be a single drop of blood visible anywhere. I sure was a smart bastard.

I lay down on the bed and waited patiently for the pieces of steel to cut my insides into ribbons. By the time I realised that the process of having my guts chopped to bits

319

would most likely be a very painful event, it was too late to regret what I'd done.

All that was left for me to do now was to relax and wait for the end to begin. I wasn't dead by lunchtime, and I enjoyed my meal more than on any previous day. I was still alive at dinnertime, so I enjoyed my dinner just as much.

I was resolved not to tell a single soul what I'd done until it was much too late for me to survive. I really was pleased with myself. I had chosen an ingenious way to say goodbye and good riddance to a rotten world.

A sharp, stabbing pain in the belly woke me in the middle of the night. I ignored the beads of sweat that formed on my brow and reassured myself, saying: 'Well, Ollie, be proud of yourself. Finally you've done something right.'

Then I farted. The pain disappeared, and I cursed the pea soup I'd eaten for dinner. But I was not discouraged altogether. I was cocksure that I'd end up a corpse, if not today then tomorrow. There was no way for me to back out now.

The very next morning I was called down to the office of the prison's governor, who smiled at me and said: 'I have good news for you, Weiss. Your sentence has been commuted.'

I looked straight past him and stared at a larger than life portrait of my fallen idol, Adolf Hitler, the charismatic leader dressed in a plain brown uniform adorned with nothing but the Iron Cross First Class, the bravery medal he'd earned himself in the last war.

Then the tragic irony of what had befallen my country in this second world war really hit me.

Only God or a genius could have done for Germany what Hitler had accomplished. In just a handful of years he had turned poverty into prosperity, shame into pride, despair into hope and beggars into achievers. He'd raised the spirit of a whole downtrodden nation. He'd turned sixty-odd million losers into a new and proud Volk of Vaterland-loving Germans. He gave us the Volkswagen for the working-class and the Hitlerjugend for the new generation. He shaped a timid, frightened little boy like me into a belligerent and self-opinionated monster. And he made the trademark 'Made in Germany' stand out in the world market for quality and excellence.

Then he'd turned it all into dust.

'Something wrong with your hearing, Weiss?' The voice of the governor seemed to come from miles away. 'Your sentence has been reduced from fifteen years to eight years. With good behaviour and remissions you'll be out about 1951. Do you know how lucky you are?'

'Am I, sir?' I mumbled. 'Am I lucky, sir?'

It wasn't until I got back into my cell and the door clanged shut that I laughed out aloud, insanely loud, furiously loud. And, believe you me, I felt every single fragment of that blasted razor blade ripping my insides to pieces. Jesus Christ! What had I done to myself? There would be no firing squad to face for me, and we'd lost the war already. It would only be a matter of time before I was a free man, because that's what I'd be if Germany surrendered. The devil must have possessed me when I swallowed that blade!

But, as in so many of the things I'd tried to do in my life, I failed in the attempt to end it.

Exactly two weeks later, on his birthday, the Führer gave us a present none of us expected. Our cell doors were thrown open from the ground floor all the way up to the very top. The governor stood at the bottom of the staircase with a megaphone raised to his lips. 'The Führer has pardoned all of you,' he shouted, his voice echoing from wall to wall. 'He's declared an amnesty for all of you. Congratulations! You are given another chance to make up for the crimes you committed. Your country needs you. The

Führer needs you to stand up and fight for our Vaterland. Good luck, Kameraden!'

I wasn't the only one who sniggered. Only yesterday the governor would have been happy to have any of us executed and would have thought nothing of it. All of a sudden we were 'Kameraden'. He went on ranting and raving about how fortunate we were and how grateful we were expected to be. At the end of all the drivel he broadcast through that megaphone of his, he had us shouting 'Heil Hitler' and 'Sieg Heil' as if we'd been listening to the chief liar of all — Josef Göbbels, Propaganda Minister extraordinary, who could make almost anybody forget the principles he stood for. 'Heil bloody Hitler to you all!'

When we found that we would receive full rations, new uniforms and underwear, even cigarettes and a generous measure of brandy, and that the cell doors would remain open overnight, our scepticism waned and we looked forward to celebrating.

My senses dulled by alcohol, my fears allayed by euphoria, I gave myself a solemn undertaking before I drifted off to sleep. No matter what happened, I would not fire another shot for the rest of my life. They could make me carry a rifle, but they couldn't make me pull the trigger. I had done enough fighting and shooting and killing to last me for the rest of my life.

Kurt had been right when he told me: 'You can't change the world and you can't change your destiny. As long as there are people, there will be wars. Wars are part of human nature just as death is part of life. Peace is just an interval between wars that have to be fought. You cannot change the flow of the tide. Running away like a coward or standing up to fight like a hero makes no difference to anyone but yourself. What happens is meant to happen. Neither you nor I can change the course of history, not now and not in a thousand years.'

How could I tell a dead friend that he might have been right?

Anyway, as far as I was concerned, I was through with trying to change the course of history.

14

On a perfect bright and sunny spring day, our convoy of trucks moved slowly but steadily away from the doom and gloom, putting a good distance between us and the hostile gaol with its barred windows, where contempt and pea soup, degradation and cabbage broth, deprivation and porridge were on the menu day after dismal day.

Jubilantly celebrating the demise of our questionable past, we were all caught up in the same euphoric momentum, and for the time being all the hardships we had suffered stayed locked away in the far corners of our brains.

The thirty of us, sitting on the wooden benches of one bouncing truck, were a motley congregation of army rejects. Coming from all walks of life, we were as different from each other as chalk and cheese. We had little in common other than the sallow prison complexion on our faces and the plain, unadorned new uniforms we wore.

Yet there was an obvious bond between us. Although we hardly knew each other's names, we'd suffered together and we'd been pardoned together. And all our faces were now painted with the same kind of smile.

None of us wanted to talk about the war. The songs we sang together were not of the kind that were sung in Sunday School. The cruder the lyrics, the more we enjoyed them. Why shouldn't we have wallowed in ribaldry? Isn't it true that the penis is the only friendly weapon at a soldier's disposal? Isn't it indeed his only piece of equipment that creates life rather than destroys it?

Anyway, none of us had his mind on either creation or destruction. We didn't really care about anything but the fact that Hitler had not only promised us a pardon but had kept his word.

All the signposts along the highway pointed towards Munich, the home of the famous Oktoberfest. Our imaginations ran hot and wild as we fantasised shamelessly and vociferously about cold steins of Bavarian beer and hot loins of Bavarian maidens. I'm sorry to say, my treasured Helga and all the love and the things I had promised her so long ago never entered my mind. I guess when a man gets out of gaol after enduring a lengthy period in solitary confinement, it is only natural for him to be as horny as hell.

One prune-faced little fellow tried to spoil our fun for a while. He panicked when our convoy moved off the main highway, screaming something about us going to the Dachau concentration camp. But who'd want to take any notice at all of a ratbag like that? We'd been pardoned by the Führer himself! The Führer needed us! Wasn't that what we'd been told?

When our trucks finally came to a halt, we found ourselves in a quadrangle in the middle of nowhere and miles away from the Hofbräuhaus in Munich. Little Prune-face ended up with egg on his face because there wasn't a strand of barbed wire let alone a concentration camp anywhere near our allocated quarters.

For so long I had thought that God didn't want to know me any more, but now I was certain that He'd kept His eye on me all the way through my suffering. I promised to pray to Him and thank Him for taking care of me. This would be the first night, since the day when a village idiot delivered me into the arms of the law, that I wouldn't spend cooped up in solitary confinement.

But I couldn't sleep. I got out of bed, rolled up the blackout blind that covered the window, and tried to make eye contact with the Lord who was supposed to have His kingdom somewhere beyond the Milky Way. And, perhaps only in imagination and yet so very clear, I saw Him blink at me with eyes brighter than any of those countless stars up there, as if He wanted to give me reassurance.

My conscience was in total disarray. What was I to do if I was handed a rifle and ordered to go forward and fight for 'Ein Reich, ein Volk and ein Führer'? Would I be a coward and break the promise I'd given myself? Or would I be a coward of a different kind, strong enough to refuse to take any further part in the mass murder that was called war?

In a way I was glad that Max came to stand next to me at the open window, puffing tobacco smoke into the crisp air, and telling me about the rough deal he'd got from a court martial. He had committed the same crime as me — desertion. But his reasons differed greatly from mine. His only daughter had got married, and the army refused to give him compassionate leave to give his daughter away at the wedding. He must have been extremely lucky. He hitchhiked all the way from the front line in Russia back to his home town and got there just in the nick of time. He was arrested the morning after his daughter's wedding.

'How about you?' he asked me quietly. 'What did you do to get yourself into trouble?'

I had no reason to lie to him. 'I'm through with fighting,' I confessed. 'I've seen enough blood and torn limbs to turn me into a pacifist for the rest of my living days, Max. Why can't politicians do their own dirty work? I'm quitting.'

'Have you gone crazy or something?' he said, flicking his cigarette butt into the crisp night air. 'Good heavens, Ollie, the Führer has just given you your freedom. Don't you think you owe him something for that? What are you going to do when they give you a rifle in a couple of days and send you out fighting?'

'I'm not gonna fight, Max.'

'Not even if I'm walking next to you and some bastard blows my head off?'

'I'm afraid I can't answer that question truthfully until the occasion arises. If I shot a whole enemy platoon out of sheer revenge, you'd still be dead, wouldn't you. I don't believe in an eye for an eye any more. Sorry, Max, but that's the way I feel.'

Max held his breath for a moment, then turned on his heels mumbling, 'I hope they don't put you and me in the same foxhole.'

'You never know your luck,' I whispered acrimoniously, feeling very much at odds with myself and Max and the rest of the world.

At assembly the next morning we were

informed in no uncertain terms as to what the army had in store for us. The ugly truth was that we were still nothing better than the scum of the Vaterland.

An officer told us: 'Don't even consider for one moment that Germany condones what you have done. You might be wearing the uniform of the Wehrmacht now, but we wouldn't trust any of you to carry a rifle. The Führer has pardoned you, but the army hasn't, and it never will.'

The officer paused for a moment to watch our reaction to the news. Then he continued: 'You are now part of the Strafeinheit Randt, a newly formed penal unit. The only weapons you'll carry will be picks and shovels. It'll be your job to dig foxholes and graves for our real soldiers who are brave enough to stand up and fight. Of course, once we shift you to the front line you can try to surrender to the enemy. If you do, you'll end up with a bullet in your back before you can raise your hands. And that's a promise.'

I was one of the very few people who smiled after that speech. Max and many others felt somewhat deprived of a golden opportunity to get back into the killing game and make up for lost time.

'You can always hit them over the head with a shovel,' I remarked to Max, who was not at all amused and much too angry to tell me what he really thought of me.

I thanked God for His mercy and promised Him I would turn into one of the best hole-diggers the country had ever seen. Hell, maybe God had discovered my vocation. Perhaps I should have been a hole-digger instead of a pen-pusher after I left school. Jesus, if I got through the rest of the war alive I might go back to Prenzlau and put a shiny brass shingle on the wall for everybody to see: 'Ollie Weiss. Expert Hole-Digger. Prompt Efficient Service. You Die, I Dig. Make Your Appointment Before It's Too Late!'

★   ★   ★

I still don't know whether it was the abundance of rich food or the magnitude of a rigorous training regime that put litres of fluid into my legs and made them swell up like balloons. For the life of me I still can't figure out why I suffered a kind of epileptic fit at lunchtime on the third day. When I regained consciousness and looked at all the concerned faces staring down at me, I had a certain feeling that my hole-digging career would be delayed for a while.

And I was right. I was put on a stretcher and carried all the way to the Dachau SS

Hospital, which happened to be only a fifteen minute walk from our barracks. Long before I found the time or the opportunity to thank God for His kindness, my boots were cut off my legs and my body sank into the comforting softness of a real bed. I didn't mind having a few needles stuck into me and losing a few cc's of my Aryan blood. It was a small price to pay for the unexpected luxury I enjoyed.

The doctor who came to see me asked a thousand questions, but didn't know what was wrong with me. He couldn't confirm that I'd suffered a seizure and he couldn't explain why my legs were almost twice the normal size. He shrugged his shoulders, gave me a pat on the head and left me to ponder my extraordinary stroke of luck.

It took me a while to come to terms with the fact that I, a convict, a deserter, a disgrace to the Vaterland and a condemned arsehole, had ended up in an elitist, hoity-toity place like this. What, for goodness sake, was I doing in the twenty-bed ward of an SS hospital?

Although most of the patients were hardly in good enough health to take notice of me, I felt like a fish out of water. But that didn't stop me from going to sleep and dreaming of Helga and lilac and also of ravishing busty and lusty Bavarian maidens. I prayed that when I woke up I would still be in the same ward, in the same hospital, in the same haven. And, thank heavens, I was!

It was in that hospital that I first came face to face with an inmate of a concentration camp. He was dressed in a blue and grey striped zebra suit and was pushing the coffee trolley along the aisle that divided the two rows of beds.

He looked well fed and a hell of a lot healthier than waterlogged and underfed me.

Curiosity got the better of me. I couldn't help saying hello to him and asking what life was like in that camp of his. 'You are doing all right for yourself, aren't you?'

The zebra-man handed me a cup of coffee and went on his way, almost expressionless, with just the hint of a smile at the corners of his eyes.

'You don't talk to bastards like him,' said the man in the bed next to mine, who'd lost one leg just above the knee. He was a Sturmführer. He happened to be the first SS officer I'd met.

I could have told him that my Dr Rosenbaum was not a bastard. Sure, I could have, but who was I to contradict a man who had more medals pinned to his jacket than I had teeth in my mouth? I didn't have to ask him if he was a hero. In my book anybody who'd lost a leg and kept a smile on his face was a big hero. He turned out to be a much better chess player than I'd ever be. His name was Heini. He beat the socks off me in the first two games. In between matches he told me what he was and who he was and why he had a thing going — on crutches and without — with half the nurses on our floor.

His wife had walked out on him as soon as she found out that he'd lost a leg. 'It's a pity, really,' he told me. 'She was a good cook and a great lover. But life goes on. Losing a leg and a wife is not the end of the world. There's always somebody who's worse off than you are.'

Heini lifted one of his crutches and pointed to the bed nearest to the door. 'See that poor bastard over there? He's eighteen years old, nineteen at the most. Lost both arms up to the elbows. He can't even wipe his own arsehole or blow his own nose. God only knows why they're keeping him alive. The poor devil wants to die. But he can't pick up a gun and blow his brains out, can he? Holy shit, what have I got to complain about?'

It was very quiet in the ward after dinner. Most patients lay back and waited for the darkness to cradle them into a few hours of blissful sleep — drug-induced and well deserved — sleep that would block out the pain and the suffering and the misery.

The doctors and the nurses had retired. I walked to the nearest window to watch the slow transition from day to night in the gently waning twilight. My mind went walk-about . . .

Sunset in Prenzlau. I'm sitting on my father's knee on a wooden bench on the Esplanade. Both of us are looking across the golden surface of the Uckersee.

'Look, Papa, the sun is falling into the lake.'

'Nein, mein Junge, it's not falling into the water.'

'But it is, Papa. Can't you see?'

'No, it's not. It's just having a bath so it can shine all the brighter for us tomorrow morning . . .'

Now, beyond the hospital window, the sun disappeared slowly from the horizon. And, far away, glimmering, shimmering flashes of light played hide and seek among the slow-moving clouds. At first I thought that an out-of-season thunderstorm was brewing in the distance. But it wasn't long before I recognised that the war was coming to pay us a visit in the very near future. As the night grew older, the ominous noise of war grew louder and louder.

'Let's have a game of chess or two before

the war is over.' Heini was in great spirits in the morning. I'd imagined that for a man of Heini's calibre it would be rather tough to cope with the fact that he'd ended up being on the losing side. I couldn't help talking to him about it. He just shrugged his shoulders and grinned. 'We lost the last war and we've lost this one. Don't you worry, we'll make sure we win the next one. Third time lucky, ja?'

'If you say so,' I muttered. I couldn't possibly disagree with a Sturmführer of Hitler's elite troops.

I got myself busy setting up the pieces on the chessboard. Heini drew black. I moved my king's pawn two squares forward and Heini reached out to respond. Before he had a chance to make his first move, the war came to pay us a nasty visit. We hadn't even noticed the sound of aircraft engines in the sky. The attack was as sudden as it was brutal. Peace one moment, war the next.

They came out of the sun, flying low, just skimming over the treetops. They were firing from all barrels and they used the large red cross painted on the roof of our hospital for target practice. Heini the hero moved faster than Ollie the coward!

The bullets came screaming through the windows and smashed into the sterile white walls of our ward. Among a shower of glass and mortar I dived for cover under my bed and bumped headlong into Heini, who said drily, 'What kept you so long, Kamerad?'

The strafing raid stopped as suddenly as it had began. The humming, droning engine noise dissipated in the distance. Shaken and confused, we crawled out from under our beds and gazed speechlessly at the mess that used to be our tidy, squeaky-clean ward.

Holy Moses, hadn't times changed. I recalled the spring and summer of 1942, when I'd watched our Stuka bombers home in on the panicking hordes of Russkies in full flight. I remembered how we'd jumped up and down on the floor of our fast-moving truck, cheering, yelling, shouting and Sieg-Heiling during hot pursuit, with a smell of victory tickling our nostrils, our chests swollen with pride.

Somebody yelled: 'Hey, they're coming back! Deckung!' I dropped back onto the floor faster than lightning could strike. I heard the shards of broken glass crunch under the weight of my trembling body. I thought, Isn't it ridiculous? Why am I taking cover at all? Why am I frightened out of my wits? Didn't I want to die? Hadn't I tried to kill myself? Am I scared of dying now or of being dead forever? Why can't I stand up like a man, lean out of the smashed window and wave at the murdering bastards up there? Why the hell can't I?

I was still clawing frantically at the floorboards, trying to scratch out a hole large enough to hide my face in, when Heini started to collect the chess pieces that lay strewn across the floor. He put them back into the cardboard satchel one by one, lovingly and gently wiping the specks of fragmented glass from their lacquered surfaces. 'I'll get you, you Tommy bastards,' he swore. 'One day I'll even the score. You can bet your life on it.'

I looked away from Heini and straight into the beaming face of the pudgy zebra-man, whose eyes were riveted on Heini. He didn't realise I was watching him, and his joviality fell away from his face like an ill-fitting mask. I'd never seen hatred rise so quickly in any man's face. It didn't last long, just a second or two, and the cover-up smile shrouded his true feelings once more. It seemed to me as if the zebra-man's face heralded victory rather than the defeat Heini and I and most of us were ready to accept.

★ ★ ★

Neither God nor the combined leftovers of the routed German army could prevent the front line from closing in. How long would I have to wait to make use of the English I'd learnt in school?

From the open window of the hospital ward I watched the penal unit I belonged to, the Strafeinheit Randt, abandon quarters. Soon afterwards I watched the looters move in on the vacated barracks and stores. I didn't realise Heini had gone until he arrived back with his first haul of booty.

'Take what you need, Kamerad,' he said, dumping cigarettes, cans of bully beef and God knows what on his bed. 'I've got a fair idea that we'll have lean times ahead of us. Be my guest. I'm going back for more.'

And he did. He shouldn't have, because I could already hear steel grating on steel, clattering, clamorous, menacing and spine-chilling. Nothing but tanks could create noises like that; noises that would make every infantryman's nerves stand on edge. I wished Heini hadn't gone for a second time. Most of the 'raiders' had already returned to safety when I spotted him. He was still a hundred metres or more from the hospital. He had a bottle of liquor in each hand and found it difficult to use his crutches properly.

I yelled out to him: 'Throw the bottles

away, Heini! Hurry up! Come on. Come on. Hurry.'

He recognised my voice. He stopped and looked from window to window until he found me. He waved the bottles in the air and shouted: 'Keep your shirt on, Ollie. Don't panic. Nobody's gonna shoot a cripple!'

The nurse we'd nicknamed 'Big Tits', because of her enormous and excruciatingly provocative boobs came running into our ward shouting, loud and panicky: 'We are evacuating the hospital. Everybody raus. Raus! Schnell! Off with you into the air-raid shelter. Go on, get a move on!'

I didn't move from my spot at the window and kept on shouting to Heini. He didn't have far to go now. He crossed the little footbridge that spanned a concrete-lined canal, leaving only a large open square of frostbitten lawn between him and the protective walls of the hospital.

'Hey, Weiss,' shouted Big Tits. 'You want a special invitation?'

I ignored her and kept on calling out to Heini: 'Throw the bottles away, you idiot. Throw the damned bottles away and hurry up.'

But he clung stubbornly to the booty that impeded his progress. 'It's French cognac, Ollie. I'd rather be killed than throw these

340

little treasures away.'

Then there was a single rifle shot, just one lousy shot, one blasted bullet, Heini dropped his treasured bottles first. They didn't even burst when they tumbled onto the ground. The crutches fell away from his armpits as he raised his arms and clawed at the air, searching for something to hold on to. He crumbled and fell into himself without a scream, without protest and without time to say goodbye. He came to rest between the two bottles of liquor he'd given his life for.

I flew into a rage as soon as I realised what I had witnessed. I screamed blue murder. A defenceless cripple had been shot in front of my very eyes. Was that what this stupendously brutal war was all about? Shooting the crutches away from under a crippled and unarmed man? I was insane with rage. Big Tits grabbed me and tried to calm me down. I brushed her hands away and bolted towards the door. 'I'm coming, Heini.' I shouted. 'I'm coming.'

But hands stronger than my own good intentions got hold of me and my thrashing body. And all my protesting didn't do one bit of good, not for Heini and not for me. Hemmed in and helpless, I was pushed down the stairs and into the dark and clammy and overcrowded concrete bunker only a few paces away from the hospital's side entrance. My cries of revenge drowned in that special kind of silence only fear can create.

A few minutes later the door was ripped open from the outside. White teeth, gum-chewing mandibles, strange-looking helmets and weary, bloodshot eyes were the first things I saw of my captors. Thank the Lord, they were Americans and not Russians. What a relief that was! Every soldier in the German army was undoubtedly terrified at the prospect of getting caught by the Russians and ending up somewhere in Siberia. I reached out to hug the soldier who stood closest to me. But my smile froze when I saw his index finger move towards the trigger of his rifle.

Then I heard the first sounds of American English, including phrases that had absolutely nothing in common with the Oxford English I had so eagerly studied in school. I remember the words vividly, and I must apologise for reiterating the spate of expletives that now hit me with huge force and made me cringe in awe: 'Put your fuckin' hands on your fuckin' heads, you mother-fuckin' Jerry bastards, and git outa there one by fuckin' one before I fuckin' well blow your fuckin' heads off.'

When the verbal onslaught ended, I was

one of the first to emerge from the bunker — into a totally new world. With everybody pushing from behind, I reached for the handrail to steady myself. A rifle swung towards me and aimed for a spot between my eyes. The barrel was as steady as any barrel can be. I had no problems at all with putting my shaky hands back on top of my head.

'Don't try to play no fuckin' tricks on me, Fritz,' warned my rather edgy adversary. 'You'd better git movin', you fuckin' son of a bitch!'

I'd often pondered what it would be like to surrender to one's enemy. Now I realised that my imagination was far from the terrifying truth.

I moved. All of us moved — everybody but Heini. He still lay motionless on the spot where he'd died.

The hospital and its surrounds, once so peaceful and serene, had yielded its serenity to the US Army and a milling mob of gun-toting warriors. They were everywhere, running, yelling, waving their rifles in the air, herding us together with the expertise and tenacity of well-trained sheep dogs.

The crews of the now stationary tanks sat atop their steel monsters like a captive and appreciative audience. With their cannon homing in on us, they cheered as they watched a deadly and humiliating version of cowboys and Indians.

Numbed with confusion and fear, stumbling towards nowhere in particular and following the leader blindly, I tried to work out how coldblooded and heartless a soldier would have to be not only to aim his rifle at an obviously unarmed cripple on crutches but actually to pull the trigger. This war of ours was turning all of the participants into hardhearted, remorseless murderers. I thought to myself, May God have mercy on all of us. May He bring us to our senses and restore sanity to our brains.

I had waited and yearned for my moment of surrender for so long. But now the joy of knowing I had survived turned sour. I stood there, tears welling in my eyes, watching two of the conquerors get hold of Heini's arms and drag him out of the way. The stump of his leg pointed skyward. His head, lifeless as it was, bounced across the hard ground, twisting and turning in strange angles. Oh, dear Jesus, what had gone so wrong in a world that was meant to be a paradise?

I guess that nothing, not even a court martial and solitary confinement, can be as intimidating and humiliating and debasing to any man's self-esteem as being taken prisoner of war. Without being told, I knew that my compatriots and I were completely at the mercy of strangers who obviously had the authority to blow our brains out for no reason whatsoever, whenever they felt the urge.

As a convicted and despised deserter I'd been nothing. As a prisoner of war I was less than nothing, and easy prey.

★ ★ ★

We huddled together like a scared mob of sheep. Some carried briefcases, others clutched bulging pillow cases or stuffed kitbags. My share of Heini's loot still lay abandoned on my bed in the upstairs ward.

'Line up three deep along the edge of the canal, facing me.' The voice came crisp and clear in accent-free German.

The one and only time I had followed my conscience, rather than following orders, I'd got myself into more strife than I could handle and had had to face a court martial. I'd learnt my lesson the hard way, thank you very much. I'd line up three deep all by myself if I was ordered to do so.

First we had to deposit all of our baggage next to our feet. Nurses' handbags, doctors' stethoscopes, parcels and survival packs, they all ended up on the ground.

Next we were told to empty our pockets

and turn them inside out. The only thing we were allowed to keep was a handkerchief. Obviously our captors didn't want us to have anything at all, not even a snotty nose.

After we were told to step forward, the soldiers of the US Army moved behind us and got busy kicking our discarded belongings into the canal — bags, paybooks, wallets, much treasured photos and letters, keepsakes and lucky charms and whatever else we'd carried with us. It all ended up in the drink, some of it sinking straight to the slimy bottom, other things floating, twisting and turning, drifting slowly out of view.

When at long last our antagonists were convinced that we had neither pistols nor hand-grenades hidden away somewhere, there wasn't a toothpick or a condom to share between the lot of us.

Nobody took much notice of a group of noisy, gesticulating people who approached us from the left. They were obviously celebrating the end of their war. But when they came closer I noticed that the revellers wore identical clothing. They were all dressed in blue and grey striped, pyjama-like trousers and jackets — the same as the orderly in our ward had been wearing. No one had to explain to me that they were inmates from the nearby concentration camp. As they came

346

closer I discovered that, besides wearing the same prison garb, they had identical physical features. My brain refused to comprehend what my eyes saw. All of those poor people looked like death warmed up, barely warmed up: bodies consisting of nothing but skin and bones; skeletons risen from their graves; ghosts dancing in the sunshine like animated scarecrows.

Suddenly I realised that the whispered asides I'd overheard every now and then had not been malicious rumours or wicked Communist lies and propaganda. What I saw with my own unbelieving eyes was not a bad dream that would go away and never come back. What I stared at with horror-filled eyes was a nightmare that would haunt me for the rest of my days, even more perhaps than a child's arm rising from the rubble in Stuttgart. At first I was torn to pieces by anger; anger directed at my once idolised Adolf Hitler, the fanatics of the SS, and myself. Hadn't I shouted 'Heil Hitler' just as fervently as everybody else who became obsessed with the surge towards a Thousand Year Reich?

I shuddered, tears forming in my eyes. Oh, my God, I thought, is this what the Third Reich was going to be built on?

Anger went and shame took over. All the

glory of my Jungvolk and Hitlerjugend days fell away into nothingness as I looked from one haggard face to the next and the next, searching for my Dr. Rosenbaum, my gypsies, my Helga and her father. I had prayed that they'd been put into concentration camps for their own good. And now, for my own sake, for my own peace of mind, I prayed and hoped that they were not among the survivors; prayed that they'd died long before they'd suffered a fate a thousand times worse than death. God Almighty, what would I tell my children if ever I had any offspring? What would I say to them?

The pyjama people came toward me like spooks from a past that no sane human being could possibly want to remember. And suddenly there was silence.

With bloodshot eyes sunk deep in the sockets, with hollow cheeks, with gaunt faces covered by skin the colour of death, they came, many of them with a half empty bottle of bourbon in one hand and an American handgun in the other. They swayed and they stumbled along our rows of frozen and awe-stricken faces while our Yankee captors kept their guns aimed at us. Were they still afraid of us? I couldn't have run anywhere anyway. My legs would no longer obey orders.

The pyjama people passed me, one after the other. They stared at me, glared at me, their searching, burning eyes probing my brain and my soul. I'd never seen so much agony in so many faces at the same time.

They pointed at some of our group and passed others by, perhaps just at random. Jesus Christ, this couldn't be for real. I closed my eyes, then opened them again. I was still staring the same nightmare in the face. Oh, my God, help me. Please, help me!

I was ignored: no finger had beckoned me to step forward. Roughly eighty from our group of two hundred or so had been singled out, and were now facing us, standing herded together with their backs to the hospital wall. Eighty people from all walks of life: doctors in their white coats; nurses in their spotless starched uniforms; wounded and sick comrades from the army; grimfaced and defiant-looking soldiers in black-collared battle jackets decorated with the emblems of the Führer's elite, the legendary, infamous Waffen-SS; and civilians who had happened to visit wounded relatives in the hospital.

Stupefied and petrified, sweating like a pig on the spit, I could feel goosebumps rise all over my skin. I didn't have to be an Einstein to work out what was going to happen. The harder I tried to close my eyes, the wider they opened in fear and shock.

An American soldier received his orders. He positioned his machine-gun right in front of me. He pushed his shoulder against the butt and dug the tips of his rubber-soled lace-up boots into the ground. Then, obeying his orders just as I might have done before I defected, he did his job and pulled the trigger. His body shuddred from the recoil of the deadly weapon. He kept his finger hard on the trigger. The ominous, heartless rat-a-tat-tat of the rapid-fire gun mixed with the screams that split the sky asunder and reverberated all over the country. The young machine-gunner, who wouldn't have been a day older than I, just kept on firing. The bullets slammed into the writhing mass, tearing faces, hearts, limbs and lives apart. And the killing went on and on. The liberated skeletons in their flimsy zebra suits stood and watched silently without blinking an eyelid.

As the screams died down, so did the gunfire. There was little movement left in the human mountain of bleeding flesh — flesh that had been sacrificed to compensate in some eerie way for the horrendous misery suffered by the inmates of the Dachau concentration camp. But later the question rose and lingered in my mind: Do two wrongs ever make a right?

One of the massacre's victims was still alive enough to crawl away from the mangled bodies. A bullet had ripped his belly wide open and his intestines spilled from the gaping wound. I will never, not till the last day of my life, forget his wailing screams. He used one hand to crawl away from the dead. He used the other hand to push the slippery mess of his own guts back into his open, bleeding belly. Screaming in utter agony, he begged for mercy and found none. Instead, one of the pyjama people kicked him back into the heap of prone bodies, grabbed a gun from one of the American soldiers, and shot the victim in the head.

I cried, and went on crying. And I wished I had died in Heini's place.

Later I tried to console myself with the thought that, if only half of the hundred and twenty survivors could find the courage to teach their sons and daughters that the atrociousness of war knew neither reasoning nor mercy, that it spawned no heroes and bore neither dignity nor sanity, then perhaps those eighty victims of unrestrained revenge had not died in vain.

The walking skeletons now stood in small groups. Some of them wanted all of us to die. Others passed the bottles of bourbon around, content with toasting their newfound freedom.

I honestly wanted to despise the lot of them for the massacre they'd instigated. But how could I do that? If I'd gone a thousand times through living hell as they had obviously done, wouldn't I act in the same manner? Wouldn't I scream for bloody vengeance? Of course I would.

A soldier jerked his rifle at us. 'Put your fuckin' hands back on your fuckin' heads and walk, you goddamn Nazi bastards!'

I walked, and all who were capable walked with me. I didn't know whether I should thank God for sparing my life or curse Him for letting me suffer. No matter how hard I might try to plead ignorance and innocence on my part, the overwhelming feeling of guilt and shame, I realised, would never be erased from my mind. I was German. Therefore I was guilty.

But then, on the other hand, I wouldn't have wanted to be in the shoes of the young American soldier who pulled the trigger of the machine-gun. Could he live with himself for the rest of *his* life? Could he justify what he'd done? Could he ever forget the events of that ghastly day?

Good soldiers don't think. They simply follow orders.

15

Three abreast, and carefully guarded by our captors, we walked away from the Dachau SS Hospital towards an unknown destination and a dim future — if there was to be a future.

My mind was in a state of utter chaos. The only clear thought I could muster was that nothing made any sense at all, no matter how and from which angle I looked at it.

I kept on dragging my feet, pushing all my mental and physical resources to the limit, trying to keep in touch with the man who trudged along in front of me. I was too sick to walk and too frightened to stop. I was convinced that I'd be killed if I suffered another seizure or simply couldn't keep up with the rest.

Alas, the Americans didn't kill me. They had something worse than death in store for me and all the massacre survivors: we were taken to the Dachau concentration camp. To this very day I wish that I'd been struck with blindness before my eyes saw what they saw. But it was not to be. In the bouts of nightmares that came to haunt me day after day, year after year, I kept on seeing rows of white porcelain insulators on the posts along the fence, and tall deserted watchtowers, and a huge fat chimney that towered over rows of squat buildings, and a crudely fashioned sign on the wrought-iron gate:

ARBEIT MACHT FREI

In the context, 'Work Makes [You] Free' was perhaps the ultimate perversion.

Even now, more than fifty years after the end of the war, I am still plagued by nightmares. I can still hear the incensed voice of a distraught American who screamed at me: 'Open your goddamn eyes, Fritz! Have a good look at what you have done, you murdering bastard. And then give me one damned reason why I shouldn't blow your fuckin' head off right now, you goddamn son of a bitch.'

I can still see the row of open boxcars standing abandoned on the railway track. The wooden sides of the Deutsche Reichsbahn wagons were a metre and a half high. The large sliding doors in the middle of each carriage were wide open, revealing the gruesome, macabre cargo that had apparently arrived too late at the crematorium for annihilation. Jesus Christ, will You ever forgive us, for we do not know what we have done. God Almighty, why did You let it happen?

Emaciated, naked corpses, stacked in tiers: heads, feet, heads, feet, heads, feet. God in heaven, tell me this is not true. Tell me! Arms, legs, spindly and scrawny like twisted branches of dead trees. Heads, legs. Heads, legs. Too horrendous to be real. No, no, no! I was having a nightmare in the middle of the day.

I vomited and turned away. But the bloodcurdling image of heads and feet, heads and feet, did not vanish.

'Mitgefangen, mitgehangen,' the saying goes. Caught together, hanged together. Never a truer word was said.

It was too late now to wish that the ground under my feet would open up and swallow me, boots and all. Why the hell hadn't I killed myself when I had a chance? Up to now I'd felt sorry for the eighty victims of the bestial massacre at the hospital just one hour ago. Now I envied them. Those people were the lucky ones. They didn't have to face their own conscience. They wouldn't have to justify what they'd done and what they'd failed to do.

My tears did nothing to alleviate the pain inside me.

The fresh breeze of the newly created. Thousand Year Reich had picked me up like a dry leaf. It had carried me to wherever it wanted me to go. For years on end I had happily drifted with the tide, a tide which had given me, a meek, unpretentious and timid child, more power than I'd ever dreamt of, the power to denounce my own mother to the Gestapo if I'd wanted to, a tide powerful enough to turn a black sheep white — well, almost white.

Now the last shreds of pride were gone. My conscience was in a shambles. It seemed inconceivable to me that my friends from school and the Hitlerjugend, perhaps even my own cousins and uncles, might all be guilty in the eyes of the world. And how about me? Could I stand up before a judge and declare my innocence? Of course I couldn't. I'd been much too busy saying 'Heil Hitler', too busy pretending to be a good German and an obedient disciple of Adolf Hitler.

May God have mercy on me! I'd foolishly prayed and hoped that Helga was safely tucked away in a concentration camp, together with our baby. Good Lord, had I wished such suffering on her and on my own flesh and blood?

I forced myself to have a last glance at the ghastly cargo. I screamed out in agony, thinking that Helga's skeletal remains could quite possibly be among the corpses inside one of those railway wagons.

When our grim-faced captors finally decided that we'd seen enough horror for one day, our caravan of badly shaken ex-warriors was permitted to move on. The vomit in my mouth tasted almost as rancid as life itself. Yes, now I knew why the wall of the Dachau SS Hospital was stained with the blood of eighty men and women. In fact, it was a miracle indeed that any of us was still alive.

Now, you might argue that in years past we should have listened to the rumours that surfaced at times. Maybe we did. As children of Hitler's Germany we used to tease each other with threats like: 'If you do that again I'll tell the Gestapo. And you know what they'll do to you, don't you? They'll send you straight to a concentration camp!' It was nothing more and nothing less than telling somebody to go to hell. Yet I for one should have known better. I should have taken notice of all those ugly murmurs that made the rounds every now and then. But Adolf Hitler was my God, my Jesus Christ and my salvation. Damn it, I believed in him! And my mother hated him. Wasn't that more than enough reason for me to put him on a pedestal?

A POW camp, set among sweet-smelling orange groves somewhere in beautiful California — that's what I'd dreamed of in the latter part of the war, when our likely fate was becoming clearer by the day.

Fürstenfeldbruck was nowhere near California. It took us four or five hours to walk there from Dachau. We were not the first to arrive on the freshly ploughed paddock surrounded by tanks instead of barbed wire. Intentionally intimidating, the barrels of their cannon pointed at each and every one of us. Just to make sure that we would be safely contained within the imaginary boundaries of the makeshift camp, the spaces between the tanks were rendered impenetrable by overly alert and trigger-happy Yankee sentries. It seemed laughable that such a mighty force from the US Army should be employed to guard a routed and spent riffraff of disillusioned, unarmed losers.

One thing that wasn't laughable was the firm warning that the gunners in their armoured turrets would open fire at anybody or anything that moved during the hours of darkness.

Life is a never-ending chain of experiences, some joyful, some not so pleasant and others one would rather forget in a hurry. I am not going to describe what it was like to empty one's bowels when stretched out in a horizontal position, while wishing for nothing more than a precious little piece of paper or a priceless handful of grass.

But in the morning our compound reeked worse than a pigsty.

Who knows? Perhaps our conquerors didn't want us to shit at all. Maybe that's why we didn't get any breakfast or lunch. And, come dinnertime, they had better things to do than to feed a mob of despicable, stinking, starving Nazi bastards.

Even those among us who were caught in other locations, and had been fortunate enough to retain some provisions and their water canteens, ran out of supplies before any of us have-nots grew desperate enough to beg for a mouthful of water or a bite to eat.

The number of prisoners kept on rising to more than one thousand. And God on the third day created the Red Cross. The charitable ladies arrived at the field around noon on the back of two trucks carrying huge pots of pea and ham soup. The familiar smell would have roused the dead from their graves.

I was as sick as a dog and as weak as can be, but I surged forward with the rest of my starving compatriots. Instead of shouting 'Heil Hitler' we yelped in glee and in unison, 'God bless the Red Cross!'

Alas, close as we came to having a serving of pea soup poured into our cupped hands — we had nothing in the way of eating utensils at all — our watchful captors had other plans for us. A handful of Americans rushed towards the food trucks, waving their guns in the air, commanding the drivers to stop just fifty metres from us. At the same time a volley of shots convinced us that we'd end up being hungry dead men before we got a taste of that steaming soup. We stopped surging. While we were still trying to work out what was going on, an amplified voice came thundering from a loudhailer, addressing the Red Cross women.

'These men are prisoners of the United States Army! They are our responsibility. It is up to us to feed them and to take care of them. So turn your trucks around and get the hell out of here! That's an order!'

I guess that if it hadn't been for the tank cannon sweeping across our filthy camp, the 'Liberators of Europe' would have had a rebellion to deal with.

Where there are people, there are rumours. Gossip spreads faster than dysentery. The grapevine had it that the officer in charge of our compound was a German-born Jew, who intended to run his own little concentration camp for as long as it pleased him. If the rumour was true, then, for the first time in my life, I despised a Jew.

Anger spread quickly throughout the area. Infuriated men from the Waffen-SS shouted, 'Juden raus!'

A group of Austrian braves congregated in one corner of the field and lodged their own kind of protest. 'Mir san Österreicher!' they shouted in unison. 'We are Austrians, not Germans. We are your allies. We didn't vote for Hitler. Mir san Österreicher.'

The devil denouncing the devil! What next?

Drinking water was still on the agenda. Our oppressors, who'd taken up residence in a sprawling old farmhouse just outside our compound, connected a single tap to the end of a long hose and fastened it to a wooden pole — one tap for a thousand thirsty men; one perpetual queue until nightfall when no one was game enough to rise more than a centimetre or two off the putrid soil for fear of getting shot.

At noon the defiant German women from the Red Cross showed up again to feed us. Once again they were sent on their way. But this time they weren't just told to go; they were told: 'You have no rights here. You lost the war. Now fuck off, all of you!'

And lo and behold, later in the afternoon, our zookeepers came to feed the animals. God bless their generosity! One loaf of spongy white bread to share between twenty. Concentration camp rations perchance?

'All good things must come to an end,' I told myself, carefully picking up a crumb of bread from the reeking soil. 'Do all bad things come to an end as well?'

God must have heard my prayers. On the very next morning, right after the breakfast we didn't get, they loaded us onto trucks like pigs earmarked for a quick trip to the nearest abattoir. Only we smelled worse.

A young second lieutenant supervised the proceedings in his own self-pleasing way. He employed a thin fencing sword as if it were a billiard cue. But instead of potting black or red balls he aimed at scrotums and backsides and anything else that was obviously German. He never took time out to tally his score.

Our driver and his sidekick were Negroes, just a shade darker than ebony. Their intriguing faces fascinated me. I'd never seen teeth as white as theirs before. The only black people I'd seen in my whole life were those on the line-up boards of freak shows at carnival time. I'd gawked at them as they were exhibited together with the fat ladies, the dwarfs and the Siamese twins.

But the tables had turned. Now I was the freak. As a young child I'd thrown peanuts to one of those black things that seemed to be a cross between man and ape. Now, ironically, the very black co-driver stuck his head through the window, grinned at us and threw us a fistful of Hershey bars and a few packs of cigarettes.

My first mouthful of American chocolate was tastier than the crisp skin of the finest Christmas goose. My first American cigarette made me delightfully lightheaded and dizzy. I craned my neck to catch another glimpse of the kind man's face. And I found more compassion in the shiny eyes of one Negro than I'd seen in a whole ocean of white faces from either side of the world.

Little did I know then that only a few months later I would watch black American soldiers emerge from the PX Shop in Frankfurt's Kaiserstrasse, carrying cartons of Hershey bars under their arms. They'd walk the whole length of the street and hand out a chocolate bar to every child they met. They would feast on the smiles of the surprised children and keep on walking without waiting for a 'Danke schön.' I am convinced that during those hardship-filled days many German children actually believed that Santa

Claus was black. Come to think of it, who am I to surmise that he isn't?

Our truck stopped in the first village we came to. The driver and his mate jumped from their cabin and started yelling at the curious audience they attracted, telling them to fetch some food and drink for us.

Making use of the English I'd learnt in school, I called out to the co-driver to thank him for the chocolate and the cigarettes. He grinned at me and said: 'That's all right, buddy. No trouble at all. I reckon there ain't no difference 'tween you an' me. Me bein' a fuckin' nigger an' you bein' a fuckin prisoner of war. We're both slaves of the almighty white man from the US of A!'

He lit two smokes and gave me one of them. 'Luck is on your side, pal,' he said, still grinning. 'They'll have to let you go sooner or later, and you're gonna be a free man. But me, pal, I'll always be black and I'll always be a fuckin' slave to the white man.'

He winked at me, pulled a well-chewed piece of gum out through his protruding lips, stretched it, then gathered it in again with the pinkest tongue I'd ever laid eyes on.

No tanks were needed to secure the periphery of the POW camp near Heilbronn, which was our next port of call. We disembarked outside the main gate of what was not just one compound but a whole constellation of glinting wire-netting fences and kilometre upon kilometre of strands and teased-out coils of barbed wire. The high fences divided hundreds of hectares into a maze of smaller compounds like squares on a huge chess board. We were not the first to arrive and, judging by the enormous size of the complex, we certainly wouldn't be the last. The camp was large enough to accommodate all that was left of the German army in the western sphere of the shortlived Thousand Year Reich.

God only knows why Adolf Hitler had had each and every one of his beloved Waffen-SS heroes branded with a telltale blood group tattoo, thus making it easy for our captors to separate the wolves from the sheep — or rather the bad bastards from the ordinary bastards.

Waffen-SS to the left, the rest to the right! And we never saw each other again. I still don't know what happened to the captured SS men. I guess I don't really want to know either. I'm just glad that I didn't happen to be one of them.

It was back to life under the stars once more. The earlier arrivals had already built their temporary homes, shallow foxholes covered with ground sheets or blankets to keep the morning dew at bay. I had neither spade nor spoon; not a thing to dig a hole with. It cost me my first ration of bread to borrow a spade for half an hour. My pleas for an empty bully beef tin fell on deaf ears. I ended up buying one with my second day's slice of bread. Without a receptacle of some kind I wouldn't have been able to collect the once-a-day serve of watery soup. I wondered what had happened to a thing commonly known as comradeship.

★ ★ ★

'Hitler is dead!' The rumour spread like wildfire from compound to compound.

'The Russians have conquered Berlin!'

'Unconditional surrender!'

I'd imagined for a long time how my heart would jump with joy at that news, the news all the world must have been waiting for. Now, though, I felt no joy at all. Instead of celebrating the end of the war, I mourned for all those who hadn't lived long enough to see it. Dead friends, dead enemies, dead women and dead children strewn all over Europe, their limbs torn, their hopes buried and their lives curtailed. Dear God, what a terrible price to pay for peace by victor and loser alike. What price would freedom be? What

366

would the future bring? Would there be a future?

My days and nights were filled with a mixture of reveries and nightmares — with dreams of holding Helga in my arms and beginning a brand new life; with nightmares of hollow-eyed skeletons grinning at me from the open doors of boxcars and saying over and over again what I'd been told at the end of my court martial: 'We must destroy his future! We must destroy his life!'

I didn't want to listen. I didn't deserve to be drowned in an ocean of guilt and shame, of doubts and rejection. Damn it, I had followed my conscience. God had not created us to destroy each other.

And yet, I wouldn't be able to walk through the streets of my home town with my head held high, being aware of people whispering behind my back, pointing their accusing fingers at me and saying: 'He was in gaol, you know. There goes a coward who deserted his comrades.'

People would like to believe that hardships form friendships, that suffering brings people closer together, that comradeship grows stronger in the face of adversity. Sorry to say, nothing like that happened in our POW camp. The only thing shared by all of us was the 'Donnerbalken,' the roughly cut wooden beam that straddled a long and narrow pit in the centre of our compound. The stench of calcium chloride and human waste that emanated from the primitive latrine was pretty well intolerable, almost as intolerable as the tension among the people who used it. Out in the battlefields we would have given our lives for each other. Now everybody tried to fight for his own survival. The fortunate bastards who still had precious provisions to share banded together and shared with each other. Poor buggers like me and many others who had nothing to barter with couldn't even get a small piece of paper or tissue from them. We ended up with more cackleberries on our behinds than hairs on our chests.

Eighteen men to a loaf of bread per day. Eighteen pairs of eyes keenly watching a blunt knife carve through the soft dough. Every crumb counted. Nothing was wasted. Touch a crumb that wasn't yours and risk your life. One scoop of soup per day, soup thinner than dishwater. We grazed the camp area for every green thing that emerged from the soil and put it into the liquid that was supposed to be soup. We fought greedily for a handful of coffee grounds in the waste bins behind the kitchen. Did you know that you can chew for hours on a small fistful of coffee grounds?

In spite of all the misery and hardship, there were many in our crowd who never once stopped boasting about their heroic exploits in hard-fought battles, about their foolhardy bravery and their readiness to fight the war all over again. My God, peace was only a few days old and they revelled in the glory of their memories already, just as my father had done when I was a little boy and a fascinated, gullible and impressionable listener. Sad as it was, the young boys of today would become tomorrow's soldiers — the blind were leading the blind in a never-ending circle.

I learnt a lot during the weeks I spent inside that camp. I discovered that greed and selfishness seemed to be the main factors in the fight for survival. Compassion did nothing but make you hungrier than others in a hell where, if it came to the crunch, some wise guy would steal your shallow foxhole from under you if he could.

With more time on my hands than I could cope with, I spent many, many hours sitting near the boundary fence, gazing wistfully into the distance where freedom and peace engulfed the soft hills of the undulating countryside, trying to catch a glimpse of my future. Would I be able to stand on my own feet and run my own life? With Helga or without her, would I be strong enough to grab a slice of life for myself? I was still searching for answers one day when a fellow POW came walking towards the fence and called out to a patrolling sentry outside the boundary: 'Hey, hallo! American soldier, hallo!'

The sentry came closer to the fence. 'What do ya want, Jerry?'

'Cigarette, please, sirrrr.' The man doing the begging was dressed in what used to be an honourable field-grey uniform. 'One cigarette for a nice gold ring, ja?'

He pulled the wedding band from his dirty ring finger and proffered it to the young American. 'Eine Chesterfield? One Lucky Strike, please?'

'You oughta be ashamed of yourself, you fuckin' son of a bitch,' said the American. He shook his head and walked away in disgust.

Well, this second world war was over. From now on, each of us — winner or loser — would have to start a new life all over again. It was wonderful to know that, at least in the near future, bombs would no longer rain down on a devastated Europe. It was comforting to know that the terrifying and deadly symphonies of Stalin-organ salvos would soon be replaced by the soothing sounds of real organs in real churches where real people would congregate to thank whatever god they still believed in. And bells would toll from lofty spires to spread the message of peace to all the corners of the world.

One cigarette in exchange for a wedding ring! We had truly reached the bottom of the barrel.

In the midst of tears, I thought, I am only twenty-one years old and I have lived through scores of lives already. I am nothing. I own nothing. I have no skills with which to build a future for myself. My only precious possession is my own life. No, I shall not kill myself tomorrow or any other day. I shall learn to live all over again, to live without fear, to live without hatred and prejudice . . . and to believe once again that we humans are the noblest of all beings created by the mysterious Holy Spirit I choose to call God.

Epilogue

Only a few more weeks to go until Christmas. The poinciana trees are dressed up in their magnificent coats of flame-red flowers. Slender palms sway gently to and fro in the mild, lazy breeze that blows from across the Pacific Ocean. I can hear the surf rolling in to the golden sands of the beach that stretches for miles to the north and to the south of Surfers Paradise. A kookaburra flits from branch to branch of a towering eucalyptus tree. The laughing jackass calls out to me as if to wish me a happy day. And I say thank you, and I laugh back at the happy, noisy bird.

Half a century has passed since my release from a POW camp into a shattered and unrecognisable Germany. God only knows why I tried to settle down in Frankfurt, where I knew no one and no one knew me. The only thing I was sure of was that, at least for the time being, I could not return to my home town. Most likely shame, pride and sheer obstinacy stopped me from sliding back into the folds of a family which never wanted me anyway. They would not notice the scars in my heart and the torment in my confused brain. They would just keep on despising me more than ever. Once a black sheep, always a black sheep.

Arriving in Frankfurt in my tattered uniform that needed a wash as much as I did, with forty Reichsmarks of discharge money in my pocket at a time when one single American cigarette cost ten Reichsmarks on the black market, my chances of survival didn't seem to rate highly. But somehow I did survive. And I did get married. My wife gave me the greatest gift of all, a son to love and to cherish. The Americans suddenly seemed to realise that Stalin and his Communist Russia had not been an ideal ally in a fight for freedom in the world.

The beginning of the Cold War brought fears and anxieties back into my daily life. I couldn't help wondering whether we, the terrible Germans, would be blamed for a third world war as well as for the first and the second. I picked up my son from his cot, hugged him and promised him that I would take him away from the ruins and the upheavals and the uncertainties and the new threats of war we had to face once more from day to day.

I kept my promise. More than forty years have gone by since we migrated to Australia in desperate search for a new and meaningful life and that elusive thing called freedom. Frustrations, fears and nightmares have long been buried.

I am so glad that I didn't succeed in killing myself during those troubled times when I was too scared to live and too frightened to die. Life has never been better for me than right now. I am married to the most wonderful woman in the whole world.

I blow some grey flakes of cigarette ash from the keyboard of my typewriter, which has been my dear friend and confidant through the years. For endless nights and days it has listened to me with the kind of patience only a typewriter can muster. It has shaped my innermost thoughts into words, and it has never ever laughed at me because I still can't pronounce the 'th' and the 'w' properly. It has neither condemned nor despised me for having been born in a wonderful country at the wrong time.

'Whatever did happen to Helga?' my wife asks, standing behind me, looking over my shoulder, stroking my grey hair with ever so gentle fingertips.

'I never found out, honey,' I reply, and sadness touches my heart for a fleeting moment. 'I searched high and low. Didn't leave a stone unturned. She'd simply disappeared from the face of the earth without leaving the slightest trace. Maybe she was meant to be my dream; just a dream that kept me sane through the worst years of my life.'

'And you are still dreaming, aren't you?' My wife knows me better than I know myself. She gives me a sharp tap on the head and walks towards the door. She turns around and smiles. She is beautiful when she smiles. I tell her that I love her every minute of every day. 'I know that already,' she replies, and shuts the door.

I'll never get used to celebrating Christmas in the middle of summer. Christmas without snow is only half a Christmas. Yet a Christmas here in Australia is truly a very special event for me. I don't only celebrate the birth of Christ; I celebrate my re-birth into a wonderful and tolerant country, where I found the kind of peace and freedom I yearned for ever since I stopped saying 'Heil Hitler'.

Life certainly wasn't a fairytale of rags to riches. Though I worked hard I might not have left one single tiny footprint in the sands of time.

Many years ago, when I worked and lived in Sydney, a Polish friend who'd migrated to Australia years before I did took me to visit a lonely, old German-born Jew who lived in a terrace house in downtown Surry Hills. On the mantlepiece above the fireplace in his comfortably furnished home, among vases of freshly cut flowers, stood a collection of photos in gilded frames, depicting a woman perhaps in her late forties and four teenage boys. Over a cup of coffee, the old gentleman told me that his wife and his four sons had all perished in the concentration camp of Buchenwald. His eyes reflected sorrow and compassion as he looked at me and said quietly: 'We cannot change the past, my friend. Now it is up to all of us to change the future.'

I have found my peace: not the peace that silences guns and stops the bombs from falling; not the peace my Führer Adolf Hitler wanted me to die for. My peace is within myself: in my heart, in my mind and in every single day I have the privilege of being alive.